DATE DUE

DE 17 '97			
AP 9 '98			
DE 17 '04			
MY 15 '08			
NO 25 '08			

DEMCO 38-296

GETTING THE LEAD OUT

The Complete Resource on
How to Prevent and Cope with
Lead Poisoning

GETTING THE LEAD OUT

The Complete Resource on
How to Prevent and Cope with
Lead Poisoning

IRENE KESSEL
and
JOHN T. O'CONNOR

PLENUM TRADE • NEW YORK AND LONDON

ation Data

Getting the lead out : the complete resource on how to prevent and
cope with lead poisoning / Irene Kessel and John T. O'Connor.
      p.   cm.
   Includes bibliographical references and index.
   ISBN 0-306-45525-0 (hardbound). -- ISBN 0-306-45526-9 (pbk.)
   1. Lead poisoning--Popular works.   I. O'Connor, John T., 1954-
. II. Title.
   [DNLM: 1. Lead Poisoning--popular works.   QV 292 K42g 1997]
RA1231.L4K47   1997
615.9'25688--dc21
DNLM/DLC
for Library of Congress   96-50951
                                                                CIP

ISBN 0-306-45525-0 (Hardbound)
ISBN 0-306-45526-9 (Paperback)

© 1997 Irene Kessel and John T. O'Connor
Plenum Press is a Division of Plenum Publishing Corporation
233 Spring Street, New York, N.Y. 10013-1578
http://www.plenum.com

10 9 8 7 6 5 4 3 2 1

Printed in the United States of America

For Our Children

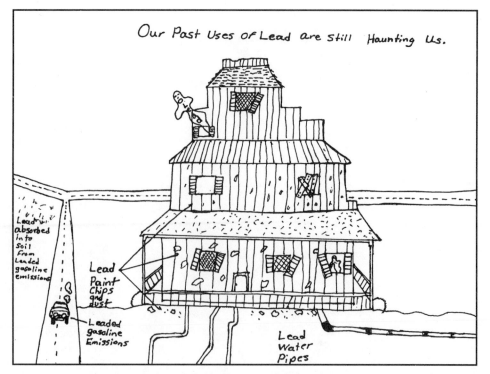

Drawing by Josh Caldwell, Age 12. Bowdon Elementary School, Carroll Co., Ga.

Foreword

Lead poisoning is one of the oldest diseases known to humankind, occurring from the time humans learned to smelt and use lead, at least 5000 years ago. The disease was recognized and described by ancient Egyptian and Greek physicians and was so widespread during the Roman civilization that more than one scholar has suggested that it significantly weakened that society and may have led to its downfall. During the medieval history of Europe, there occurred outbreaks of lead "colic" (so named for the striking abdominal pain symptomatic of adult lead poisoning) often in association with poor wine vintages, as lead was commonly used in those times to "doctor" sour wine and restore a sweet taste. The practice was so common and known to be detrimental to those who drank the wine that it was banned in the Holy Roman Empire.

In colonial America, lead was known to cause disease in printers and rum distillers, and was famous for causing "cider colic," a condition produced by drinking cider stored in pewter vessels from which lead "leached" in large amounts. Benjamin Franklin spoke of it in his correspondence with Dr. Benjamin Rush, a noted physician of the time.

Lead was first introduced as a pigment or paint early in the nineteenth century. Because lead ore in the Midwestern United States was so pure, America soon became the lead supplier to the world for this purpose, building a large and influential lead industry. By 1975, virtually every new home built in the northeastern quadrant of the United States received a coat of lead paint, which was really lead oxide suspended in linseed oil, known as "lead-in-oil." Pigments were added, and this product became famous for providing durable, mildew-resistant surfaces.

Because of the property of lead pigments to "chalk," and therefore provide an endlessly renewable surface, they were also noted for the brightness of color they produced. Even today, lead chromate is the constituent of the yellow paint that marks curbstones, fire hydrants, and highway guidelines. Sadly, little did anyone realize at the time that, in addition to flaking and peeling, the chalking of lead paint would produce deadly layers of lead chips and dust inside painted homes.

Although the adult form of lead poisoning was already well known, the first cases of childhood lead poisoning as we know it were described in 1897 by an Australian eye physician by the name of Turner. He recognized a group of cases of optic neuritis (inflammation of the nerve that leads from the eye to the brain) in a group of children from Queensland, Australia. Over the next decade, there appeared a flurry of scientific articles confirming this observation, recognizing it as due to lead and attributing it to the habit of chewing on porch railings from the verandas of Queensland homes! Thus, the entire pattern of childhood lead poisoning was fully described and published by 1905.

Why then, you must certainly ask, was the use of lead paint not banned when its dangers to children were now known? It was prohibited in Europe and Canada but not in the United States. By 1918, sufficient reports had appeared in America and Europe to persuade authorities in Belgium, France, and Germany, as well as in Canada, to restrict the concentration of lead paint to 5% lead by weight. This contrasted with American paint that sometimes contained ten times that much! As a result, while the Europeans and Canadians have not escaped unscathed, they have fared far better than us and our English counterparts who have been slow to recognize this danger. Lead paint was not finally regulated in this country until 1970 in Massachusetts and 1978 nationally by the Consumer Product Safety Commission.

Application of this paint to American homes continued from 1875 until about 1950 when, purely for economic reasons, the paint companies began to replace lead with titanium. Our best available data tells us that as a result more than 60 million homes in the United States contain potentially dangerous amounts of lead. The dilemma of reducing this danger lies in the fact that lead paint is most hazardous when the surface is disrupted; yet we cannot remove it without disrupting it. And, as the late Dr. Randolph Byers remarked to me over lunch one day when we were struggling to have the Massachusetts Lead Poisoning Prevention Act enacted into law, "Once you remove it, where are you going to put it?"

Ms. Kessel and Mr. O'Connor have done an admirable job of condensing into a relatively short book a large amount of basic information about childhood lead poisoning. Interspersed with case histories, they have outlined in a straightforward language the full dimensions of the problem facing our country.

The remarkable fact that lead was removed from gasoline in 1978 had an unexpected but substantial impact on average lead levels around the country. That, plus the efforts of hundreds of thousands of concerned parents, health workers, housing advocates, and others throughout our communities in forcing the government to attack the problem in all its forms including toys, food, water, and industry has resulted in a significant reduction in the frequency with which we now see this problem compared to in 1970. Then, fully 25% of the preschool children living in the area surrounding Boston's Children Hospital had lead levels high enough to warrant treatment by the then criteria,which were twice as high as they are today. The same was true or worse in many of the industrialized cities in the United States.

So we've come a long way but not far enough. Much remains to be done and the price of any relaxation of safeguards will be the intellectual function of future generations. Our thanks to Ms. Kessel and Mr. O'Connor for this effort. It all helps.

John W. Graef, M.D.
Chief Emeritus and Senior Consultant
Lead and Toxicology Program
Children's Hospital
and
Associate Clinical Professor of Pediatrics
Harvard Medical School

Boston, Massachusetts

Acknowledgments

We express our appreciation to the following individuals who reviewed and contributed to this book:

James Bryson, Lead Paint Abatement Coordinator, U. S. Environmental Protection Agency, Region I

Matthew Chachere, J.D., Northern Manhattan Improvement Corporation

Nick Farr, Director, National Center for Lead Safe Housing

John Graef, M.D., Chief Emeritus of Lead and Toxicology Program, Children's Hospital, Boston

Anne Guthrie, Deputy Director, Alliance To End Childhood Lead Poisoning

David Guthrie, Public Health Advisor, Lead Poisoning Prevention Branch, National Center for Environmental Health, Centers for Disease Control and Prevention, U. S. Department of Health and Human Services

Marco Kaltofen, P.E., Boston Chemical Data, Inc.

Marianna Koval, J.D., licensed lead-based paint inspector/risk assessor, Lead Safe Home, Inc., Brooklyn

Neil Leifer, J.D., Thornton, Early and Naumes, Boston

Dennis Livingston, Community Resources, Inc., Baltimore

Catherine McVay Hughes, New York Public Interest Research Group (NPIRG)

Sandra Shaheen, Ph.D., Longwood Neuropsychology, Boston

We also thank all of the individuals who are working to fight lead poisoning, both in public agencies and in private organizations, many of whom have provided valuable information and insight for this book. In particular, we thank Michael Shannon, M.D., David Bellinger, Ph.D., and Beth Holleran, LISCW, of Children's Hospital, Boston; John Rosen, M.D., of the Albert Einstein College of Medicine, Montefiore Medical Center; Benjamin Hiller, J.D., of Moquin and Daley; Burton Nadler, J.D., of Petruccelly & Nadler; Neil Gendel of Lead Poisoning Prevention Project, Consumer Action, San Francisco; Harold Goldstein, Ph.D., of Northeastern University; Frank Smizik, J.D.; Michael Withey, J.D., of Trial Lawyers for Social Justice; Arthur Bryant, J.D., of the Association of Trial Lawyers of America's Lead Paint Litigation Group; Joseph Ponessa, Ph.D., of Rutgers Cooperative Extension; Stephanie Pollack, J.D., of Conservation Law Foundation; Ellen Silbergeld, Ph.D., of the University of Maryland Medical School, Baltimore; Mary Jean Brown, R.N., Sharon O'Brien Carter, Case Management Coordinator, and Kathy Maloof, LISCW, of the Massachusetts Department of Public Health; Paul Mushak, Ph.D., of Pb Associates; Audrey L. Seyffert, Administrator of Pupil Services of the Natick Public School System, Natick, MA; Annette Grace, R.N., M.S.C.S., and N.P. of Harvard Pilgrim Health Care; Susan Sawyer, R.N., of Dimick Community Health Center; Karen Tewhey of the Head Start Program, Boston; Maurci Jackson and the other parent advocates of United Parents Against Lead; and Peg Brier for her delightful illustrations, Paul Sherman for his computer graphics, and Charles Rhodes, Beverly Rich, and Martin Kessel for their research and editing assistance.

Finally, we thank Erika Goldman, Arun Das, and David Bahr at Plenum for their support throughout this project.

Contents

Introduction

Maurci Jackson was working on her ceramics late one night, after 15-month-old Maurissa had gone to sleep. Hearing a noise from the bedroom, Maurci found that the baby had gotten out of bed and had put a chip of paint in her mouth, which she was trying to spit out. Maurci rinsed out the baby's mouth and used a towel to remove any remaining bits of paint. The next morning she took Maurissa to the doctor, who tested her for lead poisoning. He found an elevated level of lead in Maurissa's blood, over 30 micrograms per deciliter—more than three times the level that is considered to be safe.

The doctor prescribed chelation therapy, a treatment that would remove some of the lead from the baby. It was an ordeal. Maurissa was given two shots a day for periods of 3 or 5 days. She screamed as her mother had never heard her scream before. The pain was excruciating. Although the treatment did lower the level of lead in Maurissa's blood, the level went back up after the treatment was over. It had to be repeated several times over 8 months until the blood lead level finally lowered, but never below a safe one.

No one explained to Maurci that returning a chelated child to the same lead-contaminated environment would result in poisoning her again. She was told only to keep the home clean—so she did. She increased vacuuming and dusting. She was not told that lead dust is so fine that normal vacuuming and dusting do more to spread the toxic lead by putting it back into the air than they do to remove it.

Maurci, in the meantime, had done some reading on nutrition and was carefully providing iron supplements and cooking with cheese and yogurt. She took Maurissa for retesting every 2 to 3 months, and the levels were lower. Maurci promised her child she would never have to endure those painful shots again.

Finally, after about a year, the landlord sent some workers to the apartment to remove the lead paint. They scraped it off, with no precautions to protect themselves, the home, or its occupants. Two men finished the scraping and sanding, with fans in the windows for ventilation, which resulted in the dust blowing from the bedroom to the adjoining rooms of the apartment.

Maurissa's scheduled follow-up lead screening happened to be a few days after the paint removal work was started. The level of lead in her blood had gone back up—even higher than it had been when she was poisoned the year before! Maurissa had to be brought in, crying and protesting, for those awful shots again.

The doctor, after learning of the landlord's recent efforts, insisted they move from the apartment immediately. The rugs, the furniture, even the stuffed animals were contaminated and would have to be left behind. Maurci was told that some damage may have already been done to the development of Maurissa's brain. Removing the child from the sources of lead and treating her with a chelating drug would prevent any additional injury, but no treatment could reverse any damage that had already occurred.

Maurci was furious that this could have happened. Why wasn't she told that removing lead paint without proper precautions could expose a child or a pregnant woman to dangerous levels of lead? It would only have taken a brief comment or a simple informational brochure, but even that was never given to her. She was outraged that the individuals who had done the work weren't trained to do it in a safe manner. Why was lead paint even present in her home, if lead is such a dangerous toxin?

Maurci was determined to do all she could to prevent others from having to endure what she went through. She turned her energy to educating, organizing, and advocating for lead poisoning prevention.

The ordeal of daily injections that Maurissa went through is not the typical treatment for lead poisoning. Other less traumatic means of administering chelating drugs are more commonly used. However, other aspects of this family's experience are indeed typical of lead-poisoned families. Needless exposure to lead and inadequate knowledge to protect one's children are all too common.

Maurci's story and those of many other lead poisoning victims and advocates are the inspiration for this book. Providing increased awareness as a tool to fight lead poisoning is our shared mission.

Lead poisoning is one of the most common and preventable pediatric health problems in the United States, according to the Department of Health and Human Services, Centers for Disease Control. Although the problem has existed for centuries, we are only now beginning to realize its real impact on the health and well-being of children. The average level of lead in children's blood is lower now than it was 25 years ago, before lead paint was prohibited from use in homes and the phasing out of lead in gasoline. However, the problem of lead poisoning is receiving more and more attention because we are learning that lower and lower blood levels of lead can affect children's health, and especially the development of the brain.

The repercussions of lead poisoning reach far beyond its impact on any individual child and family. The cognitive impairment of a large segment of our society lowers their productivity and effectiveness as citizens and puts an increased burden on our educational, health, social, and penal systems.

Each year, more than 1½ million children have elevated blood lead levels in this country. In most cases of lead poisoning there are no obvious symptoms to alert a parent. Yet these children are at risk for behavioral problems, learning disabilities, and reduced IQ because of exposure to this invisible toxin, which is all around us.

The major cause of lead poisoning is lead-based paint. A child does not, however, have to eat paint chips to become lead poisoned. Any time lead-based paint is disrupted there is a potential for lead poisoning—whether the paint is rubbed against, sanded or scraped, chewed on, or simply falling off.

Urban families living in older housing are disproportionately affected by lead poisoning. Nevertheless, lead poisoning cuts across geographic and socioeconomic boundaries. A middle-class family renovating an old Victorian in a rural area might find their toddler poisoned from the fine lead dust generated from scraping and sanding the paint—IF the proper precautions are not taken. A preschooler might be exposed to dangerous levels of lead in a suburban park or playground where the removal of old paint from an adjacent building has left toxic paint chips in the soil or the sandblasting of a nearby bridge has spewed lead dust into the air—IF the lead dust from these activities is not well contained.

A child can be exposed to lead through a number of other sources as well. Drinking water can be contaminated with lead from household plumbing, or from an old water cooler or antique kettle. A ceramic mug, if not properly glazed or fired, may leach dangerous amounts of lead into a toddler's morning orange juice. A young child could become lead poisoned by chewing on pool cue chalk or imported mini blinds. Lead emitted by automobiles burning leaded fuel years ago still contaminates soil near well-traveled roads, which, in turn, contaminates vegetables grown in that soil. Sources of lead are everywhere. Parents can only make efforts to control or avoid these sources if they are aware of them.

The best defense against lead poisoning is information.

In this book, we will explain the nature and sources of lead poisoning and discuss the basic measures for minimizing the associated risks and damage. In separate chapters we will deal with each major source of lead poisoning in depth and present concrete steps you can take to control each particular source.

If you have a child who has been lead poisoned, you may have a number of concerns. You will need to make important decisions regarding how best to care for your child. You may need to deal not only with treating lead poisoning but also with overcoming any neurological impacts lead has had on your child as well as the psychological repercussions on you and your family. We will give you enough basic information to be able to deal in an informed way with a medical doctor treating lead poisoning, a contractor removing lead paint from your home, or a special education director designing a program in your child's public school.

For those who are interested in taking a more aggressive posture toward lead poisoning, we will discuss fighting lead poisoning on both personal and community levels. We will explain what is involved in bringing a lawsuit to redress personal injury caused by lead poisoning. We will advise you as to how you can make a difference in your community by organizing. Finally, we will summarize some of the public policy issues concerning lead poisoning.

In the appendixes, we present an extensive resource section, including state-by-state and subject-by-subject breakdowns of useful names and addresses for more information and support.

Lead poisoning is a needless tragedy. The key to preventing this tragedy is awareness. With the proper knowledge, and action based on that knowledge, we can protect our children from this ubiquitous poison. As a society, we can eliminate lead poisoning with an enlightened public policy and the commitment of adequate resources. As parents, we can provide our children the best care possible with a good understanding of how to prevent and cope with lead poisoning.

PART ONE

Understanding Lead Poisoning

Lead poisoning is one of the most common and preventable pediatric health problems in the United States.
U. S. Department of Health and Human Services, Centers for Disease Control and Prevention

CHAPTER ONE

Lead Poisoning: A Background

The latest official government figures on lead poisoning show that about 1.7 million young children, or about 8.9% of preschoolers in the United States, have levels of lead in their blood that are considered to be of concern.[1]

Blood levels of lead have been declining in the United States over the past several decades, largely because of the phaseout of leaded gasoline. However, at the same time, we have learned from scientific studies that lower and lower

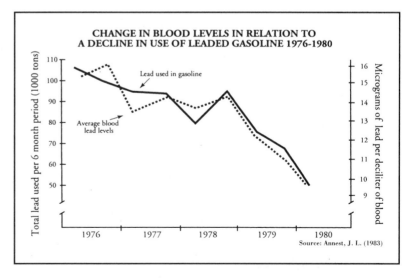

**CHANGE IN BLOOD LEVELS IN RELATION TO
A DECLINE IN USE OF LEADED GASOLINE 1976-1980**

Lead used in gasoline

Average blood
lead levels

Total lead used per 6 month period (1000 tons)

Micrograms of lead per deciliter of blood

1976   1977   1978   1979   1980

Source: Annest, J. L. (1983)

levels of lead, previously believed safe, actually have serious health effects. Recent studies have found that even amounts of lead believed to be safe a few years ago might cause damage to young children's developing brains, decreasing IQ and causing behavior and learning problems. And it is unclear to what extent this damage is reversible.[2]

Because of its detrimental effect on the intellectual potential of each new generation, lead poisoning has been called "the most common and societally devastating environmental disease of young children."[3] It affects so many people that it threatens the intelligence level and well-being of the nation as a whole.

Lead poisoning is totally preventable. This is because lead can be easily identified in the body, and in the environment. We understand how people get lead poisoning and what we need to do to eradicate the disease.

What Is Lead Poisoning?

Lead poisoning is a disease caused by exposure to and absorption of lead. It is identified by measuring the blood level of lead in an individual. Lead poisoning affects virtually every system in the body, and especially the developing brain and nervous system of unborn and young children.

Lead is a very, very strong poison. An extremely small amount of lead can cause serious harm to a child. The blood concentration of lead that might cause coma, convulsions, and even death in children is 100 micrograms per deciliter. This is comparable to half of a drop of a contaminant in a bathtub full of water. Even concentrations of lead in the blood that are 1/10th that strong, or equivalent to 1/20th of a drop of a contaminant in a bathtub full of water, have been found to be associated with detectable damage to the development of the brain.

The threshold of 10 micrograms per deciliter is a level at which a number of harmful effects of lead have been identified. This is referred to as the LEVEL OF CONCERN. Federal figures show that about 9% of children aged 1 to 5 had such a level from 1988 to 1991. Fifteen micrograms per deciliter is of somewhat greater concern, as a larger degree of harmful effects are documented. Under 3% of young children had this blood lead level. Even fewer, about 1%, had levels of 20 or more micrograms per deciliter and about 0.5% had levels of 25 or over.[4]

There is no clear level of blood lead that identifies a child as LEAD POISONED. The term is used differently in different contexts. The term LEAD POISONED is used by the U. S. Department of Housing and Urban Development (HUD) to refer to a child who has had a measured blood lead level of 20 or over, or one who has two consecutive measurements of 15 or over. The U. S. Centers for Disease Control does not use a single definition for lead poisoning but rather considers different levels of blood lead as calling for different responses. Some state and local laws define lead poisoning at higher levels than the HUD definition. Some medical works use the term LEAD POISONED to describe a child with a blood lead level of 10 or above.

In this book, we will refer to children with a level of 10 or slightly above as having ELEVATED BLOOD LEAD LEVELS or BLOOD LEAD LEVELS ABOVE THE LEVEL OF CONCERN.

Lead Poisoning Affects People in All Geographic Areas

The number of children with elevated blood lead levels has exceeded a shocking 50% in many urban areas.[5] Lead poisoning, however, is not limited to our cities. It occurs everywhere, including suburbs, small towns, and rural areas.

Parts of the country with older homes have a greater problem with lead from paint, for example. Areas with very cold climates are also likely to have a higher concentration of lead in paint, increasing the likelihood of dangerous levels of exposure to children. In the western United States, the risk of exposure to lead from pottery might be higher than in the east. Certain ethnic groups are exposed to lead in their traditional remedies. Communities in the vicinity of lead smelters and other lead-emitting industries are exposed to greater amounts of lead from such industrial sources. Some water districts may have water that is more corrosive, and prone to contamination with lead, than others. Also, some water systems still have lead water mains, which may contaminate drinking water.

Lead Poisoning Affects Persons of All Socioeconomic Groups

Children living in older houses where the paint is deteriorating are at the greatest risk of lead poisoning. Therefore, the burden falls disproportionately on poor, inner-city, minority families. However, children in middle-income families are also vulnerable.[6] Seven percent of white children living under favorable economic conditions were found to have high blood lead levels in the mid-1980s.[7]

Lead paint does not have to be peeling or flaking to pose a threat. Even in well-maintained homes, lead paint can create toxic dust without being visibly disturbed. Any lead-painted surfaces that are subject to friction and abrasion can generate lead dust. When windows are opened and closed, for example, the paint on the window rubs against the paint on the frame and creates very fine particles that fall to the windowsill and the floor. Children pick up this dirt both directly and via toys and pets.

Remodeling or renovating an older home poses one of the greatest threats of lead poisoning. Many severe cases of lead poisoning have resulted when upper- or middle-income families have renovated older homes.[8]

Lead in drinking water also affects households of all income levels. The concentration of lead in drinking water is a function of the characteristics of the water and the presence of lead in the pipes, solder (joining the pipes together), and plumbing fixtures in the home as well as in the pipes bringing the water into the home. Likewise, sources of lead poisoning such as ceramics and crystal can present dangers to any family that is not aware of the threat.

The myth that only poor inner-city minority children can be lead poisoned has resulted in the delayed diagnosis of numerous cases of lead poisoning.

Rebecca Rex moved into her dream house when she was 2 months pregnant, and threw herself into fixing up the 75-year-old suburban home. She was aware of the dangers of lead paint and even knew that she might be especially susceptible because of her pregnancy. She took all of the precautions she was able to find out about to protect her unborn child. She religiously used a painter's mask and gloves when she sanded and scraped the paint from the walls. Unfortunately, she was not aware that a paper mask provides no protection from the fine particles of lead produced when a lead-painted surface is disrupted, and that gloves do no good at all, as lead gets into the body through the mouth and nose (by ingestion and inhalation) and not through the skin.

Rebecca's baby always cried, and never slept longer than an hour and a half at a time. She alternated between having diarrhea and being constipated for days at a time. One day Rebecca happened to pick up a brochure at Toys R Us entitled "Safety Tips." It listed a number of symptoms of lead poisoning—every one of them described her child. She immediately asked her pediatrician to screen the baby for lead poisoning.

But she had to endure eight more months of this before the test was finally done. "Lead poisoning doesn't happen to people like you," she was told by her physician, who refused to perform the lead test for her child. The suburban Texas pediatrician believed that lead poisoning afflicts only poor minority children in inner cities. Once the problem was acknowledged and treated as lead poisoning, she saw improvement within weeks.[9]

THE HEALTH EFFECTS OF LEAD POISONING

Lead travels through the blood to virtually every organ in the body. The parts most noticeably affected are the central nervous system (including the brain), the kidneys, and the blood-producing organs. Lead also affects the digestive and reproductive systems.

Although large amounts of lead can affect anyone, three groups are the most vulnerable to lead poisoning: young children, pregnant women, and certain workers.

Young Children Are Especially Vulnerable to Lead Poisoning

Why Young Children Are Vulnerable

Young children are more vulnerable to lead poisoning because they come into closer contact with sources of lead in the environment. Children spend a lot of time on the floor or ground, thus exposing themselves to lead in dust and soil. They ingest lead-contaminated dirt or dust when they touch their hands to dust on the floor or other hard surfaces, or dirt in an outside play area. They might also mouth toys that are dusty or dirty, or pet a dog or cat that has been in contact with contaminated dust or dirt. Very young children may ingest lead when they explore their environment and relieve teething discomfort by mouthing lead-painted objects and surfaces.

In addition to the fact that they tend to take in more lead than adults, a larger percentage of the lead that enters a child's body is actually retained (absorbed). Fifty percent of the lead ingested by an infant is absorbed, compared to only 5 to 15% of that ingested by an adult.[10]

Specific Health Effects in Children

Lead can have a number of adverse health effects, depending on the amount of lead the child has absorbed.

The most alarming danger of lead is the damage it can do to a child's developing brain and nervous system. Even amounts of lead that were considered harmless a few years ago have been shown in scientific studies to cause learning disabilities and behavioral problems.[11] A number of studies have found that for each 10 micrograms per deciliter over the threshold of 10 or 15 micrograms per deciliter of lead in a child's blood, IQ is lowered about one to three points.[12]

Lead is a very potent poison. It affects the brain because it interferes with essential aspects of the development of the architecture of the brain as well as with the biochemical connections between cells of the brain.

Only the most severe and long-term exposure to lead, in the cases of certain individuals who are more vulnerable for any of a number of reasons, actually causes enough damage to result in mental retardation.[13] However, low and moderate levels of exposure, or brief exposure at higher levels, could exacerbate a preexisting developmental delay, or limit the rate of improvement of such a condition.[14]

In a recent study, which followed children with mildly elevated levels of dentin (tooth) lead in early childhood, adolescents were found to fail at school seven times as often as those with lower lead levels, and to be six times more likely to have reading disabilities.[15] Moderately

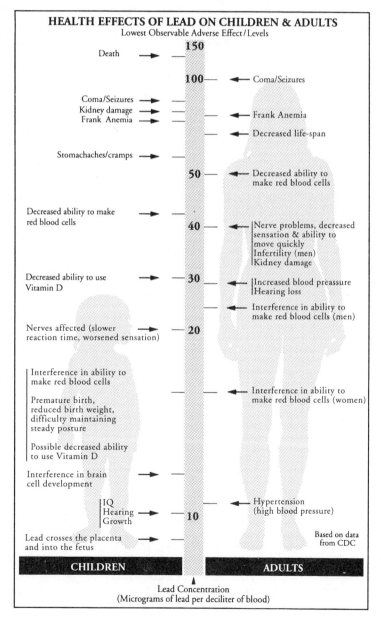

HEALTH EFFECTS OF LEAD ON CHILDREN & ADULTS
Lowest Observable Adverse Effect/Levels

- Death → 150
- 100 ← Coma/Seizures
- Coma/Seizures →
- Kidney damage →
- Frank Anemia → ← Frank Anemia
- ← Decreased life-span
- Stomachaches/cramps →
- 50 ← Decreased ability to make red blood cells
- Decreased ability to make red blood cells →
- 40 ← Nerve problems, decreased sensation & ability to move quickly / Infertility (men) / Kidney damage
- Decreased ability to use Vitamin D → 30 ← Increased blood preassure / Hearing loss
- ← Interference in ability to make red blood cells (men)
- Nerves affected (slower reaction time, worsened sensation) → 20
- Interference in ability to make red blood cells
- Premature birth, reduced birth weight, difficulty maintaining steady posture
- ← Interference in ability to make red blood cells (women)
- Possible decreased ability to use Vitamin D
- Interference in brain cell development →
- IQ / Hearing → / Growth — 10 ← Hypertension (high blood pressure)
- Lead crosses the placenta and into the fetus →

Based on data from CDC

CHILDREN | **ADULTS**

Lead Concentration
(Micrograms of lead per deciliter of blood)

elevated blood lead levels affect the way nerves communicate in a young child. As a result, lead exposure can cause minor impairments in hearing, balance, attention, and learning new material in a young child.[16] Because of these physiological effects, schoolchildren exposed to lead when they were younger may exhibit disruptive behavior in the classroom, daydream, have difficulty staying seated, and be fidgety.[17]

Lead poisoning has been associated in scientific studies with various types of problematic behavior. Specific behaviors that have been associated with moderately elevated blood lead levels include sleep problems, depression, hyperactivity, and aggression. THESE NEUROLOGICAL EFFECTS CAN RESULT EVEN WHEN THERE ARE NO DETECTABLE SYMPTOMS OF LEAD POISONING. There is concern that because of these effects lead poisoning might contribute to delinquent behavior.[18] The mechanism for this effect is not fully understood, but clinicians suspect that the lead may negatively impact parts of the brain so as to contribute to increased impulsivity and decreased self-control. These characteristics, combined with social factors, can result in poor judgment and coping skills which may be associated with juvenile delinquency. Although lead has been shown to directly trigger aggressive behavior in laboratory animals, this effect has not been established in humans.[19]

At blood lead levels of 15–20 micrograms per deciliter lead interferes with the production of vitamin D, as well as of heme, a component of hemoglobin, the part of the blood that transports oxygen throughout the body, including to the brain.[20] At levels over 20–30 micrograms per deciliter, studies have shown that nerve conduction can be slowed.[21] These moderately elevated levels can also prevent children from growing properly and attaining what would be their normal height.[22]

At higher levels, additional physiological symptoms can occur. At over 50 micrograms per deciliter a child can suffer from colic. Possible kidney damage should be evaluated when a child has such an elevated blood lead level. Although mild anemia is observed at lower blood lead levels, it can be more serious at over 70 micrograms per deciliter, and is aggravated by medical treatment (chelation therapy).[23]

Thanks to broad screening and increased awareness of lead poisoning and its causes, in only a small fraction of a percent of cases of lead poisoning—those with extremely high levels of lead (over 80–150 micrograms per deciliter)—does a child go into convulsions or a coma.[24] Although this condition of lead encephalopathy, untreated, usually leads to death, since the 1950s medical treatment with chelation therapy has reduced the mortality rate to 1–2% in even these extremely rare cases.[25]

Unborn Children Are Also Particularly Vulnerable

Pregnant Women Need to Be Protected from Exposure to Lead

The lead toxin passes through the placenta to the fetus where it can have far-reaching effects on brain development. Therefore, pregnant women need to be protected from exposure to lead in order to protect unborn children from harm.

The fetus can be harmed not only by lead that the mother is exposed to during pregnancy but also from lead that is stored in her bones from exposure earlier in her life. During pregnancy, the body has an increased need for calcium. The needed calcium is often released from the bones, especially when the mother's diet does not provide an adequate amount. Because lead closely resembles calcium chemically, it can mistakenly be released into the blood along with the calcium and passed in this manner to the fetus.[26]

This transfer has been shown to begin when a woman is around 12–14 weeks pregnant, and to peak in the third trimester, when more calcium is needed for building the bones of the fetus.[27] Blood lead levels that might result in no symptoms in the pregnant mother could cause severe damage to the unborn child. It is not surprising that the fragile and very quickly developing fetus is more susceptible than either adults or children to very small amounts of lead.

Specific Health Effects

According to a 1988 federal government survey, 400,000 babies were born with high blood levels each year in the early 1980s.[28] Lead poisoning in unborn children can cause premature birth, low birth weight, and birth anomalies including neurological damage, as well as miscarriage and still births.[29] Research has shown that women who were lead poisoned as children, thus having an increased chance of stored lead being passed to the fetus during pregnancy, also have an increased risk of having children with learning disabilities.[30]

There is also scientific evidence that lead poisoning of the father before procreation may result in abnormalities in the sperm.[31] Lead can suppress the circulation of testosterone. This disrupts the stimulation of the testes, which in turn alters the functioning of the sperm and interferes with its ability to penetrate and fertilize the egg.[32]

Certain Workers Are Vulnerable to Lead Poisoning

Workers who are exposed occupationally to large amounts of lead suffer disproportionately from lead poisoning.

Contractors who are licensed to remove lead paint are trained about the proper precautions to protect themselves from lead on the job. However, if they fail to use the respirators and protective clothing properly, then they might be exposed to dangerous levels of lead on a daily basis.

In other occupations, the enforcement of federal safety standards is left to the employer. In cases where there are under ten employees, these guidelines are not enforced routinely. Even in cases where the recommended safety measures are complied with, it is not clear whether the level of exposure permitted is actually safe. Workers who may be exposed to dangerous levels of lead include: construction workers, painters, carpet layers, and workers in battery recovery, plastic, smelting, insecticide, and electronic component plants.

These workers may bring lead dust back home where children and other family members are often exposed.

For a brief discussion of dust from occupational exposure as a source of lead in the home environment, see Chapter 2.

This book deals with lead poisoning that is not related to occupational exposure.

For information on lead poisoning from occupational exposure, see the resources listed in

Appendix B under Occupational Safety. *For a more complete list of occupations that present a danger of lead poisoning, see Appendix C.*

Other Adults Can Also Be Affected

Although the above three groups are the most common victims of lead poisoning, other adults can also suffer adverse effects from lead poisoning. Women are particularly vulnerable during pregnancy, lactation, and old age. At these times, lead tends to be released along with calcium into the blood from storage in the bones.

Lead poisoning can cause high blood pressure, especially in men.[33] Other symptoms of lead poisoning in adults are kidney malfunction, infertility, loss of hand coordination and strength, peripheral nerve damage, and hearing problems.[34] Lead can also interfere with the formation of red blood cells, causing anemia.[35] The more research that is done, the more we discover that ever lower levels of lead cause medical problems.

CHAPTER TWO

The Sources of Lead Poisoning

LEAD IN THE ENVIRONMENT

Lead poisoning is referred to as an environmental disease because it is caused by exposure to lead in our daily surroundings. Although we cannot see, taste, or smell it, lead is everywhere in our environment. It is not just in the obvious places, such as the emissions from a lead smelter or the peeling paint in an old house, but also in our air, water, soil, and dust.

Even if we were to eliminate all uses of lead, most of the hundreds of millions of tons of lead already present in our air, soil, plumbing, and homes would remain there.[1] Lead is PERSISTENT in the environment. Because lead is an element, once it is mined from the ground, it does not degrade as do organic materials, but rather remains in the environment forever, whether it is in use or disposed of in some way. Our soil is full of it. Our walls are painted with it. Our plumbing is made or joined with it. And our industries still use tons of it every day.

We are still haunted by the ghosts of our past uses of lead. In spite of the phasing out of leaded gasoline and prohibitions and controls on lead-based paint and other uses of lead, overall lead consumption was down only 2% from 1970 to 1989 and figures for the early 1990s show consumption actually increasing slightly from that date.[2] Although lead-based paint has been banned from use in housing units, more than 64 million homes in this country still bear the lead paint they were painted with before 1978.[3]

Because we cannot get rid of the huge quantity of lead in our environment, we need to be alert to its hazards so that we can protect ourselves and, especially, our children.

SUMMARY OF SPECIFIC SOURCES

Lead is found everywhere in our environment. The following is a summary of the most common sources of lead poisoning. Those that are the most important are discussed further in later chapters.

Lead-Based Paint Is the Largest Source of Lead Poisoning

Lead in Household Paint

Lead-based paint accounts for the overwhelming majority of lead poisoning cases nationally. Three million tons of old lead-based paint line the walls and fixtures of about half of all homes in this country.

Normal wear and tear, friction from opening and closing windows, and sometimes flaking and peeling of old paint, produce dust over the years, which is ingested unknowingly by small children. Eating paint chips and gnawing on windowsills can produce very severe cases of lead poisoning.

Renovating old houses can result in very dangerous lead exposure, particularly in do-it-yourself operations. Whenever you disrupt paint—that is, whenever you sand, scrape, or strip a surface that has been painted with lead-based paint or perform any demolition or removal of windows or other building parts attached to a lead-painted wall, even if it is covered with other paint or wallpaper—you could be putting lead dust into your living space where it can be ingested by children if you do not take the proper precautions.

The same dangers presented by lead in paint and dust in the home might threaten our children in other settings as well. To ensure that your children are not exposed to dangerous levels of lead in paint and dust, you should be aware of any hazards present in their school or day care as well as at friends' and relatives' homes where they spend a lot of time.

Paint used for commercial and industrial buildings, automobiles, boats, and other exterior uses still contains lead.

Toys, Furniture, and Other Items with Lead-Based Paint

Toys and furniture sold before 1976 may have been painted with lead-based paint. Stripping old furniture can create very high levels of lead dust. Imported toys are still occasionally identified and recalled by the U. S. Consumer Product Safety Commission (CPSC) because they contain dangerous levels of lead paint. Playground equipment may be painted with lead-based paint. Such equipment in a number of city parks around the United States has been recently found to present a hazard to young children.[4] *For information on product safety and recalls, contact the CPSC, listed in Appendix B under* Product Safety.

Imported articles that are intended for decorative use rather than as toys may contain lead paint. Christmas tree ornaments or other types of miniatures or knickknacks may expose small children to lead if they are chewed on or mouthed. *For a more detailed discussion about lead in paint and dust, see Chapter 10. For a discussion of how to identify and control lead paint hazards, see Chapters 11 to 13.*

House Dust Can Be Contaminated with Lead

When lead-based paint deteriorates or is worn away via normal wear and tear, fine lead dust is generated. This dust settles on the floor and hard surfaces where young children come into contact with it during the course of normal play and hand-to-mouth contact. Lead dust can also be produced by lead-bearing soil being tracked into the home.

Parents Can Bring Lead Dust Home from Work

Workers in many types of factories, smelters, and construction trades are exposed to high doses of lead daily. They bring lead dust into the home on their clothing, skin, hair, and shoes, thus exposing their children to lead. If contaminated clothing is not laundered separately, it can contaminate the rest of the family's clothing. *For a list of occupations that present a risk of lead exposure, see Appendix C.*

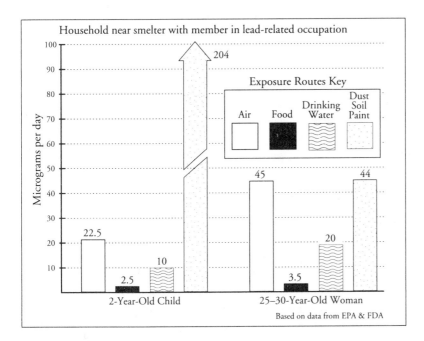

Lead May Contaminate Our Drinking Water

Plumbing Systems

Water can eat away at and release lead from plumbing systems. The characteristics of the water, such as its pH and hardness, affect how corrosive it is, and therefore how much of the lead it carries away. Lead pipes have not been used for decades, but many homes are still connected to municipal services containing old lead pipes. Although lead solder has been outlawed for use in residential plumbing systems since 1986, it nonetheless joins together the copper pipes in many homes. Brass faucets can still contain up to 8% lead. These lead sources can be present in our water distribution systems or in our homes themselves.

Pumps, Fountains, Kettles

Submersible water pumps with lead parts can contaminate drinking water from private wells. Old kettles used for boiling water, or samovars (used for making tea by some Middle Eastern and Russian immigrants), can put lead into water. Drinking fountains can contain lead liners or lead solder joining seams together, contaminating the water that schoolchildren drink.

Water Supplies

Water supplies can be contaminated with lead from industrial emissions and runoff from landfills where batteries or computer monitors have been dumped. *For a more detailed discussion of lead in drinking water and how to protect your family from it, see Chapter 16.*

Lead Is in Our Soil

Although we no longer use leaded gasoline, our soil has been contaminated from decades of exposure to emissions from cars and trucks burning leaded fuel. Lead is also added to the soil from paint that falls or is scraped from houses and other structures and equipment painted with lead-based paint. In some cases, industrial emissions and pesticides are also present. The net result is large quantities of lead in our soil. *For a more detailed discussion of lead in soil and how to protect your family from it, see Chapter 14.*

Lead May Get into Our Food

Vegetables grown in soil contaminated with lead are likely to contain lead. In recent years, this problem has been greatly alleviated because of increased awareness and the phaseout of leaded gasoline. However, lead still occasionally enters our food from cans containing lead solder at the seams or from storage or service in improperly glazed ceramics. Old, homemade, or imported ceramic cups and mugs used for juice or hot drinks are still a threat. Wine may be contaminated from the foil wrap on the bottle. Wine and other alcoholic or acidic beverages can also absorb lead from storage in leaded crystal. Some calcium supplements and traditional Chinese, Hispanic, and other ethnic remedies and cosmetics continue to poison children with lead. *For a more detailed discussion of lead in food and how to protect your family from it, see Chapter 15.*

Lead Is in Our Air

Millions of tons of lead have been emitted into the earth's atmosphere every year. In 1980, for example, the total was 5.7 million tons. A half million tons was from natural sources, such as dusts, volcanic eruptions, and vegetation. The vast majority, about 4.7 million tons, was from human activities.[5] In this country, over 7 gigagrams are emitted annually. This is a huge improvement over the situation 20 years ago, when over 200 gigagrams were emitted each year.[6] Unfortunately, however, the lead that has been emitted over the decades is still present in our environment, and much of it remains as a health threat in the soil.

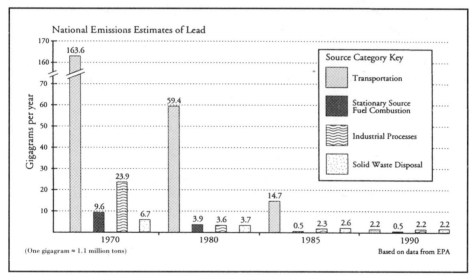

National Emissions Estimates of Lead

Source Category Key

Transportation

Stationary Source Fuel Combustion

Industrial Processes

Solid Waste Disposal

(One gigagram ≈ 1.1 million tons)   Based on data from EPA

Industry

Heavy metal production contributes a great deal of lead to the atmosphere. Lead smelters (where lead metal is retrieved either from the lead ore that is mined from the earth or from recycling lead-acid batteries or scrap metal) are among the worst of the industrial polluters in this country. Although there have been federal limitations on how much lead a lead smelter can emit into the air, most smelters in the United States have not complied with those limits.[7] And the limits themselves have been found by the EPA to be inadequate. An unregulated smelting furnace can typically emit between 28 and 77 tons of lead into the air yearly. Using technologies that are now available, this amount can be cut to less than 1 ton a year.[8] New

regulations on emissions from secondary lead smelters could reduce emissions by lead smelters by 75%.[9]

Gasoline

Over the past several decades, leaded gasoline has been the greatest source of lead in our air. Four to five million tons of leaded gasoline were burned before 1986 in the United States.[10]

Leaded gasoline remains a serious hazard for those living or spending time in other countries, as well as for those Americans living on the Mexican border.

Waste Disposal

The unregulated transportation, handling, and incineration of wastes containing lead and lead-contaminated materials results in the dispersal of lead dust into the air.

Bridges and Other Large-Scale Exterior Paint Removal

The uncontained sandblasting of bridges or any exterior structure bearing lead-based paint can temporarily add hazardous amounts of lead to the air in the immediate vicinity and in communities just downwind from the work site.

Some Hobbies Involve Contact with Lead

Toxic levels of lead exposure can occur while doing some types of arts and crafts activities, such as stained glass or jewelry making, enamel work, pottery glazing, antique ceramic doll painting, metal sculpture soldering, antique furniture refinishing, or fishing weight or ammunition making.[11] Lead that is used in arts and crafts supplies must be appropriately marked. Always check labels for any precautions regarding working with materials containing lead.

There Are a Number of Other Possible Sources of Lead in Our Environment

Children's Art Supplies

In 1994, the U. S. Consumer Product Safety Commission recalled several brands of crayons made in China because they were found to contain lead.[12] When buying crayons, paint sets, chalk and modeling clay, or any art supplies, look for a statement on the label that they conform with ASTM D-4236, a voluntary industry safety standard.

Toys

Miniature solid lead figures sold as toys present a hazard when handled by small children. Toy soldiers and small figures for use with model railroad sets are examples.

Ammunition

Very high levels of lead are present in the air at pistol ranges. This results both from the lead bullets themselves and from materials used to propel the bullets.[13] Lead shot used for duck and game hunting can result in contamination of aquatic ecosystems and the food they produce.

Fishing Sinkers/Curtain and Carpet Weights

Lead fishing weights, as well as lead curtain or carpet weights or any other lead objects, are a source of lead exposure to persons who handle them. Lead may enter the body when hands come into contact with the mouth or food after handling any lead object. Lead can also be ingested when the teeth are used as pliers to attach fishing sinkers to the fishing line.

Very small fishing weights may no longer be made of lead because they can be ingested by waterfowl and contaminate soil where aquatic plants grow. Once entering the food chain, they further contaminate birds of prey and aquatic life feeding on these animals and plants.[14]

Ceramic Doorknobs and Bathtubs

Cases of lead poisoning have been attributed to lead leaching into bathwater from old ceramic bathtubs.[15] Other ceramic objects, such as doorknobs, may also contain lead.

Plastics

Many plastics contain lead, which can be ingested if chewed. Lead is added to plastic both as a pigment and as a stabilizer, to protect the plastic from deterioration in sunlight. It tends to be used in products designed for outdoor environments.

Miniblinds

In June 1996, the U. S. Consumer Product Safety Commission reported that nonglossy vinyl miniblinds from China, Taiwan, Indonesia, and Mexico contain lead. The lead, which is added to stabilize the plastic, deteriorates from exposure to sunlight, leaving lead dust on the surface of the blinds, which can be ingested by young children who touch the blinds. Ingesting the dust from just one square inch of the blinds each day, a child could become lead poisoned in just a couple of weeks to a month.

Miniblind manufacturers agreed to change the way the blinds are manufactured. Miniblinds that have been purchased since July 1996 should be safe. Check that they bear labels like "new formulation," "nonleaded formula," "no lead added," or "new! nonleaded vinyl formulation."[16]

Sources from Other Countries

Industrial pollution is not as well regulated in some other countries. As a result, a young child who spends his or her first months or years in an Asian or Latin American country may already be poisoned from lead sources such as proximity to a smelter, or the mother's occupational exposure to lead. Adopted children from these countries have been found in some cases to have high lead levels when they come to this country.[17]

Miscellaneous Sources

The above list is by no means exhaustive. Lead often shows up in surprising places. Decals on T-shirts and designs on drinking glasses have been found to contain lead. Sailboat keels and votive candlewicks are made of lead. Isolated cases of lead poisoning have been attributed to such varied sources as pool cue chalk, an old fishing buoy floating in a child's wading pool, chewing on electrical wire insulation, and moonshine made in an old lead-soldered radiator.[18]

Inside Environmental Sources of Lead Poisoning

Outside Environmental Sources of Lead Poisoning

Pesticides used
in orchards and crops

Industrial
emissions

Flaking
lead paint

Ammunition &
fishing weights

Pet becomes carrier
of contaminated soil

Lead paint
removal

Vegetables grown in
contaminated soil

Leaded gasoline exhaust

THE CUMULATIVE EFFECT OF LEAD

Lead is persistent and cumulative. It does not degrade. Once lead is absorbed into a person's body, it remains there and accumulates. Therefore even small exposures can pose a risk. When bone has already stored lead from previous exposures, lead from new exposures will be more likely to remain in the blood and travel to other tissues, such as the brain, where damage is done.

Even if a child is never exposed to a single large dose of lead, all of the tiny amounts a child is exposed to can add up to trouble. For instance, the average child living in a town near a smelter may have a blood-lead level of 8 micrograms per deciliter from exposure to emissions. A relatively small exposure to lead paint, therefore, will bring his or her blood lead level over the threshold of concern of 10 micrograms per deciliter. Likewise, a child who drinks lead-contaminated water will be much more likely to suffer toxic effects if exposed later to lead-contaminated soil or dust.

PART TWO

Preventing Lead Poisoning

Childhood lead poisoning is entirely preventable.
U. S. Department of Health and Human Services, Centers for Disease Control
and Prevention

CHAPTER THREE

Basic Prevention

Lead poisoning is entirely preventable. It stands apart from other diseases in that its causes are not only understood but also totally within our control.

As a society, we can protect all of our children from being lead poisoned by adopting policies to eliminate lead from our environment. Dramatic steps have already been taken by prohibiting the use of lead-based paint and lead solder (for joining pipes) for residential use and phasing out leaded gasoline. However, until we create an effective system and commit the necessary resources to remove the lead that still covers the walls and woodwork in our homes, the threat of lead poisoning remains. *For a discussion of public policy addressing lead poisoning, see Chapter 19.*

CONTROLLING LEAD HAZARDS

As a parent, the best way to minimize the risk of lead poisoning to your child is to eliminate sources of lead from your child's living environment. *For a discussion of controlling lead paint and dust hazards, see Chapters 10 through 13.*

Although paint and dust are the most common sources of lead poisoning, there are a number of other sources contributing to the disease. Lead poisoning can be caused by several sources acting in combination, or occasionally by just one less common source, such as water in baby formula, a ceramic mug, or a traditional remedy. *For a discussion of simple preventive measures to reduce exposure to lead from soil, food, and water, see Chapters 14 to 16. For a summary of steps you can take to protect your child, see Appendix I.*

TEMPORARY MEASURES TO REDUCE THE RISK

Until you are able to take these more definitive steps, however, there are a number of simple preventive measures that are generally recommended as good practices to provide your family the best possible care.

Reducing the Amount of Lead Dust in the Home

Wash or Wet Mop Hard Surfaces in Your Home

Dirt tracked inside and dust from wear and tear on painted woodwork are ready sources of lead poisoning for your children. Sweeping and dusting can send hazardous lead dust into the air to be breathed by your family or simply settle again on hard surfaces where it can be picked up by children's hands and toys.

Washing and wet mopping are much more effective in removing lead dust. Horizontal surfaces are especially important because they tend to collect dust. Wet mop uncarpeted floor surfaces, including porches and decks. Wash other hard surfaces that might collect dust, such as windowsills and baseboards. There are a few products made especially for removing lead dust that seem to be especially effective, but these are too expensive to be practical for regular use by most people. Washing or wet mopping with any household detergent is very effective in removing lead dust. Even washing with water alone is much better than dusting or sweeping. Rags, mops, and sponges used for this purpose may be contaminated with lead, and should not be used for cleaning dishes or eating surfaces. Regularly waxing floors will also help keep the dust down.

Using two buckets will prevent spreading around the lead that you mop up. One bucket should be used for water for cleaning and one for the water for rinsing. Some lead poisoning prevention advocates recommend using three buckets, one for washing, one for rinsing, and one for squeezing the mop out. That way you aren't putting the lead from the mop back into the water you are using to clean with. Squeeze the mop out in a wringer that sits over the bucket rather than submersing it in the rinse water each time, so that you don't get lead from the water back onto the mop. Other advocates suggest simplifying the process by using a spray bottle with the detergent solution and then rinsing with water from a bucket.

The standard recommendation of most public agencies has been to wash hard surfaces with a solution of TSP (trisodium phosphate), sold at hardware stores, or a phosphate-containing automatic dishwashing detergent. Phosphate was believed to be effective for dissolving lead dust.

Doubts have been raised recently, however, regarding whether high phosphate products are any more effective than normal detergents. Recent scientific studies suggest that the phosphate content of a cleaning product does NOT significantly affect its effectiveness in removing lead.[1]

In addition to TSP not being significantly more effective in cleaning up lead dust, there are a number of other reasons why its use is not advisable. It is very caustic relative to other cleaning products which have also been found to be effective.[2] TSP is prohibited in some areas because it is harmful to the environment. It can also damage the finish on woodwork or furniture. Your eyes and the skin on your hands can be hurt if you don't take the right precautions.

If you do use TSP, you should protect your hands with plastic gloves and your eyes with protective eyeglasses. TSP dumped down the drain may pollute water and damage aquatic ecosystems. Particularly if you live near a lake and have a septic system, it would be safer to dispose of the wash water in your flower garden or lawn than down the drain. It will not damage plants. Businesses licensed to use sewer systems might actually be prohibited by the terms of their licenses from disposing TSP down the drain.

Vacuum with a High-Efficiency Particulate Air (HEPA) Vacuum Cleaner

Sweeping spreads dust around. Even vacuuming puts fine dust back into the air. In a regular vacuum cleaner, the filter allows small dust particles to pass through it. The best solution is to use a HEPA-vac, a special type of vacuum cleaner equipped with a HEPA filter. This type of vacuum cleaner is very effective at removing lead dust particles, which are very, very small, because it has an exhaust that does not allow fine particles to escape. An "ultra low particulate air" (ULPA) vacuum has the same effect.

If you do not have access to a HEPA-vac (or ULPA), a wet vacuuming system or a cleaner that uses water in the filtering process is better than a regular vacuum cleaner, as it creates far less dust. *For information on specific HEPA vacuum cleaners, see Appendix G.*

If you do use a regular vacuum cleaner, have another member of the household do the vacuuming when you are pregnant. Children (and pregnant women) will inhale less dust if vacuuming is done when they are not home and the windows are left open. It is recommended that you allow the dust to settle at least an hour before children (or pregnant women) come back in the room.

Keep Your Rugs and Carpets Clean

Carpets provide surface area for collecting toxic lead dust. Small rugs should be washed regularly. Larger carpets can be sent out to be cleaned. They should be taken up when the house is empty. As an alternative, carpets should be cleaned with a shampooer that vacuums up the dirty water. Ordinary vacuuming puts fine lead dust right back into the air. Even using a HEPA-vac usually fails to remove all of the lead dust. Finally, plastic carpet runners may help to keep dust away from children.

Removing carpeting, especially if it is old and worn, should be considered as an option. Using washable area rugs is a healthier choice than wall to wall carpeting in a number of respects. In addition to being problematic for the control of lead dust, rugs collect dust mites, mold, and mildew, which cause allergic reactions in a large portion of the population. Synthetic carpets also can pose a risk of serious respiratory and neurological effects.

Remove Your Shoes in the House, or Wipe Them before Entering

You can reduce the amount of lead-contaminated soil that gets into the house by either having household members and guests remove their shoes when they enter the house, or keeping a heavy-duty mat by the door for them to wipe their shoes on when they come inside.

Replace Your Heating and Air Conditioning Filters

Forced air heating and air conditioning systems can collect a lot of dust. If you have forced hot air or central air conditioning, change the filters regularly to avoid contaminated dust being put back into your living environment.

Keep Any Dust from Lead-Related Work or Hobbies out of the House

If you (or any member of your household) have a job where you come into contact with lead, wash well and change your work clothes before, or on, arriving home. If you handle fishing weights or work with arts and crafts materials containing lead, be sure not only to keep those materials away from your children's living quarters but also to protect your children from any lead dust on you by washing well and changing clothes before entering the family's living space. Clothing contaminated with lead dust should be laundered separately from the rest of the family's clothing.

Keep All Objects that Your Child Puts in His or Her Mouth Clean

Toys and stuffed animals also collect dust, which can be transferred to your child when he or she plays with them. Keep children's toys away from under the window, as a good deal of lead dust often comes from windows. Clean them often to cut down on the accumulation of lead dust that your child is exposed to. Wash stuffed animals in the washing machine and hang them out to dry.

Wash pacifiers and bottles if they fall on the floor or ground. The dust they pick up from the floor may contain lead. Snap-on holders on the baby's clothing prevent pacifiers from falling on the floor and getting dirty.

Handling Hot Spots

If you have areas of peeling or flaking paint, any way of keeping your children away from the hazard is worth taking. There are a number of simple, inexpensive, temporary measures that can keep a young child from chewing on or touching a lead-painted surface that is peeling.

☐ Move a piece of furniture in front of a peeling spot on the wall.
☐ Cover a peeling spot with duct or masking tape, or contact paper.
☐ Remove a small area of peeling, flaking paint with tape using the following method:

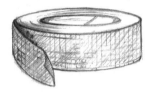

- Lay down a sheet of plastic or paper beneath the spot to catch any small chips that might fall.
- Press a piece of wide sticky tape onto the spot and carefully remove the tape along with the scraps of paint that stick to it.
- Fold up and carefully dispose of the tape and the material used to cover the floor and catch the scraps.

NOTE: Do not scrape peeling, flaking paint without taking the proper precautions. Removing lead paint without appropriate containment of lead dust and worker protections can do more harm than good. *See Chapters 12 and 13 for a discussion of methods to remove paint and precautions to take.*

Keeping the Lead out of the Child's Mouth

Make Sure Your Children's Hands Are Washed Often

Much of the lead that children end up ingesting is transferred when they touch their hands to their mouths or food after touching dirt or dust contaminated with lead. Thus, one of the most effective ways to keep children from ingesting lead is to keep their hands clean. Wash your children's hands (or teach them to wash their hands) before meals or sleeping so that the dirt and dust they may have gotten on them does not get into their mouths. This is especially important when they come inside from playing outside. Particularly in spots near roads, or near older painted buildings, dirt can have a high concentration of lead from years of automobile exhaust and peeling house paint.

Maurci Jackson, Director of United Parents Against Lead (UPAL), taught her children nursery rhyme-style verses to help them to remember the basic safety rules for preventing lead poisoning. She found her daughters reminding each other to wash their hands using this verse she wrote for them:

> *Wash your hands before you eat*
> *Wash your hands before you sleep*
> *Wash your hands after outdoor play*
> *Wash your hands throughout the day.*[3]

Likewise, keeping their fingernails short and clean will cut down the lead-contaminated dust and dirt that could be transferred to children's food or directly into their mouths. Washing children's faces before eating and sleeping, especially the area around the mouth, can also reduce the total amount of lead dust from their environment that ends up in their mouths.

Provide Safe Objects for Your Child to Teethe On

Keep an eye on small children and teach them not to chew on windowsills or other surfaces that might be painted with lead-based paint, such as crib or chair rails. Distract them with a safe unpainted or plastic object to teethe on instead. If they continue to use painted surfaces for teething, cover these surfaces with cloth or remove them from their reach. Put corner guards on door frames and other chewable edges to avoid this problem.

NUTRITION

A healthy diet goes a long way in reducing the damage from exposure to lead sources by keeping lead from being absorbed by the body. *For a discussion of specific nutritional measures, see Chapter 6.*

CHAPTER FOUR

Diagnosing Lead Poisoning

The symptoms of lead poisoning are difficult to identify: there may be neurological damage without any noticeable symptoms. The only way to know whether your child is lead poisoned is via a blood lead level screening. Because a child is at greatest risk of lead poisoning between the ages of 12 and 36 months, this is the most critical time to screen your child for lead.

SYMPTOMS

Even though lead poisoning can cause serious harm, it often goes undetected because there are no obvious symptoms. Lead poisoning is sometimes called the silent disease. Even fairly severe cases show symptoms that are difficult to identify because they are the same for many other diseases—irritability, stomach pains, dizziness, constipation, vomiting, muscle weakness, and lack of appetite.[1]

Lead poisoning has no FINGERPRINT, or BEHAVIORAL SIGNATURE. That is to say there is no specific set of symptoms that identify a child as lead poisoned, as there would be for, say, attention deficit hyperactive disorder (ADHD). Neuropsychological symptoms vary from individual to individual. The change in intelligence seems fairly consistent throughout a number of studies, but this is probably because IQ testing integrates the assessment of skills

Kim and her family moved into a Little Italy-type neighborhood in Cleveland where a friend offered them a good deal on an apartment in an old duplex. It appeared to be in good condition. Only the window wells and threshold drew their attention as in need of repair on the initial walk-through of the apartment. They asked the landlord to repair the wells, but he did not, feeling that his tenant was just as able to take care of it, so the matter slid. In the meantime, the house next door (about a dozen feet away) had exterior paint falling off it and onto the driveway area (composed of brick and soil).

Within a couple of months, their 2-year-old's behavior changed dramatically. Previously cuddly and good-natured, Joel now had mood swings like an alcoholic, was violent, stopped napping, was irritable, and woke in the middle of the night. The pediatrician told Kim to discipline the child more consistently, and characterized the problem simply by commenting, "He's a boy, he's two—two strikes against you." He gave her information on discipline and referred her to a psychologist to work on parenting skills.

Three months later, she brought the child back, reporting "no improvement." At that point, the doctor evaluated the child for ADHD and tested for lead. Although regular lead screening was required by law for Medicaid children in Ohio, this had not previously been done for either Joel or Kim's older child when they had been on Medicaid until the year before. When she got the results—48 micrograms per deciliter, a highly elevated blood lead level—Kim cried for hours and hours. She found a two-page entry on lead poisoning in a medical encyclopedia and every symptom corresponded to their child. Why hadn't she been informed about lead poisoning sooner?[6]

from across the domains. More specific neuro-psychological tests examine a more focused area of mental functioning, and do not turn out to be so consistent among different lead-poisoned children.[2]

Practitioners at Children's Hospital in Boston have found an association between the age when the child is exposed to lead and the neurological effect. If the lead exposure occurs under age 2 when language is rapidly developing, linguistic skills will be affected. If lead exposure occurs at ages 4 to 6, when higher-level skills are developing, then such abilities as impulse control and complex problem solving seem to be affected. Of course in real cases of lead poisoning, exposure times are not always known and don't necessarily fit into neat categories but could include 2 or 3 different levels of damage.[3]

Neurological damage is especially difficult to observe, especially for a younger child. Some types of damage might not be observable until the child is called on to perform organizational tasks and produce academic output, which might not be until as late as third grade.[4]

Because of the broad range of normal behaviors in early childhood, it can be difficult to associate specific behaviors with lead poisoning. If there is a history of lead poisoning, extra vigilance is required to detect possible neurological damage indicated by what might be mistaken as "terrible twos," for example.[5]

THE ONLY WAY TO KNOW IF A CHILD HAS AN UNSAFE BLOOD LEAD LEVEL IS TO HAVE HIM OR HER SCREENED.

SCREENING

Lead screening is a very simple and quick precaution that indicates the amount of lead a person has absorbed from the environment, by measuring the level of lead in the blood. Screening can be invaluable in alerting you to the importance of taking measures to avoid additional exposure, and in some cases, to pursue critical treatment.

Lead screening is done by testing a person's blood, measuring the concentration of lead

Over the winter, Elena was often constipated. She experienced unexplained vomiting several times. Her mother, Melissa, assumed it was attributable to a flu that had been around that season, or to something she ate. The 2-year-old went from sleeping 12 hours a night straight through to waking up four or five times a night. At first this happened only occasionally, but by the end of the year it happened every night.

The doctor said it was "just a phase she is going through." Melissa and her husband were getting divorced, so Melissa attributed the child's symptoms to the psychological stress in the household. Elena, who had been a quiet child until this time, was now loud, and mean—she was biting, pulling hair, and the like. Melissa tested her daughter for food allergies, but none were found.

Finally, about 6 months after the symptoms presented, Elena was screened for lead poisoning, which was routine for the Head Start program she was enrolled in. "We have a problem," was how the pediatrician presented the results to her, explaining that Elena was in a medical state of emergency and must report the following morning for medical treatment (chelation therapy). Her lead level was in the high 40s and lead deposits in the joints, kneecaps, and brain indicated that levels had been in the 60s.[7]

it contains. The lead in a person's blood, or BLOOD LEAD LEVEL, is usually measured in micrograms of lead per deciliter of blood (μg/dl).

As scientists discover adverse health effects of lead associated with lower and lower blood lead levels, the level that is considered to be of concern becomes ever lower. Only a few years ago it was believed that up to 25 μg/dl was a safe level. Today a young child with a level of 10 μg/dl or greater is considered by the U. S. Department of Health and Human Services to be at risk, because studies have found that children with blood lead levels as low as 10 μg/dl can suffer adverse effects.

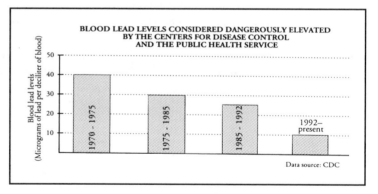

Finger Stick/Capillary Blood Lead

A capillary blood test is given on a routine basis by most practices to test the level of lead in the blood. A small amount of blood is drawn from a child's finger (or an infant's heel) and analyzed by a laboratory to determine how much lead it contains.

This FINGER STICK test gives a good indication of whether the child is at risk for lead poisoning. However, it is simply a screen, not a definitive test. Finger sticks may provide a false-positive result, that is, the test often shows a higher level of lead than is actually present in the blood. This effect can be minimized by careful use of proper sampling technique.

The State Laboratory in Massachusetts, for example, has found that of all finger stick readings over 15 μg/dl, about one-half actually turn out to be that high when retested using a

venous blood test. Of those indicating over 23 μg/dl, only about one-third are confirmed when retested. In spite of this drawback, however, the finger stick is generally preferred for screening, according to Mary Jean Brown at the Massachusetts Lead Program, not only because it is simpler to administer for medical staff but also because the procedure itself is often less traumatic for both the child and the parent.[8] Other programs find that with a good phlebotomist (specialist in drawing blood) venous blood sampling can be done in less time and less painfully.[9]

The false positives occur because of contamination from lead dust on a child's skin or from the environment of the laboratory. If the finger stick test is high, then blood should be drawn from the vein to confirm that the lead level is truly elevated.

Over the next few years you may be presented with a new screening option. ESA, a company in Massachusetts, is developing a point-of-care testing instrument for healthcare providers, with a CDC grant. The new apparatus will measure the lead in a blood sample taken by finger stick in only 10 minutes. This offers the advantage of indicating right away if the child should be retested, so that a venous sample can be taken during the same doctor or clinic visit if necessary.

Venous Blood Lead

The other screening method currently used is a VENOUS blood test, or the testing of blood taken from a child's vein. Some practices use the venous test on a regular basis to avoid having the false positives from finger stick tests and the need to retest. Finger sticks might be used, for example, only when a child will not sit still for the venous test.

The blood obtained by either of these methods is analyzed by a laboratory using either atomic absorption spectrometry (AAS) or anodic stripping voltammetry (ASV). AAS is sometimes found to be more reliable, because of lack of expertise in using ASV. However, if a laboratory handles large volumes of samples with ASV, this method can also be very reliable. As far as a parent is concerned, the best approach is to go to a medical practitioner you trust, who will, in turn, use a laboratory he or she has confidence in.

Regardless of the method of analysis and the competence of the laboratory, different laboratories come out with somewhat different results for the same sample. Variations of up to 5 μg/dl between one laboratory and another are not considered unusual or problematic. This does mean, however, that if a child's blood lead level is being followed to see if it is responding to environmental intervention or medical treatment, it is best to use the same laboratory for each follow-up test.[10]

EP Level

Screening by measuring a chemical in the blood [erythrocyte protoporphyrin (EP)] was the standard method as recently as the early 1990s, before the level of concern was lowered to 10 µg/dl. This measures the amount of the chemical in blood that is transformed into hemoglobin, the component of blood that transports oxygen in the body. When lead is present, it disrupts the process of hemoglobin formation and leaves these cells in an incomplete state.[11]

The percentage of cells that are in this condition can be a good indication of the presence of lead in the blood over a certain level. EP testing does not adequately identify most cases of blood lead levels below 25 µg/dl. EP tests are, however, a good indicator of iron levels in the blood, and are still used to detect iron deficiency. They are also used as a double check for high blood lead level test results. If screening indicates levels of lead that are inconsistent with what the EP test shows, then the laboratory knows that the sample should be analyzed again.[12]

Tooth, Hair, and Bone Testing

Testing of hair and fingernails is not recommended for diagnosis of lead poisoning because levels of lead do not correlate with those in the blood.[13] Measuring the lead in a child's baby teeth that have fallen out can give some information about how much lead a child had accumulated up to that time, but does not reflect the amount that the child is being exposed to and absorbing at the time the test is done.[14]

X-ray fluorescence (XRF) measurements of lead in bone are sometimes used to assess the effects or timing of long-term lead exposure. However, they may fail to show current exposure, even in cases of very high lead exposure. Although these tests can give an indication of a problem, they are not the accepted standard and should not be relied on in terms of indicating whether a child should be treated for lead poisoning. They reflect past exposure and accumulation of lead in the body, rather than the threat presented by current exposure.[15]

When Should Your Child Be Screened?

The CDC (Centers for Disease Control and Prevention of the U. S. Department of Health and Human Services' Public Health Service) is expected to change its policy from UNIVERSAL screening to one which would allow state and local health officials to choose either a UNIVERSAL or a TARGETED screening approach. The federal policy would provide guidance to state and local authorities who could continue to design their own programs responsive to their own situations and priorities. *To find out what the recommendation is in your state, contact your state lead program, listed in Appendix A.*

Through 1996, the CDC recommendation was that every child be screened for lead poisoning at least at the ages of 1 and 2. The new policy is expected to be that all children be screened only in areas that are considered to be at HIGH RISK if state or local officials do not develop customized criteria. This would be determined by either the results of data from lead screenings (at least 12% of 1- and 2-year-olds to have elevated blood lead levels), or the percentage of the housing that was built before 1950 (over 27%). Each state would decide which areas are high risk within that state.

The guidelines suggest that children who do not live in these areas be screened only if the individual child is considered to be AT RISK. This is determined by asking the parent a set of questions about the lead sources the child might be exposed to.

Children who are AT RISK should be screened at 12 and 24 months. Blood lead levels tend to be the highest during the second year of a child's life. If a child who is from 3 to 5 years old has never been assessed, he or she should be assessed at least once. All Medicaid patients should be screened at 1 and 2 years of age unless they are in a low-risk area. If an area is determined to be at very low risk, then neither screening nor assessment is recommended.[16]

If a child is found to have a blood lead level over 10 μg/dl, he or she should be rescreened every 3 to 4 months. If the level is over 15 μg/dl, both the frequent screening and additional follow-up are called for. However, if two consecutive measurements under 10 μg/dl or three under 15 μg/dl are obtained, then screening may decrease to once a year.[17]

A recent study suggests that blood lead levels vary by season and may be higher in the summer than in the winter. To ensure that your child is not at risk, it is best to do the screening during the summer months.[18]

The targeted screening approach is based on the fact that lead poisoning is environmental in origin and its incidence in a specific geographic area is related in great part to the age and condition of local housing stock. Given a limited pool of resources, it is logical to focus efforts where the problem is most serious.

In spite of the new government policy, some advocates still recommend that every child be screened. The factors addressed in the questions recommended by the CDC are not the only ones that increase a child's risk for lead poisoning. Exposure to any one of the numerous sources described in Chapter 2 may elevate the level of lead in a child's blood and threaten her or his health.

Many states either already have or will soon implement periodic screening programs for children under 6 years old.[19] A few states have laws mandating universal screening of young children. That is to say, lead screening is required as part of a routine physical examination. Even in this case, many children are missed, especially those who do not have routine medical visits.[20] In states that participate in Medicaid's Early and Periodic Screening, Diagnostic, and Treatment (EPSDT) program, which provides a variety of preventive services, patients are given lead screening routinely.[21] Some Head Start programs also give regular lead tests to their participants. However, in most instances throughout the country, the decision to screen for lead poisoning is left to the discretion of healthcare providers and parents.

In addition to protecting the health of the individual child who is tested, screening for lead poisoning serves an important public function. By knowing where the greatest risk for lead poisoning exists, public health administrators can better understand the sources of the disease and direct resources toward those who are most affected. Just as an individual parent can better protect his or her child with more information and better awareness, we as a society are better able to deal with lead poisoning with more information about whom it affects.

> *NOTE: If your child has a high reading from a lead screening, don't panic! Not every high test result means that the child is actually lead poisoned. There may have been a laboratory error or the sample might have been contaminated.*

What Does It Mean if My Child Has an Elevated Blood Lead Level?

False Positives

If your child gets a high reading from a finger stick test, do not panic. Lead screenings may yield FALSE POSITIVES. This means that the results WRONGLY indicate that a blood lead level is elevated. This is why it is referred to as a SCREEN rather than a test. If your results are high, it tells you that the blood lead level MAY be elevated and you should be retested. Even if you get a high reading from a venous test, you might want to repeat it to confirm the results. Laboratory errors do occasionally occur, even when the methods are reliable and the laboratory is competent.

Follow-up for Elevated Blood Lead Levels

Once you have confirmed that the reading actually does reflect the level of lead in your child's blood, your response will depend on exactly how high that blood lead level is. The CDC recommends the following[22]:

A blood lead level above 10 is a red flag. Your child may be at risk so you should be on your guard. He or she should return for follow-up screening, as recommended in the above section, to make sure the level does not go up any further. You should be careful about your child's diet, the cleanliness of the home, washing hands before eating, and other measures to reduce lead exposure. *The basic measures you can take to protect your child are set out in Chapters 3 and 6 and summarized in Appendix I. Controlling lead hazards in the environment is discussed in Chapters 5 and 12 through 16.*

If your child's blood lead level is over 15 or 20 μg/dl, both medical management and environmental intervention are called for. A public health nurse will speak to you about lead poisoning, its potential sources, and ways to reduce blood lead levels. Your child should be retested regularly and tested for iron deficiency and your home examined for sources of lead. Depending on what is found, medical treatment and/or control of lead poisoning sources might be appropriate. *Measures that are recommended in response to an elevated blood lead level are discussed in Chapters 5 through 16.*

Depending on your state and/or locality, specific requirements for removing lead paint may exist. In some locations, such as Massachusetts or New York City, an inspector may be sent to your home to investigate the cause of the poisoning, and you may be required to take

What Do the Results of a Lead Screening Mean?

BLOOD LEAD LEVEL		WHAT IT MEANS	FOR MORE INFO, SEE
I.	Less than 10 μg/dl	OK.	
IIA.	Between 10 and 14 μg/dl	Test again more frequently.	Chapter 4
IIB.	Between 15 and 19 μg/dl	Test again more frequently.	Chapter 4
		Test for iron deficiency.	Chapter 7
		Be careful about cleaning and diet.	Chapters 3 and 6
		Try to find and control lead source.	Chapters 5 and 11
III.	Between 21 and 44 μg/dl	Have a complete medical evaluation.	Chapter 7
		Investigate and eliminate lead source.	Chapters 5 and 11
IV.	Between 45 and 69 μg/dl	Begin medical treatment, investigate, eliminate lead source within 48 hours.	Same as above
V.	Over 70 μg/dl	Begin medical treatment, investigate, eliminate lead source IMMEDIATELY.	Same as above

μg/dl = micrograms of lead per deciliter of blood.

measures to control the lead hazards in your home. *Identification and control of lead hazards in the home are discussed in Chapters 5 through 16.*

If your child's blood lead level is over 45 μg/dl, medical treatment (chelation therapy) will be prescribed. Some practices will recommend chelation at lower levels than this. *Chelation therapy is discussed in Chapter 7.*

PART THREE

Treating Lead Poisoning

First get the child out of the lead,
then get the lead out of the child.
John W. Graef, M.D., Chief Emeritus, Lead and Toxicity Program, Children's
Hospital, Boston

CHAPTER FIVE

Environmental Investigation and Intervention

THE INVESTIGATION

Children are lead poisoned by absorbing lead they are exposed to in their environments. So the first thing to do in response to an elevated blood lead level is to identify and eliminate or reduce the child's exposure to the sources of lead that have caused the elevated blood lead level.

Sources are identified through an investigation of the child's home. An investigation consists of a detailed questionnaire, a visual inspection of the premises, with a special eye to potential hazards, and possibly testing for lead content of paint, dust, ceramics, etc.[1]

The investigation of a home for lead sources may be done by the local health department or lead program. However, that is not the only option and sometimes not an option at all. State and local health departments often do not have the jurisdiction to intervene unless a child's blood lead level is 20 or 25 $\mu g/dl$ or greater.

According to lead consultant Marianna Koval, many state and local health departments are struggling to provide basic services in a time of massive budget cuts. As a result, a state or local health department may have ill-trained staff and use old, inaccurate testing equipment. Unfortunately, sometimes relying on a health department can be dangerous.

For example, the New York City Department of Health visits the home of any child who has a blood lead level of 20 μg/dl or greater. The inspector, however, will only test those painted surfaces for lead that are peeling, chipping, or deemed to be in "imminent disrepair." Such surfaces that test positive for lead will be ordered to be abated (removed or covered). But no hazards assessment is conducted. And New York City law permits the lead-poisoned child in many cases to remain in the residence during the dangerous abatement process. So, in many cases, poor testing results in false positives that prompt unnecessary and dangerous abatements. Such "help" from the Department of Health can cause your child to become more severely lead poisoned, require you to spend tens of thousands of dollars without need, and prevent you from knowing and eliminating your child's initial source of lead exposure.[2]

If you are not offered the services of a risk assessor/lead paint inspector by a public health agency, or if you are concerned about the kind of service they are able to offer, you can hire a private risk assessor/lead paint inspector. Some individuals who call themselves CONSULTANTS also serve this function. Choose a risk assessor/lead paint inspector very carefully, paying special attention to the training he or she has received and his or her experience in investigating the source of lead exposure of a child with an elevated blood lead level. *For a discussion of how to choose a lead paint inspector/risk assessor, see Chapter 11.*

A standard risk assessment, done solely for purposes of prevention, where there is no actual case of lead poisoning, involves inspecting the home for lead paint hazards and testing for lead in dust and soil. This is followed by a detailed listing of what needs to be done to fix or control the lead hazard. The process is described in Chapter 11.

If there is a lead-poisoned child living in the home, a more thorough investigation should be done. In addition to doing a risk assessment of paint, dust, and soil hazards, other potential sources are checked for, including soil, dishes, toys, deteriorated paint on furniture, and water. The investigator considers other buildings the child may have spent substantial time in, including day cares and friends' or relatives' homes, as well as less common sources of lead poisoning, such as makeup, traditional Chinese, Hispanic, or other ethnic remedies, or a porcelain bathtub.

Lead Hazard Assessment Questionnaire

The following sample questionnaire, used by HUD, clearly explains what the environmental investigation process is all about.

CONTROLLING LEAD SOURCES

In the simplest case, the lead source is simply removed from the home. A ceramic mug or traditional remedy responsible for lead poisoning can be handled in this way. If the source is water, the child can be given filtered water rather than drinking straight from the tap. In the case of lead paint in a day-care facility or babysitter's house, the family could find alternative accommodations for child care. Measures you can take to control various sources of lead poisoning are discussed in detail in Chapters 13–16.

In the majority of cases, the hazard is the lead paint and dust in the child's home. In this
(*text continued on p. 52*)

RESIDENT QUESTIONNAIRE
FOR INVESTIGATION OF CHILDREN
WITH ELEVATED BLOOD LEAD LEVELS

THE RESULTS OF THIS QUESTIONNAIRE WILL BE USED FOR TWO PURPOSES:

- TO DETERMINE WHERE ENVIRONMENTAL SAMPLES SHOULD BE COLLECTED.
- TO DEVELOP CORRECTIVE MEASURES RELATED TO USE PATTERNS AND LIVING CHARACTERISTICS (E.G., FLUSHING THE WATER LINE IF WATER LEAD LEVELS ARE HIGH, MOVING THE PET'S SLEEPING AREA IF IT APPEARS THE PET IS TRACKING IN LEADED DUST, AND SO FORTH).

THE INVESTIGATOR SHOULD ALWAYS RECOMMEND TEMPORARY MEASURES TO IMMEDIATELY REDUCE THE CHILD'S EXPOSURE TO LEAD HAZARDS.

GENERAL INFORMATION

1. WHERE DO YOU THINK THE CHILD IS EXPOSED TO THE LEAD HAZARD? _____

2. DO YOU RENT OR OWN YOUR HOME?   RENT   OWN   (CIRCLE)

    IF RENTED, ARE THERE ANY RENT SUBSIDIES?   YES   NO   (CIRCLE)

    IF YES, WHAT TYPE: (CHECK)

    _____ PUBLIC HOUSING AUTHORITY

    _____ SECTION 8

    _____ FEDERAL RENT SUBSIDY

    _____ OTHER (SPECIFY): _____

    LANDLORD INFORMATION (OR RENT COLLECTOR AGENT)

    NAME: _____

    ADDRESS: _____

    PHONE: _____

3. WHEN DID YOU/YOUR FAMILY MOVE INTO THIS HOME?

    COMPLETE THE FOLLOWING FOR ALL ADDRESSES WHERE THE CHILD HAS LIVED DURING THE PAST 12 MONTHS:

DATES OF RESIDENCY	ADDRESS (INCLUDE CITY AND STATE)	APPROXIMATE AGE OF DWELLING	GENERAL CONDITION OF DWELLING: ANY REMODELING OR RENOVATION? ANY DETERIORATED PAINT?

4. IS THE CHILD CARED FOR AWAY FROM THE HOME? (THIS WOULD INCLUDE PRESCHOOL, DAY-CARE CENTER, DAY-CARE HOME, OR CARE PROVIDED BY A RELATIVE OR FRIEND.)

    IF YES, COMPLETE THE FOLLOWING:

Type of care	Location of care (name of contact, address, and phone number)	Approximate number of hours per week at this location	General condition of structure. Any deteriorated paint? Any recent remodeling or renovation?

Lead-Based Paint and Lead-Contaminated Dust Hazards

1. Has this dwelling been tested for lead-based paint or lead-contaminated dust? yes no (circle)
   If yes, when? Where can this information be obtained? _____

2. Approximately what year was this dwelling built?   If unknown, was the dwelling built before 1950? _____

3. Has there been any recent repainting, remodeling, renovation, window replacement, sanding, or scraping of painted surfaces inside or outside this dwelling unit? If yes, describe activities and duration of work in more detail.

   _____

4. Has any lead abatement work been conducted at this dwelling recently? yes no (circle)

5. Where does the child like to play or frequent? (Include rooms, closets, porches, outbuildings.)

6. Where does the child like to hide? (Include rooms, closets, porches, outbuildings.)
   Complete the following table:

Areas where child likes to play or hide	Paint condition (intact, fair, poor, or not present)*	Location of painted component with visible bite marks

*Paint condition: Note location and extent of any visible chips and/or dust in window wells, on window sills, on the floor directly beneath windows. Do you see peeling, chipping, chalking, flaking, or deteriorated paint? If yes, note locations and extent of deterioration.

Assessment: (check)
_____ Probable lead-based paint hazard.
_____ Probable leaded dust hazard.

ACTION: (CHECK)

_____ OBTAIN RECORDS OF PREVIOUS ENVIRONMENTAL TESTING NOTED ABOVE.

_____ XRF INSPECTION OF DWELLING (CIRCLE ONE): LIMITED   COMPLETE.

_____ PAINT TESTING—DETERIORATED PAINT: ADD ANY ADDITIONAL AREAS TO FORM 5.3.

_____ LEADED DUST SAMPLING OF HOME: ADD ANY ADDITIONAL AREAS TO THE LIST OF ROOMS TO BE SAMPLED, USING FORM 5.4.

_____ OTHER SAMPLING (SPECIFY): _____

WATER LEAD HAZARDS

1. WHAT IS THE SOURCE OF DRINKING WATER FOR THE FAMILY? (CIRCLE) MUNICIPAL WATER PRIVATE WELL   OTHER (SPECIFY): _____
   (THIS INFORMATION WILL BE USED TO HELP DETERMINE RESPONSIBILITY AND METHODS OF CONTROLLING LEAD EXPOSURES FROM WATER.)
   IF TAP WATER IS USED FOR DRINKING, PLEASE ANSWER THE FOLLOWING:

2. FROM WHICH FAUCETS DO YOU OBTAIN DRINKING WATER? (SAMPLE FROM THE MAIN DRINKING WATER FAUCET.)

3. DO YOU USE THE WATER IMMEDIATELY OR DO YOU LET THE WATER RUN FOR AWHILE FIRST? (IF WATER LEAD LEVELS ARE ELEVATED IN THE FIRST FLUSH, BUT LOW IN THE FLUSHED SAMPLE, RECOMMEND FLUSHING THE WATER AFTER EACH PERIOD THE WATER HAS REMAINED STANDING IN THE PIPE FOR MORE THAN 6 HOURS.)

   _____

4. IS TAP WATER USED TO PREPARE INFANT FORMULA, POWDERED MILK, OR JUICES FOR THE CHILDREN?
   IF YES, DO YOU USE HOT OR COLD TAP WATER?
   IF NO, FROM WHAT SOURCE DO YOU OBTAIN WATER FOR THE CHILDREN?

5. HAS NEW PLUMBING BEEN INSTALLED WITHIN THE LAST 5 YEARS?   YES   NO   (CIRCLE)
   IF YES, IDENTIFY LOCATION(S).
   DID YOU DO ANY OF THIS WORK YOURSELF?   YES   NO   (CIRCLE)
   IF YES, SPECIFY. _____

6. HAS THE WATER EVER BEEN TESTED FOR LEAD?   YES   NO   (CIRCLE)
   IF YES, WHERE CAN TEST RESULTS BE OBTAINED?

DETERMINE WHETHER THE DWELLING IS LOCATED IN A JURISDICTION KNOWN TO HAVE LEAD IN DRINKING WATER IN EITHER PUBLIC MUNICIPAL OR WELL WATER. CONSULT WITH STATE/LOCAL PUBLIC HEALTH AUTHORITIES FOR DETAILS.

(CHECK) _____ AT RISK   _____ NOT AT RISK

ASSESSMENT: (CHECK)

_____ AT RISK FOR WATER LEAD HAZARDS.

ACTIONS: (CHECK)

_____ TEST WATER (FIRST-DRAW AND FLUSH SAMPLES).

_____ OTHER TESTING (SPECIFY): _____

_____ COUNSEL FAMILY (SPECIFY): _____

LEAD IN SOIL HAZARDS

(USE THE FOLLOWING INFORMATION TO DETERMINE WHERE SOIL SAMPLES SHOULD BE COL-LECTED.)

1. WHERE OUTSIDE DOES THE CHILD LIKE TO PLAY?
2. WHERE OUTSIDE DOES THE CHILD LIKE TO HIDE?
3. IS THIS DWELLING LOCATED NEAR A LEAD-PRODUCING INDUSTRY (SUCH AS A BATTERY PLANT, SMELTER, RADIATOR REPAIR SHOP, OR ELECTRONICS/SOLDERING INDUSTRY?) YES   NO   (CIRCLE)
4. IS THE DWELLING LOCATED WITHIN TWO BLOCKS OF A MAJOR ROADWAY, FREEWAY, ELEVATED HIGHWAY, OR OTHER TRANSPORTATION STRUCTURES?
5. ARE NEARBY BUILDINGS OR STRUCTURES BEING RENOVATED, REPAINTED, OR DEMOLISHED?
6. IS THERE DETERIORATED PAINT ON OUTSIDE FENCES, GARAGES, PLAY STRUCTURES, RAILINGS, BUILDING SIDING, WINDOWS, TRIMS, OR MAILBOXES?
7. WERE GASOLINE OR OTHER SOLVENTS EVER USED TO CLEAN PARTS OR DISPOSED OF AT THE PROPERTY?
8. ARE THERE VISIBLE PAINT CHIPS NEAR THE PERIMETER OF THE HOUSE, FENCES, GA-RAGES, PLAY STRUCTURES? IF YES, NOTE LOCATION.
9. HAS SOIL EVER BEEN TESTED FOR LEAD? IF YES, WHERE CAN THIS INFORMATION BE OBTAINED?
10. HAVE YOU BURNED PAINTED WOOD IN A WOODSTOVE OR FIREPLACE? IF YES, HAVE YOU EMPTIED ASHES ONTO SOIL? IF YES, WHERE?

ASSESSMENT: (CHECK)

_____ PROBABLE SOIL LEAD HAZARD.

ACTIONS: (CHECK)

_____ TEST SOIL. COMPLETE FIELD SAMPLING FORM FOR SOIL (FORM 5.5). OBTAIN SINGLE SAMPLES FOR EACH BARE SOIL AREA WHERE THE CHILD PLAYS.

_____ ADVISE FAMILY TO OBTAIN WASHABLE DOORMATS FOR ENTRANCES TO THE DWELLING.

_____ COUNSEL FAMILY TO KEEP CHILD AWAY FROM BARE SOIL AREAS THOUGHT TO BE AT RISK.

(SPECIFY): _____

OCCUPATIONAL/HOBBY LEAD HAZARDS

USE THE INFORMATION IN THIS SECTION TO DETERMINE IF THE CHILD'S SOURCE OF LEAD EXPOSURE COULD BE RELATED TO THE PARENTS', OLDER SIBLINGS', OR OTHER ADULTS' WORK ENVIRONMENT. OCCUPATIONS THAT MAY CAUSE LEAD EXPOSURE INCLUDE THE FOLLOWING:

*   PAINT REMOVAL (INCLUDING SANDBLASTING, SCRAPING, ABRASIVE BLASTING, SANDING, OR USING A HEAT GUN OR TORCH).
*   CHEMICAL STRIPPERS.
*   REMODELING, REPAIRING, OR RENOVATING DWELLINGS OR BUILDINGS, OR TEARING DOWN BUILDINGS OR METAL STRUCTURES (DEMOLITION).
*   PLUMBING.
*   REPAIRING RADIATORS.

- MELTING METAL FOR REUSE (SMELTING).
- WELDING, BURNING, CUTTING, OR TORCH WORK.
- POURING MOLTEN METAL (FOUNDRIES).
- AUTO BODY REPAIR WORK.
- WORKING AT A FIRING RANGE.
- MAKING BATTERIES.
- MAKING PAINT OR PIGMENTS.
- PAINTING.
- SALVAGING METAL OR BATTERIES.
- MAKING OR SPLICING CABLE OR WIRE.
- CREATING EXPLOSIVES OR AMMUNITION.
- MAKING OR REPAIRING JEWELRY.
- MAKING POTTERY.
- BUILDING, REPAIRING, OR PAINTING SHIPS.
- WORKING IN A CHEMICAL PLANT, A GLASS FACTORY, AN OIL REFINERY, OR ANY OTHER WORK INVOLVING LEAD.

1. WHERE DO ADULT FAMILY MEMBERS WORK? (INCLUDE MOTHER, FATHER, OLDER SIBLINGS, OTHER ADULT HOUSEHOLD MEMBERS)

NAME	PLACE OF EMPLOYMENT	OCCUPATION OR JOB TITLE	PROBABLE LEAD EXPOSURE (YES/NO)

2. ARE WORK CLOTHES SEPARATED FROM OTHER LAUNDRY?
3. HAS ANYONE IN THE HOUSEHOLD REMOVED PAINT OR VARNISH WHILE IN THE DWELLING? (INCLUDES PAINT REMOVAL FROM WOODWORK, FURNITURE, CARS, BICYCLES, BOATS)
4. HAS ANYONE IN THE HOUSEHOLD SOLDERED ELECTRIC PARTS WHILE AT HOME?
5. DOES ANYONE IN THE HOUSEHOLD APPLY GLAZE TO CERAMIC OR POTTERY OBJECTS?
6. DOES ANYONE IN THE HOUSEHOLD WORK WITH STAINED GLASS?
7. DOES ANYONE IN THE HOUSEHOLD USE ARTISTS' PAINTS TO PAINT PICTURES OR JEWELRY?
8. DOES ANYONE IN THE HOUSEHOLD RELOAD BULLETS, TARGET SHOOT, OR HUNT?
9. DOES ANYONE IN THE HOUSEHOLD MELT LEADS TO MAKE BULLETS OR FISHING SINKERS?
10. DOES ANYONE IN THE HOUSEHOLD WORK IN AUTO BODY REPAIR AT HOME OR IN THE YARD?
11. IS THERE EVIDENCE OF TAKE-HOME WORK EXPOSURES OR HOBBY EXPOSURES IN THE DWELLING?

ASSESSMENT: (CHECK)
_____ PROBABLE OCCUPATIONAL-RELATED LEAD EXPOSURE.
_____ PROBABLE HOBBY-RELATED LEAD EXPOSURE.

ACTIONS: (CHECK)

_____ COUNSEL FAMILY (SPECIFY):

_____ REFER TO (SPECIFY): _____

CHILD BEHAVIOR RISK FACTORS

1. DOES CHILD SUCK HIS/HER FINGERS?   YES   NO   (CIRCLE)
2. DOES CHILD PUT PAINTED OBJECTS INTO THE MOUTH?   YES   NO   (CIRCLE)
   IF YES, SPECIFY: _____
3. DOES CHILD CHEW ON PAINTED SURFACES, SUCH AS OLD PAINTED CRIBS, WINDOW SILLS, FURNITURE EDGES, RAILINGS, DOOR MOLDING, OR BROOM HANDLES?
   IF YES, SPECIFY: _____
4. DOES CHILD CHEW ON PUTTY AROUND WINDOWS?
5. DOES CHILD PUT SOFT METAL OBJECTS IN THE MOUTH? THESE MIGHT INCLUDE LEAD AND PEWTER TOYS AND TOY SOLDIERS, JEWELRY, GUNSHOT, BULLETS, BEADS, FISHING SINKERS, OR ANY ITEMS CONTAINING SOLDER (ELECTRONICS).
6. DOES CHILD CHEW OR EAT PAINT CHIPS OR PICK AT PAINTED SURFACES? IS THE PAINT INTACT IN THE CHILD'S PLAY AREAS?
7. DOES THE CHILD PUT FOREIGN, PRINTED MATERIAL (NEWSPAPERS, MAGAZINES) IN THE MOUTH?
8. DOES THE CHILD PUT MATCHES IN THE MOUTH? (SOME MATCHES CONTAIN LEAD ACETATE.)
9. DOES THE CHILD PLAY WITH COSMETICS, HAIR PREPARATIONS, OR TALCUM POWDER OR PUT THEM INTO THE MOUTH? ARE ANY OF THESE FOREIGN MADE?
10. DOES THE CHILD HAVE A FAVORITE CUP? A FAVORITE EATING UTENSIL? IF YES, ARE THEY HANDMADE OR CERAMIC?
11. DOES THE CHILD HAVE A DOG, CAT, OR OTHER PET THAT COULD TRACK IN CONTAMINATED SOIL OR DUST FROM THE OUTSIDE? WHERE DOES THE PET SLEEP?
12. WHERE DOES THE CHILD OBTAIN DRINKING WATER?
13. IF CHILD IS PRESENT, NOTE EXTENT OF HAND-TO-MOUTH BEHAVIOR OBSERVED.

ASSESSMENT: (CHECK)

_____ CHILD IS AT RISK DUE TO HAND-TO-MOUTH BEHAVIOR.

_____ CHILD IS AT RISK FOR MOUTHING PROBABLE LEAD-CONTAINING SUBSTANCE (SPECIFY): _____

_____ CHILD IS AT RISK FOR OTHER (SPECIFY): _____

ACTIONS:

_____ COUNSEL FAMILY TO LIMIT ACCESS OR USE OF (SPECIFY):

_____ OTHER (SPECIFY): _____

OTHER HOUSEHOLD RISK FACTORS

1. ARE IMPORTED COSMETICS SUCH AS KOHL, SURMA, OR CERUSE USED IN THE HOME?
2. DOES THE FAMILY EVER USE ANY HOME REMEDIES OR HERBAL TREATMENTS? (WHAT TYPE?)
3. ARE ANY LIQUIDS STORED IN METAL, PEWTER, OR CRYSTAL CONTAINERS?
4. WHAT CONTAINERS ARE USED TO PREPARE, SERVE, AND STORE THE CHILD'S FOOD?

ARE ANY OF THEM METAL, SOLDERED, OR GLAZED? DOES THE FAMILY COOK WITH A CERAMIC BEAN POT?

5. DOES THE FAMILY USE IMPORTED CANNED ITEMS REGULARLY?

6. DOES THE CHILD PLAY IN, LIVE IN, OR HAVE ACCESS TO ANY AREAS WHERE THE FOLLOWING MATERIALS ARE KEPT: SHELLACS, LACQUERS, DRIERS, COLORING PIGMENTS, EPOXY RESINS, PIPE SEALANTS, PUTTY, DYES, INDUSTRIAL CRAYONS OR MARKERS, GASOLINE, PAINTS, PESTICIDES, FUNGICIDES, GASOLINE, GEAR OIL, DETERGENTS, OLD BATTERIES, BATTERY CASINGS, FISHING SINKERS, LEAD PELLETS, SOLDER, OR DRAPERY WEIGHTS?

7. DOES THE CHILD TAKE BATHS IN AN OLD BATHTUB WITH DETERIORATED OR NONEXISTENT GLAZING?

ASSESSMENT: (CHECK)

_____ INCREASED RISK OF LEAD EXPOSURE DUE TO _____

ACTIONS: (CHECK)

_____ COUNSEL FAMILY TO LIMIT ACCESS OR USE (SPECIFY): _____

_____ OTHER (SPECIFY): _____

ASSESSMENT FOR LIKELY SUCCESS OF HAZARD CONTROL MEASURES

1. WHAT CLEANING EQUIPMENT DOES THE FAMILY HAVE IN THE DWELLING? (CIRCLE)
    BROOM, MOP AND BUCKET, VACUUM (DOES IT WORK?), SPONGES AND RAGS

2. HOW OFTEN DOES THE FAMILY:
    SWEEP THE FLOORS?
    WET MOP THE FLOORS?
    VACUUM THE FLOORS?
    WASH THE WINDOW SILLS?
    WASH THE WINDOW TROUGHS?

3. ARE FLOOR COVERINGS SMOOTH AND CLEANABLE?

4. WHAT TYPE OF FLOOR COVERINGS ARE FOUND IN THE DWELLING? (CIRCLE *ALL* THAT APPLY)
    VINYL/LINOLEUM   CARPETING   WOOD   OTHER (SPECIFY): _____

5. CLEANLINESS OF DWELLING (CIRCLE ONE):
    CODE: 1 = APPEARS CLEAN, 2 = SOME EVIDENCE OF HOUSECLEANING, 3 = NO EVIDENCE OF HOUSECLEANING, 4 = _____, 5 = _____, 6 = _____, 7 = _____

[PICK THE BEST CATEGORY BASED ON OVERALL OBSERVATIONS OF CLEANLINESS IN THE DWELLING.]

1. APPEARS CLEAN.
2. SOME EVIDENCE OF HOUSECLEANING.
3. NO EVIDENCE OF HOUSECLEANING.

NO VISIBLE DUST ON MOST SURFACES.
EVIDENCE OF RECENT VACUUMING OF CARPET.
NO MATTED OR SOILED CARPETING.
NO DEBRIS OR FOOD PARTICLES SCATTERED ABOUT.

Few visible cobwebs.

Clean kitchen floor.

Clean doorjambs.

Slight dust buildup in corners.

Slight dust buildup on furniture.

Slightly matted and/or soiled carpeting.

Some debris or food particles scattered about.

Some visible cobwebs.

Slightly soiled kitchen floor.

Slightly soiled doorjambs.

Heavy dust buildup in corners.

Heavy dust buildup on furniture.

Matted and/or soiled carpeting.

Debris or food particles scattered about.

Visible cobwebs.

Heavily soiled kitchen floor.

Heavily soiled doorjambs.

Assessment: (check)

_____ Cleaning equipment inadequate.

_____ Cleaning routine inadequate.

_____ Floor coverings inadequate to maintain clean environment.

Actions: (check)

_____ Counsel family to limit access or use (specify): _____

_____ Provide cleaning equipment.

_____ Instruct family on special cleaning methods.

_____ Flooring treatments needed.

_____ Other (specify): _____

case, the child has to remain out of the home until it can be either totally abated or cleaned up and repaired enough so as to become safe. It is very important that a lead-poisoned child not stay in a home while any type of work is being done that disrupts lead-painted surfaces. If a child returns home before it has passed a clearance test for lead dust after the work is done, the child's condition may be made worse than it was before the abatement. *For a discussion of lead paint abatement and interim measures for controlling a child's exposure to lead paint and dust, see Chapter 13.*

Making the home safe for a lead-poisoned child should be a priority. This can take as little as a day or a few days, or, in the case of more extensive lead hazards, weeks or even months. In the meantime, accommodations have to be made for the child. Ideally, the family can find friends or relatives to stay with.

Note for landlords: Some states and localities require landlords to abate lead from rental property if it is occupied by a child who is lead poisoned. In some cases the landlord might also be required to provide alternate living quarters during the time it takes to get the job done. *For the requirements in your state, contact your state lead program, listed in Appendix A.*

CHAPTER SIX

Nutrition and Lead Poisoning

HOW LEAD FROM THE ENVIRONMENT GETS INTO OUR BODIES

Most of the lead that enters our bodies does so by way of our mouths, through ingestion. Adults ingest lead predominantly in water and food. Children, on the other hand, usually ingest more from dust and soil, as their normal daily activity brings them into contact with the ground and involves hand-to-mouth contact.

The amount of lead that we breathe in is usually relatively small. In some cases, however, hazardous amounts of lead can be inhaled, such as when there is a lot of lead dust in the air, from a house being deleaded or renovated.

Much of the lead that we ingest or inhale passes through our bodies and is eliminated as waste, without hurting us. The lead that stays in our blood has a half-life of about a month. This means that when lead enters the body, a significant portion of it remains in the blood for 48–72 hours. Then the majority finds its way to the SOFT TISSUE, the liver, spleen, heart, kidneys, muscles, lungs, and brain, where it remains for a few months. This is the lead that is an immediate threat to our health.[1]

The body sends lead in place of certain essential nutrients that it resembles in chemical structure—iron, calcium, and zinc. However, the lead is not able to carry out the critical functions of the minerals it replaces. Not only does lead interfere with good health by taking the place of essential nutrients in the body, but it actually interferes with the work these nutrients do. In the blood, for example, higher levels of lead interfere with the formation of red blood cells.[2]

Of the lead that remains in our bodies, a large proportion is stored in our bones. It can then be released at a later time. It has not been scientifically established how long this lead remains in a child's skeleton, although it is assumed to be a number of years.[3]

The lead that is not eliminated as waste, but rather remains in the body, is referred to as being ABSORBED. The proportion of lead that stays in the body, called the RATE OF ABSORPTION, depends on several factors.[4]

- Smaller particles tend to be absorbed more than larger particles.
- Young children tend to absorb more lead than adults.
- Lead tends to be absorbed more on an empty stomach than a full stomach.
- Lead consumed in liquids tends to be absorbed at a higher rate than lead consumed in solids.
- The amount of lead absorbed can be affected by nutrition. More lead is absorbed with inadequate intake of iron, calcium, vitamin C, or zinc.

THE ROLE OF GOOD NUTRITION

KEY
☐ **Fat** (naturally occurring and added)
▼ **Sugars** (added)

These symbols show fat and added sugars in foods.

Fats, Oils, & Sweets
USE SPARINGLY

Milk, Yogurt, & Cheese Group
2-3 SERVINGS

Meat, Poultry, Fish, Dry Beans, Eggs, & Nuts Group
2-3 SERVINGS

Vegetable Group
3-5 SERVINGS

Fruit Group
2-4 SERVINGS

Bread, Cereal, Rice, & Pasta Group
6-11 SERVINGS

Regular and healthy meals and snacks will reduce the amount of lead the body absorbs. A diet based on the U. S. Department of Agriculture's food pyramid is not only best for your family's overall health but also provides the specific nutrients important for minimizing the damage that lead can do to your body. The food pyramid is a diet based on breads, cereals, and other grains (whole grains if possible), fruits and vegetables, low-fat dairy products, lean meat, fish and poultry, and legumes (dried peas and beans).[5]

Specific types of food play a very important part in fortifying the body against lead poisoning. Pay particular attention to feeding your children diets low in fat and high in iron, calcium, zinc, and Vitamin C. This will reduce the amount of lead your children's bodies absorb, and minimize the risk created by whatever lead they may be exposed to.[6]

Calcium and iron slow the lead
From going throughout your body and to your head
Fatty foods taste real swell
But healthy foods will keep us well.[7]

Another rhyme from Maurci Jackson, about good nutrition to protect children from lead poisoning.

A Low-Fat Diet Helps Protect against Lead Poisoning

To reduce the amount of fat in the diet, serve foods that are baked, broiled, boiled, or steamed rather than fried. Avoid fatty snack foods, such as potato chips, donuts, and pastries. Choose low-fat or nonfat dairy products and use as little oil, margarine, and butter as possible.

Adequate Calcium in the Diet Helps to Keep Lead from Being Absorbed

Lead is very similar in chemical structure to calcium, and so is mistaken for calcium by the body. When the body is lacking in calcium, it mobilizes lead in place of calcium and sends it through the blood, and into the organs and finally the bones, right alongside the calcium. Eating foods rich in calcium, or taking calcium supplements, will help keep this from occurring.

Include foods rich in calcium such as dairy products and dark green vegetables. The following chart shows how much calcium is contained in some of the best food sources for this mineral. The federally recommended daily amount of calcium for an infant is 360 milligrams (mg) and for a child, 800 mg. A pregnant or lactating woman should have 1200 mg daily. The specific number of milligrams shown is the amount provided by the specific amount and type of food named, but other foods in the listed categories are also good sources.[8]

Canned fish WITH bones (3 oz Atlantic sardines)	372 mg
Nonfat milk (1 cup)[a]	302 mg
Whole milk (1 cup)[a]	290 mg
Kale (1 cup raw)	206 mg
Firm tofu (2½″ × 2¾″ × 1″ block)	154 mg
Blackstrap molasses (1 tablespoon)	137 mg
Broccoli (1 cup raw)	136 mg
Peanuts (1 cup roasted)	107 mg
Dried fruits (1 cup raisins)	90 mg
Garbanzo beans (½ cup dry, cooked, drained)	47 mg
Egg	28 mg
Baked potato	14 mg
Lean beef (3 oz ground)	10 mg
Poultry (1 chicken breast)	9 mg

[a]Note: If your child does not drink milk, because of lactose intolerance or any other reason, you can now buy enriched soy milk which contains the same amount of calcium.

If you are not able to get enough of these foods in your child's diet to add up to a healthy dose of calcium daily, you might want to use a supplement. The calcium should be present in the stomach at the same time as the lead to be effective, so taking a supplement before bed is not helpful.[9] Just be sure that the supplement does not itself contain lead. *For discussion of lead in calcium supplements, see Chapter 15.*

Iron Deficiency Can Aggravate the Damage from Exposure to Lead

Lead is often associated with an iron deficiency. When lead poisoning patients are iron deficient, they absorb more lead. Also, there may be similar mechanisms by which iron deficiency and lead affect growing cells, including brain cells.[10]

A young child (under 3) should get at least 15 mg of iron daily. The recommended amount for ages 4 through 10 is 10 mg. A 30- to 60-mg supplement is recommended for pregnant and lactating women. Good food sources of iron include the following[11]:

Organ meats (3 oz beef liver)	7.5 mg
Sunflower seeds (½ cup)	5.0 mg
Roast beef (relatively lean, 3 oz)	3.2 mg
Blackstrap molasses (1 tablespoon)	3.2 mg
Baked potato with skin	2.7 mg
Spinach (½ cup, cooked)	2.0 mg
Peas (½ cup)	1.5 mg
Tuna fish (3¼ oz canned in water)	1.5 mg
Nuts (½ cup peanuts)	1.5 mg
Poultry (1 chicken breast)	1.3 mg
Egg	1.0 mg
Fish (3 oz haddock)	1.0 mg
Raisins (1 oz)	1.0 mg

Many parents find it especially difficult to get enough iron in their child's diet. Adding orange juice to meals can increase a child's absorption of iron especially from vegetables.[12] Some people recommend using cast-iron cookware to increase the child's intake of iron.

Supplements are commonly used in treating a child with elevated blood lead levels and may help in reducing the risk of lead poisoning. There is concern on the part of some parents that giving too much iron might be toxic. However, although an overdose of iron supplements can be a serious matter, the body protects itself from dietary iron by passing through any iron that is not readily absorbed.[13]

Vitamin C Should Be Taken to Help the Absorption of Iron

An adequate amount of vitamin C in your diet helps you to absorb iron efficiently, especially the form of iron that is contained in vegetable sources.[14] The recommended allowance for a child is 45 mg. The allowance for a pregnant woman is 80 mg, and for a lactating woman, 100 mg. The following are good food sources of vitamin C[15]:

Broccoli (1 cup fresh)	140 mg
Collards (1 cup fresh)	144 mg
Brussels sprouts (1 cup fresh)	135 mg
Citrus fruits and juices (1 cup orange juice)	120 mg
Bell pepper (green or red)	94 mg
Strawberries (1 cup fresh)	88 mg
Tomato (medium)	28 mg
Potato with skins	26 mg

Zinc Deficits Can Increase the Amount of Lead the Body Absorbs

A shortage of zinc also increases the absorption of lead, because the body does not distinguish between the various similarly structured elements in the stomach. Also, in the case of a child who is being treated for lead poisoning, the amount of zinc that is excreted is increased by chelation therapy and should be replenished with zinc in the diet, or in the form of a supplement.[16] You can ensure an adequate intake of lead by eating whole grains and legumes or beef (or organ meats) regularly. The recommended daily amount is 5 mg for an infant, and 10 mg for a child. A pregnant woman should have 20 mg a day, and a lactating woman, 25 mg. Some of the best food sources for zinc are shown below[17]:

Oysters (¼ cup)	5.5 mg
Beef (3 oz)	4.9 mg
Sunflower seeds (½ cup)	4.0 mg
Cashews (½ cup)	3.6 mg
Beans (1 cup lima beans)	2.2 mg
Clams, shrimp (3 oz)	1.5 mg
Whole wheat bread (2 slices)	1.0 mg
Dairy products (8 oz milk/1 oz cheese)	1.0 mg
Poultry and fish (3 oz)	1.0 mg
Brewer's yeast (1 tablespoon)	0.6 mg

For a more complete table of nutritional values of foods, see Appendix D.

CHAPTER SEVEN

Medical Evaluation and Treatment

THE MEDICAL PRACTITIONER

Go to a Medical Practitioner Who Is Experienced and Competent in Treating Lead Poisoning

Even if you have a regular family doctor, he or she might refer you to a lead poisoning program if your child has an elevated blood lead level. Or after assessing your doctor's knowledge in this area, you may choose to look for the kind of expertise you would find in a specialized practice. Not every pediatrician is equally informed about and experienced in treating lead poisoning. You might find another medical practitioner, such as a nurse practitioner (NP), a physician's assistant (PA), or a doctor of osteopathy (DO), who has the requisite knowledge. Ask about his or her experience with lead poisoning and discuss the concepts contained in this book to get a good idea of the individual's knowledge.

One of the most reliable places to find a good lead poisoning clinic is at an academic hospital, one associated with a medical school or university. Your local board of health might be able to make a recommendation for you. Other people who deal with lead-poisoned children, such as attorneys or social workers, might also be helpful.

If you are unable to find an experienced clinician in the area, or if you simply prefer staying with a pediatrician you are familiar and comfortable with, even though he or she does not have expertise in treating lead poisoning, you might want to consider contacting an expert, even in another part of the country, who can advise your pediatrician regarding treatment decisions and procedures.

Ann and Jonathan Bader undertook the removal of the old exterior lead paint in the fall, about 6 months after moving into their newly purchased craftsman-style home in a suburb of Madison, Wisconsin. Jonathan scraped the paint off with a high-temperature heat gun and smoothed the surface with an electric sander, in accordance with HUD guidelines which had been given to them. They took precautions to protect their three young children from the lead paint chips, such as closing the windows on the side of the house where they were removing paint and spreading out tarps to collect the chips that fell to the ground.

But just to be sure they were safe, a couple of weeks into the process, Ann, a nursing assistant at a local hospital, decided to have the children's blood lead levels tested. They were pleased when the pediatrician reported that the test results showed only "trace" amounts of lead in the children's blood. He advised that as long as they washed lead-contaminated work clothing separately from the family's clothes and cleaned up well after the work, everything would be fine. They found out later that what the doctor considered insignificant "trace" levels were, in the case of their youngest daughter, 35 μg/dl, a level now considered very high and even then well over the acceptable limit of 25. The doctor, although a competent physician, was simply not informed about lead poisoning.

They continued their work, reassured that all was well. Jonathan would enter the house with his clothing so covered with lead dust that you could see it flying off of his shirt when he patted his chest. He would pick up his crying daughter and hold her close to him, totally unaware that he was poisoning her. This continued for another couple of months, until the point where the paint removal was virtually completed, the wood was primed, and it was becoming too cold to continue work that season. They had a follow-up blood lead level test, just to make sure everything was still OK—but it wasn't. Their youngest daughter had a blood lead level of almost 60—considered a medical emergency. The middle child's level was in the high 30s, also considered very dangerous, and even the oldest child, at 18 μg/dl, was well above the 10 μg/dl level of concern set by the U. S. government. The physician had not reported the results of the first test, as was required by law. But this one was so alarmingly high that the laboratory immediately brought the state health department in to assess the situation. The Baders were advised to, and did, move out of their house before beginning medical treatment in order for it to be effective.

Ann and Jonathan did some reading about lead poisoning and its treatment and were concerned about the prospect of their children being chelated with EDTA, which was the most common drug used for treating lead poisoning at the time (in the early 1990s). By phoning all over the country in search of someone with experience using the new oral chelator, succimer, Ann was able to solicit the support of Dr. Julian Chisolm, who advised the Baders' pediatrician in how to administer this drug to their two youngest daughters. Several courses were needed. The blood lead level did go down, but never reached what is considered a normal level (beneath 10 μg/dl). Fortunately, they were covered by an employer's health plan for the thousands of dollars spent on the medicine. Damage had clearly been done, in terms of their youngest daughter's cognitive development, which manifested itself in the form of attention problems and poor performance on a kindergarten readiness test. They have been seeing improvement, however, and are hopeful that with the proper intervention and support, both at home and at school, their daughters will be happy and productive in spite of the tragedy, although it took 5 years for the youngest child's blood level to go all the way back to normal.[1]

Work with Your Medical Practitioner

Your pediatrician, or whatever medical practitioner you are working with, should be regarded as a resource rather than an authority figure. The care of your child is ultimately your responsibility. Write down any questions you might have the night before a medical visit and take notes on your conversation. If the practitioner hasn't answered a question to your satisfaction, ask again, and make sure you understand the answer before you leave.

Any medical intervention presents some potential for trauma or negative side effects for a young fragile child. A parent must always be vigilant. You know your child better than anyone does. If you have a question or concern, speak up or you won't be heard.

MEDICAL EVALUATION

If a child has a blood lead level of 20 µg/dl or greater, the CDC (U. S. Centers for Disease Control and Prevention) recommends that a complete medical evaluation be done.

The parent is interviewed regarding the history of the child's symptoms and previous screening results, as well as factors such as diet, past and present occupations of family members, and a variety of environmental information.

A complete physical examination is given, focusing on the areas that may be affected by lead poisoning. This can include neurological, psychosocial, language development, and neurobehavioral assessments. The child may be tested for iron deficiency, as inadequate iron can cause a child to absorb more lead, and make the lead that is absorbed more damaging. An iron supplement will be given if the child is deficient in iron.

In cases where the parent thinks the child might have swallowed paint chips or a lead object during the preceding day or so, the stomach can be x-rayed to see if there is any foreign matter present.

An additional test may be given if the child's blood lead-level is over 20 µg/dl but below 45 µg/dl, the level at which pharmacological treatment is clearly recommended by the CDC. Some practices will use a mobilization test (or provocation chelation test) to help determine the best course of treatment for the child. A drug is given to the child and the urine is collected for a number of hours afterwards. The amount of lead which is excreted in the urine will be an indication of the effectiveness of the drug in removing lead from the child's blood. This information is used in combination with other factors to decide whether to treat the child with a course of this drug.[2]

CHELATION THERAPY

Lead poisoning is treated with drugs only when blood lead levels are very high or when they are not effectively lowered either by dietary changes or supplements or by controlling environmental sources. The treatment, called CHELATION, prevents the disease from progressing and alleviates acute symptoms.

Chelation can be expensive and painful. It does not undo damage that has already been done to the brain, nor does it get all of the lead out of the body. It is not a substitute for controlling lead hazards. In fact, chelation is only effective if the child lives in a lead-safe home.

Chelation Binds to Lead in the Blood and Helps the Body Eliminate It

CHELATION (kē-lā'-shən) is a medical treatment for removing heavy metals from the body. The word comes from the Greek word CHELOS meaning lobster claw. A chelating drug, which is taken either orally, by injection or intravenously, grabs onto the molecules of lead and creates a chemical shell to neutralize them. This makes the lead easier to excrete so that 10 to 50 times the normal amount can be eliminated from the body in urine, feces, or bile. The result is a decrease in the blood lead level.[3]

Chelation does not remove all of the lead in the body. There is no evidence that chelation reduces the amount of lead that is stored in the bones, which represents an estimated 70% of the total lead in a child's body.

It does, however alleviate overt symptoms in the extremely rare case when lead poisoning is so severe as to be symptomatic. It also prevents the disease from progressing. Older children (4 to 6 years old) are more difficult to chelate because the lead stored in their bones has become part of the bony matrix and more tightly bound than in a younger child (1 to 2 years old).[4]

Depending on the specific drug used, chelation may require weeks of hospitalization and can be very painful. It can also be expensive. Each treatment can costs hundreds of dollars. In some states, medical insurance must cover these expenses, but in others it may not. These drugs can have short-term side effects including fever, vomiting, headache, rashes, diarrhea, and loss of appetite. Kidney damage is a particular concern with intravenous chelating agents.[5]

Dehydration may also result if the patient does not drink plenty of water during the treatment. Specifically it is recommended that a child drink (or be given intravenously) one and a half times MAINTENANCE FLUIDS. That amount is determined according to the age and weight of the child.[5]

Four Different Drugs Are Used for Chelation

BAL (Dimercaprol)

BAL is reserved for the most severe situations, with blood lead levels over 70 or 80 μg/dl. It is quick and removes lead directly from the brain, but is highly toxic, resulting in side effects up to 50% of the time. It is given by means of injection, usually every 4 hours. The active ingredient is dissolved in peanut oil, so the injections can be dangerous for a person who is allergic to peanuts or peanut oil. It may also react seriously in combination with medicinal iron.

EDTA (Edetate Disodium Calcium)

EDTA (or CaNa$_2$ EDTA) has the advantage of being more effective at higher blood lead levels (over 45 μg/dl) than the oral chelators but the disadvantage of requiring hospitalization because it is administered intravenously. Although possibly the safest of the four chelators, the drug is toxic and draws the lead out through the kidneys, so it can harm the latter organs, and requires close monitoring.

Succimer (DMSA)

The most popular chelator is one that has been introduced over the last few years, namely, succimer (or CHEMET, by brand name). Although not quite as effective as EDTA or BAL, it is much easier to administer. Many practitioners also consider it safer than the other chelators, though this is open to question, given the limited experience we have with the drug. At moderate levels of lead poisoning, under 45 or 50 µg/dl, it is generally preferred. Succimer can be taken orally, so it is less intrusive, and usually doesn't require hospitalization.

Chelation even by succimer, however, is not a totally painless experience for the child. The drug has a very strong odor and taste, resembling that of rotten eggs and motor oil. It has to be taken with juice or some strong-tasting liquid or soft food to mask the taste, but even so can be nauseating. In some cases the child will not be able to keep it down, and must resort to one of the other chelators. In addition to GI tract upset, succimer can potentially cause liver damage and a fall in the white blood count. A child taking this medication must be monitored to guard against these adverse effects with examinations every 2–4 weeks.

> When 3-year-old Elena was found to have very high levels of lead in her blood, the doctor prescribed the oral chelator, Chemet. However, she was not able to take the medicine, vomiting whenever it was given to her.
>
> So she had to be hospitalized and was given a 5-day course of EDTA intravenously three times a day. This was very hard on her veins. Because of the high calcium content, the veins would collapse and a new one had to be punctured the next day. And there was no response—the blood lead level went neither up nor down.
>
> It was discovered that the hospital had overmedicated her. Because of the small size of a young child, the determination of the dosage can be very sensitive. Elena seemed very unresponsive and still. The hospital staff did not seem alarmed, but her mother Melissa sensed something was wrong. Elena only wanted to sleep and was difficult to awaken. Melissa finally learned that her child had become dangerously dehydrated.
>
> It was a frightening experience, seeing one's child in that state and feeling powerless. Later a nurse commented that the child had been in danger of dying. The whole experience was terrifying.[6]

D-Penicillamine (Cuprimine)

D-Penicillamine is given at lower blood lead levels, under 30 or 45 µg/dl, depending on the practitioner. In many areas it is not used because of concerns about potential toxicity and inexperience in its use. It can bring about side effects found with penicillin, such as rashes and nausea, which can be minimized by gradually increasing to the desired dosage. This drug is not officially approved for treating lead poisoning by the FDA because of the federal government's concern that it could be used unscrupulously by industries who want to cover up the fact that they are exposing workers to illegally dangerous levels of lead by using this treatment to maintain acceptable blood lead levels. According to Dr. John Graef at Children's Hospital in Boston, however, it is a relatively efficacious and safe option.[7]

Chelation Is Used Only in Limited Circumstances

The CDC has published guidelines for providing medical services for lead poisoning.[8] It is suggested that when a child has a slightly elevated blood lead level, efforts be directed only at finding and controlling the source of the poisoning, and at assessing and improving the child's diet. *These guidelines are summarized in Appendix E.*

Chelation therapy is recommended by the CDC to be used only in extreme cases where the blood lead level is over 45 μg/dl. It is generally not used in cases where levels are under 25 μg/dl. However, different lead treatment programs have different approaches toward this matter depending on their own level of confidence and experience.

As in the case of a child with any of a number of other diseases, a clinician will assess the best course of action. Each situation presents a unique set of circumstances, including:

- The characteristics of the individual child
- The source of the poisoning
- The duration of the exposure
- The severity of the poisoning
- The living environment of the child, including
  —the physical environment and
  —the social and cultural environment
- the resources available, in terms of
  —the experience and competence of the healthcare providers and
  —other services, such as social workers and alternative housing options

In Massachusetts, where the problem is one of the worst in the country, the attitude is more aggressive than the standard CDC recommended protocol. At Children's Hospital in Boston, for example, chelation is often used if environmental and nutritional intervention have failed to reduce the blood lead level below 20 μg/dl. Chelation can be unnecessary, once the other steps are taken. Where the exposure has been short term and the blood lead level is in the low 20s, or even in the 30s, if you just remove the lead source and WAIT, you may well see the blood lead go down to an acceptable level on its own over the course of a month.[9]

It cannot be emphasized enough that GETTING THE CHILD OUT OF THE LEAD comes before GETTING THE LEAD OUT OF THE CHILD. A child's blood lead will go right back up to dangerous levels if the child returns to the same lead hazards. In fact, some chelating agents can actually make the situation worse in such a case, as they increase the rate at which lead ingested by a child is absorbed (retained by the body rather than being excreted). Abatement of lead in the child's environment is absolutely necessary for the treatment to have any effect. Lowering of blood lead levels from chelation therapy can give the clinician a false sense of security, and leave the family with the sense that the problem is under control, when it actually is not.

In addition, some clinicians find that public health agencies will respond much more satisfactorily to a higher blood lead level. Taking steps to lower the blood lead level before the source of the problem is dealt with could actually be a disservice to the child. A lower blood lead level could make it more difficult to get services to eliminate the lead hazard, so the child could end up being exposed to more lead and being hurt more in the long term than if the treatment had not been given.[10]

Where Chelation Is Given

Hospitalization can be both very expensive and very traumatic for a young child and his or her family. Because of the recent availability and popularity of oral chelators, hospitalization for chelation is not as common as it was a few years ago. However, there are still instances where it is advisable.

In cases where a child is symptomatic, which is the rare exception, there might be danger of serious damage. Very severe poisoning can even be lethal if not treated, and such severity of toxicity could evolve in as little as 24 to 48 hours.

In cases of extremely high blood lead levels, over 70 or 80 μg/dl, the potential damage to the kidneys from the type and quantity of drugs needed to bring the blood lead down to an acceptable level calls for the child to be under close medical surveillance.

In cases where the clinician is unsure whether the family situation is one that will guarantee that the child is reliably given medication as prescribed, hospitalization might be necessary.

It is critical that a child who is chelated NOT be reexposed to the same lead sources that caused the poisoning. If the home presents a continuing hazard to the child and there is no alternative housing available, hospitalization might be used to protect the child from being repoisoned. Insurance companies, quite justifiably, often object to hospitals being used in this way. Some lead programs make temporary lead-free housing available to patients undergoing chelation and their families. These SAFE HOUSES provide the same protection as do hospitals and are a far preferable solution when they are available.[11]

EFFECTIVENESS OF CHELATION

Chelation therapy is generally accepted as the best treatment to remove some of the lead from a child with a high blood lead level. Although there is no treatment available that will get all of the lead out of a child's tissues, chelation does often increase the amount of lead that is excreted from the body. It is difficult to measure how effective it actually is, since a small percentage of the lead in a child's body is present in the blood, and the blood is the only part that is generally measured.

The efficacy of chelation has not been scientifically quantified. It continues to be used because it is effective in stopping the progression of the disease. It removes the most highly toxic fraction of lead, that which is circulating in the blood.

The Effectiveness of Chelation Is Evaluated in a Number of Ways

Blood Lead Level

The standard way to measure the effectiveness of chelation is to conduct repeated tests of the level of lead in the child's blood. As a general rule, blood lead levels go down when a child is chelated. It can be confusing to determine exactly how much lead is being eliminated because a child may be reexposed to lead, or lead from other parts of the body may be released from storage in the bones once some of the lead is eliminated.

The Rebound Effect

Chelators remove lead directly from the blood and soft tissues. After each treatment, the blood lead level will usually rise again, either from lead taken out of storage from other locations in the body, or from lead in the environment. As long as the child is removed from the source of lead, the blood level will gradually decrease. The treatment will often need to be repeated several times to remove this lead migrating from other parts of the body into the blood.

ZPP/EP

Another way to measure lead in the body is via ZINC (OR ERYTHROCYTE) PROTOPOR-PHYRIN (ZPP or EP). This MEDICAL MARKER is not affected by the rebound effect as is the blood lead level. ZPP is an index of the level of lead or iron deficiency or both, as is EP, discussed in Chapter 4 on diagnosing lead poisoning. This index can be useful in indicating the length and severity of exposure to lead, especially when blood lead is above 35 μg/dl. Generally, if the child is in a lead-safe environment, then the measured level of ZPP (or EP) will go down as the blood lead level goes down.[12]

> Hemoglobin, the component of blood that transports oxygen, is a long molecule (like a snake, or a very long spear) and the heme is the BUSINESS end of the molecule (as is the head of a snake). The heme is shaped like a cross with an iron atom at the center, without which it is not stable. It is assembled in hundreds of steps, the final one of which is the insertion of the iron atom. If there is insufficient iron, or the enzyme responsible for getting the iron into the heme is disabled, or interfered with by lead, then zinc will take its place, to stabilize the heme molecule. Thus, the number of these would-be hemes with zinc instead of iron (ZPP) is a measure of how much lead is present in the blood (or absence of iron, which can also be tested for).

REVERSIBILITY OF DAMAGE FROM LEAD POISONING

Although chelation therapy can alleviate some of the symptoms of lead poisoning, such as lack of appetite, colic, and anemia, it appears that learning disabilities, behavior problems, and the impairment of the intelligence may not be so readily reversed. There is, however, enough evidence to make one hopeful that the damage is at least to some extent reversible. Recent research has shown that cognitive ability increases when blood lead levels are decreased, at a rate of one IQ point for every decrease of 3 μg/dl.[13]

There is an argument that a child who is poisoned as an infant is more likely to recover more completely than a child poisoned at 4 or 5 because the brain is more resilient in infancy. The difference between the effect of lead on the brain of an infant and that of an older child can be illustrated by a comparison between the effects of a bull in a china shop and one in a pottery studio. If the china is thrown around and broken, it's much more difficult to fix than if soft, not yet formed and fired clay were tossed around and damaged. The latter has not yet reached its final solid form, and the final product might well show no effect at all from the damage, with the proper intervention.[14]

On the other hand, it is possible that injury to certain processes that are developed early on may adversely affect other parts of the brain's development which might depend on these early processes.[15]

There is more clarity regarding the reversibility of medical damage done by lead poisoning. When lead is removed by chelation, any damage to the kidneys or the production of heme and vitamin D is reversed.[16]

Whether or not any specific damage already caused by lead poisoning can be reversed, chelation, by getting the toxin out of the body, prevents further damage from occurring.

PART FOUR

Coping with Lead Poisoning

You need to get past the anger and guilt and move on with the work of helping the child.
Many a lead poisoning nurse and social worker

CHAPTER EIGHT

Getting Appropriate
Educational Services

THE ROLE OF THE NEUROPSYCHOLOGIST

Lead Affects the Functioning of the Brain

Lead poisoning causes changes in the chemistry of the nervous system. These changes in turn affect the nerves and the communication between cells. This can result in detectable differences in the way the brain functions. Thinking, learning, memory, and the ability to focus attention can be adversely affected. The speed at which the muscles respond can be slowed. Hearing can be mildly impaired, as can the ability to listen and to speak. The sense of balance, as well as motor and hand–eye coordination, can be disturbed.

Numerous studies throughout the world have shown that children who have suffered from lead poisoning have lower IQs on standardized tests as a result, relative to children with acceptable levels of lead.[1] But IQ testing does not always predict how well a child will do in school when there are known or suspected changes in the brain (because of lead or any other condition).

A Neuropsychologist Analyzes the Effect on the Individual Child

A neuropsychologist can help predict and ameliorate learning disabilities. Neuropsychologists administer standardized individual testing of thinking, memory, language, motor, and listening skills. Neuropsychological testing can help determine whether a problem is developmental and can be outgrown. A neuropsychologist can help make recommendations to parents, teachers, and other specialists for remediation.

Does the Blood Lead Level Reflect the Damage Done to the Brain?

The standard way of measuring the severity of a case of lead poisoning is the blood lead level. The CDC has set certain levels to indicate a child's risk of damage from lead poisoning. The blood level of lead is a fairly accurate measure of how much lead a child has been exposed to in the days and weeks preceding the test. This is useful as far as the medical practitioner is concerned, because it indicates immediate danger from high lead levels and the urgency of the need to eliminate sources of lead in the child's environment.

However, the blood lead level does not reveal the total amount of lead that a child has absorbed and may be present in the rest of the body. The blood contains only a small percentage of the lead in the body. The amount that has been absorbed by the child but does not show up in the blood can be important in determining the range of effects of lead on that child.

The Amount of Time the Child Was Exposed Is Also Important

A neuropsychologist evaluating a child should try to find out how long the child has been exposed to lead, because this can be an indicator of how much lead has been absorbed. This knowledge is important in predicting the future effects that lead may have on learning ability and behavior. The length of time the child has been exposed is referred to as CHRONICITY. X rays taken at the time of treatment or estimates based on EP testing may indicate chronic exposure. EP measures the ERYTHROCYTE PROTOPORPHYRIN in the blood to assess the effect over time of lead's interfering with the production of hemoglobin (the part of the red blood cell that transports oxygen to the cells of the body).

The Age at which the Child Is Poisoned May Influence the Type of Damage

An additional factor that may influence the effect that lead has on the brain is the age at which the child was exposed. Scientific research has shown that different parts of the brain, serving different functions, develop most rapidly at different times. Therefore, lead's interference in the development of the brain may damage different specific functions depending on when exposure occurs and which part of the brain is at a critical stage of development at the time. A 9-month-old infant who has a blood level of 30 μg/dl for 6 months might suffer damage different from that of a 27-month-old who also has had a blood lead level of 30 μg/dl for 6 months.[2]

EARLY INTERVENTION AND HEAD START

Early intervention and Head Start programs help to analyze any developmental delays or learning disabilities a child might have, and provide specialized services to overcome those difficulties so the child will be as well prepared as possible to begin school.

These programs assist children with many types of developmental difficulties to get treatment as quickly as possible. If the family has no medical insurance, staff will help them look for insurance. If a parent is unable to get an immediate appointment for a child who needs medical attention, they will help in this effort as well. They may have family advocates who help with transportation, for example, or even translating if that is needed. They will give the physician background information on the child, and help the family make connections with the proper resources.

Early intervention programs provide services free of charge to help children from birth to age 3 from families of all income levels.

Head Start deals primarily (90%), but not exclusively, with children from ages 3–5 of low-income families. The program guidelines call for 10% of the children served to be disabled. The program is carried out in a NORMALIZED preschool classroom (not only children with disabilities).

In the case of a child with a high blood lead level, staff will monitor the child's development using screening tests as well as careful observations, where specific milestones are noted. Speech and language are screened separately and the child is referred out for a formal assessment if a delay is found.

Head Start has the advantage of offering a broad range of services including:

- Speech and language therapy
- Occupational therapy
- Physical therapy
- Nutrition, health, and safety support from para-professionals
- Mental health consultation for behavioral issues
- Play therapy

Head Start gives the parent an opportunity to be involved in decision making, not only about individualized programs. Parents participate, for example, in hiring and firing, curriculum committees, and the budgetary process.[3]

SERVICES OFFERED BY THE PUBLIC SCHOOLS

Because of the effects that lead poisoning has on the development of the brain and different skills controlled by various parts of the brain, children who have been lead poisoned often have difficulties in school. Lead-poisoned children are more likely to be easily distracted or to have a hard time sitting still. Various types of learning disabilities may result from the damage done to the brain by lead. Organizational skills or higher-order thinking skills might be impaired. Language skills or hearing might be less well developed than in a child who has not been exposed to lead.

These problems are not insurmountable, however. The fact that a particular type of task is more difficult for your child than for the average child does not mean that he or she will never be able to master that task. It may mean that it will take a greater effort to teach the child or that a specific approach will be necessary for the child to learn well. But there is help available for children with learning disabilities and other types of difficulties that hinder their ability to do well in school. And federal law guarantees you the right to get that help.

Preschool Screening

If you have any concerns about developmental delays your child might have as a result of lead poisoning (or for any other reason) that might affect his or her readiness for public school, you can request that the school department conduct a preschool screening beginning at age 3. Screening is similar to that provided in the Head Start program, described in the last section. Follow-up assessments are done when necessary. The need for special services can then be determined. You will be advised of what special preschool programs are available. You and your school department will also be able to better assess which special services may be helpful in supporting your child once he or she enters kindergarten and later grades.

The Right to a Free, Appropriate Public Education in the Least Restrictive Environment Possible

Every child has the right not only to a free public education, but to an education that is appropriate for that child's needs. If your child needs specific services or accommodations in order to learn, because of ANY disability, then you have the right to get those services and accommodations from your public school system.

The right to a FREE APPROPRIATE PUBLIC EDUCATION (FAPE) is guaranteed by two separate federal laws. State laws can require even more special services than are mandated by the federal laws, but no state can offer less than these federal laws require.

A child with special needs must be given appropriate services either in the regular classroom or, only if necessary, in a different setting. If the services your child needs are not provided in your school system, the school district may have to pay for those services to be provided elsewhere. However, any services that CAN be provided within the district, within the child's regular school, and within the regular classroom SHOULD be so provided, so that the environment in which the child is taught is not any more restrictive than necessary. This is referred to as the requirement for the LEAST RESTRICTIVE ENVIRONMENT (LRE).

Whether a child does need special services and, if so, which special services are appropriate, is determined through a collaborative effort among the parents, school officials, and any psychiatrist, neuropsychologist, or other professional the family or the school system has hired to help. Individuals who specialize in advocating for a special needs child can also be engaged for this purpose. In some states, educational advocates are provided by the state department of education free of charge.

The law gives every child with a suspected disability the right to have that special need evaluated and to receive special services if appropriate. The parent has the right to be notified regarding the identification, evaluation, and placement of the child. Special procedures must be provided by the school system to impartially settle any disagreement the parent might have regarding how the school system is handling the situation.

Types of Services Available to Accommodate a Child's Educational Needs

Special Education

Certain disabled children have the right to an education specially designed to meet their unique needs. The federal INDIVIDUALS WITH DISABILITIES IN EDUCATION ACT (IDEA)[4] requires that any child who falls into certain specific categories of disabilities, which adversely affect educational performance, be offered specially designed instruction so that he or she will benefit from education. Related services, such as counseling or occupational therapy, need to be provided if they are necessary for the student to benefit from that specially designed instruction.

In order to qualify for special education services, the unique needs of the child who requires specially designed instruction must be due to a specific disability. The federal law lists specific disabilities that are covered. The list includes hearing impairments and SPECIFIC LEARNING DISABILITIES. A learning disability is defined as "a disorder in one or more of the basic psychological processes involved in understanding or in using language, spoken or written, which disorder may manifest itself in imperfect ability to listen, think, speak, read, write, spell, or do mathematical calculation." Learning problems are not considered "learning disabilities" if they are primarily caused by mental retardation; emotional disturbances; visual, hearing, or motor handicaps; or environmental, cultural, or economic disadvantages. Some states include additional categories that qualify for special education services.

Lead poisoning may cause minor hearing impairment or learning disabilities, which might make a child eligible for special education services. Attention deficit may also be associated with lead poisoning. The U. S. Department of Education has advised that ADHD students may be eligible under the OTHER HEALTH IMPAIRMENT category if problems of alertness negatively affect academic performance. Approximately 50% of ADHD students actually qualify for special education.[5] School districts and states vary in their approach to this.

A broad range of services can be included. Often an aide, also called a teacher assistant or a paraprofessional, is provided to assist the child in the regular classroom. Other special services range from counseling and occupational therapy to modification of academic work and special one-on-one sessions in a learning center separate from the regular classroom.

Section 504

A child whose impairment does not make him or her eligible under the special education laws might still be covered under another federal law, referred to as SECTION 504. Section 504 of the federal REHABILITATION ACT OF 1973[6] requires public schools to provide full participation in and benefits from any program or activity (of the public schools) to any student who has any physical or mental impairment that substantially limits any major life activity. MAJOR LIFE ACTIVITY is defined as including learning. So, if your child has any impairment which limits his or her ability to learn or otherwise function normally at school, you may have the right under Section 504 to obtain services necessary to accommodate your child in the regular classroom in the public schools.

Modifications that are provided under Section 504 include coordination between teaching and nursing staff to administer medications when necessary, or accommodations in the academic setting, such as providing a calculator to a child who has trouble with memorization of math facts, or special assistance from an aide.

Other Modifications within Regular Classrooms

Even if your child does not have a disability that would legally qualify him or her for special services or Section 504 accommodations, you may still get help for a child with problems in school. In many cases, simple measures can be taken in the classroom to overcome slight difficulties a child might have in paying attention or remembering assignments. You can enlist the assistance of the classroom teacher, principal, school nurse, or a counselor to choose and carry out appropriate modifications.

A child who is easily distracted, for example, could be placed in the front of the classroom so that the teacher can stand near him or her and occasionally give some type of cue for attention. A child with poor auditory memory might need directions and assignments to be written on the blackboard. This type of modification could be undertaken by the school system without going through any of the procedures required under federal laws applying to more serious disabilities.[7]

THE ROLE OF THE PARENT

Ask for Help

Parents of children with special needs are often reluctant to ask for this type of help. There is a tendency to pretend that an issue doesn't exist or that it will get better by itself. Some parents are afraid that asking for special treatment will stigmatize their child. However, the sooner you address the issue and intervene on behalf of a child who is presenting a learning problem in school, the better off the child is.

Advocate for Your Child

Do not assume a child is getting all of the services he or she needs. Pursue all of the available resources aggressively, either by yourself or through an educational advocate. The services are there, and you have the legal right to receive those that are appropriate for your child. But no matter how well meaning and hard working a special education staff is, they cannot give each child the amount of personal attention that is required. Nor can any one professional be totally knowledgeable about every special need. The ultimate responsibility remains with you as a parent to advocate for your child.

You can do a lot yourself to contribute to your child's development and help overcome his or her handicap. Giving your child plenty of nurturing and stimulation can help. You can provide your child developmental opportunities that can help to compensate for any disadvantage regardless of its cause. *For names of publications and organizations for more information and support regarding obtaining special services from public schools, see Appendix B, under* Special Education.

CHAPTER NINE

The Psychosocial Impacts
of Lead Poisoning

EMOTIONAL IMPACTS

Denial

It is not uncommon for parents to want to avoid dealing with the issue of lead poisoning. There are so many things to worry about, why should they have their child screened for lead and maybe give themselves another issue to deal with? Or once they know their child has an elevated blood lead level, they may feel that because they cannot afford a full-scale abatement of their home, they are powerless to do anything about it, so why try?

It is natural to avoid, or refuse to believe or think about a crisis or a stressful situation. This response, referred to as DENIAL by psychotherapists, can be a useful coping mechanism when the stressful situation is one that cannot be changed. It serves no purpose to fixate on something that one can do nothing about.

However, we sometimes also react this way to situations we COULD do something about. In this case denial can prevent us from doing anything to help alleviate the problem. It helps us in the short term by sparing us the stress of thinking about a problem. But, by preventing us from addressing and solving the problem, it can hurt us in the long term.[1]

We are surrounded by environmental toxins. For the most part, we can do little or nothing to avoid them. In many cases, if we live in populated areas, we must accept the fact that we, and our children, are breathing polluted air, unless we are willing to pick up and move far away from our friends and jobs. We may try to be careful about the additives in the food we buy and the latest contaminant that is found in our water supply. But if we worry about each and every detail, we could drive ourselves crazy. So to one extent or another, each of us chooses our battles and ignores other potential health threats.

Lead poisoning, however, can be distinguished from most other environmental threats in two very important ways. First, it is very easy to know how much lead a child is absorbing from the environment, and therefore how great the risk is for that child, simply by testing the child's blood. Second, lead poisoning is preventable. In many cases, we can remove sources of lead from the child's environment and thus reduce the threat of lead poisoning. Even in cases where lead sources cannot be completely avoided, there are a number of reasonable steps that we can take to reduce the threat to our children.

In spite of this difference, however, the attitude of avoidance and denial might be carried over into responding to lead poisoning. Because there are so many things to worry about, why should we perhaps create another issue to deal with?

Guilt

The overwhelming sense of responsibility created by being a parent and the all-consuming desire to give our children what is best can make the experience of lead poisoning very difficult to handle psychologically. Ultimately, we feel we have the obligation to protect our children from anything bad. We must be all-knowing and all-powerful or we are bad parents.

Some parents of lead-poisoned children have a hard time getting past the feeling that they should have done more. Maybe they knew that there was lead paint and that lead paint was dangerous, but they did not take all of the precautions that they could have. In some cases, they did not know what precautions to take or how important they were. Even with the latter knowledge, the task of turning a hazardous environment into a safe one may seem impossible, unaffordable. Our lives can be very complicated, and often seem overwhelming, with the broad array of responsibilities a parent has. We have to do what we feel is reasonable.

It's not the parent's fault. It was not you, the parent, who manufactured lead-based paint. It was probably not you who applied it to the home you lived in 20 or more years ago. And if you did, it was certainly without the knowledge that it might poison your child. You cannot take personal responsibility for the failure of our public policy to protect families from this poison.

The best thing a parent can do for his or her child is to accept what has happened as simply an accident and get on with the work of helping the child to recover and overcome whatever damage may have been done.

Stress

Lead poisoning can create financial stress in a family. Especially when lead poisoning is caused by exposure to paint and dust from housing, removing the source of exposure can be

Before moving into their new Victorian, the Sausers were required to remove the old paint, in order to qualify for a low-interest loan from an innovative neighborhood organization. Within 6 months of moving into their new suburban home, Jonathan changed from a model child to one who seemed to be "possessed." Previously he had slept soundly through from 8:00 at night until 9:00 in the morning. Now he couldn't get to sleep at night. His mother, Margaret, would typically stay with him from 8 until midnight before he would finally fall asleep. He was easily frustrated and would throw himself against a wall, pick himself up, and throw himself against the wall again. Margaret tried dietary changes, eliminating artificial ingredients that had been associated with hyperactivity. No change.

Although her pregnancy with Jonathan had gone smoothly, her next pregnancy was difficult. At 3 months she experienced bleeding and at 5 months went into premature labor which necessitated her leaving work, staying at home, and "keeping her feet up," as much as one can with a 2-year-old at home, for the rest of the pregnancy.

Cameron was born 4 weeks early, but he was 95th percentile on the height and weight charts. At about 8 months when he first started crawling around on the floor, he was still about 75th percentile.

But then something changed. At 10 months he was only at 25th percentile. The doctor suggested that she substitute formula for breast milk. As per the doctor's orders, she boiled the water every morning, straight from the tap, and mixed up the formula for the day's bottles. She didn't know that she was increasing the chances of lead contamination from the tap water both by using the water that sat in the pipes all night and by boiling the water, which concentrated the lead.

When Cam was a little over 1 year old, Margaret's sister suggested screening the children for lead, a procedure that was routine where she lived, in Massachusetts, but not widely practiced in Michigan. It took weeks to convince the doctor, because he "saw no need" to subject the children to this procedure. They were finally tested. Both children were lead poisoned.

Everything she had been doing for her children was poisoning them. The baby's growth problems, she learned later, were caused by the lead dust that permeated the home from sanding and scraping the old paint from the exterior and interior of the newly purchased house. She had tried to make a beautiful, comfortable home for her family, but it turned out she was poisoning her children with lead dust.

The problem was only exacerbated when she boiled the water for the baby's formula, concentrating the lead that the baby ended up consuming in the formula.

Lead still covered the sun porch where the children played. She knew by now that it would do more damage than good to remove it without elaborate precautions, which they could not afford. Whatever she did, she was poisoning her children. She was overwhelmed by a feeling of guilt.[2]

very expensive. In the case of a family who own the home, they might have purchased an older home in poor condition specifically because they could not afford one in better condition. The inability to pay for abatement may necessitate them moving, which is expensive in and of itself. Often saddled with medical expenses, which may or may not be covered by insurance, parents may end up in bankruptcy or needing to take on additional part- or full-time jobs. The extra time demands of taking care of and advocating for a child with developmental disabilities are only made more difficult by this set of circumstances.

Lead poisoning can create a lot of psychological stress in a marriage. If one parent doesn't blame him- or herself, the other parent might be blamed. Why wasn't he or she more careful and better informed? Professionals advise couples to be aware of this danger and make extra efforts to keep communications open and try to get past what has already happened and work together toward a solution and toward helping the child.

Stigma

Afraid of being cited for code violations for peeling paint, Rita May started melting the lead paint off the exterior of her 1905 Victorian using a heat gun and sanding when she got to the base. She was unaware of the hazards presented by lead-based paint, and remembers getting headaches after using the heat gun to melt the paint. She did stop the work when she became pregnant, in case of any detrimental effects on the fetus. But, unknowingly, she tracked lead-contaminated soil into the house on a daily basis.

After a prolonged effort to get the local health department to inspect the house, she was finally able to bring state inspectors in and lead paint was identified on the exterior. The only "help" they could offer, however, was advising her to undertake lead abatement work that was unaffordable for her. A social worker approached the local authorities on Rita's behalf, asking if there was any financial assistance available to help her pay for removing the lead paint. The response was simply, "We don't have a lead problem in this county."

When her daughter, who had been very fussy and difficult from birth, was 18 months old, Rita had her screened for lead poisoning. She was shocked to learn that her blood lead level was 34 μg/dl, over 3 times the level of concern. Feeling that others could learn from her experience, Rita shared her story in the local newspaper. Her colleagues at the county health department, where she worked as a registered nurse, treated her differently after this. She was blamed for giving the town a bad name and causing property values to drop. Rita was so harassed in town that she had to move. Police officers knocked on her door time after time, complaining about cardboard boxes being left on the porch or weeds growing too long in the yard, even demanding that she get rid of her old station wagon because it was "unsightly."

Rita's daughter was diagnosed at age 2½ as hyperactive. Rita was advised by a friend to ask Medicaid for assistance in dealing with the hyperactivity. She approached them teary eyed, weary from dealing with a difficult child, but hopeful of finding some help. They accused her of being "mentally unstable" because she was acting emotionally. They sent a social worker to Rita's home who identified such "offenses" as unfolded laundry and a cluttered house, and removed her daughter from the home for 10 days. Using both lead poisoning and the clutter in the home as justification, they put Rita on a child abuse and neglect registry. This would impede her from being hired for any nursing or child care position for a 10 year period.[3]

Lead poisoning can create a stigma against the family of the victim. There is a natural tendency to want to deny a problem. Often, the person pointing out a problem is blamed for the negative repercussions of calling attention to that problem. In the case of lead poisoning, an individual who points out that homes in a particular neighborhood may have high concentrations of lead might be blamed for her child being lead poisoned and for upsetting neighbors and bringing down property values.

The family that is actually the victim of lead poisoning may be blamed as if they were the culprit. In a lawsuit against a landlord for lead poisoning from paint on the premises of rental property, a classic defense is that the parent did not watch the child closely enough, and thus it is the parent's fault that the child ingested paint and became poisoned.

Fear of the Unknown

Fear of the unknown may send a parent of a lead-poisoned child into a state of near panic. The experience is totally new. Anything could happen. Questions bombard the parent: "How will I know what to do?" "Will I lose my house?" "Will the state take away my child?"

It is normal to be afraid of the unknown. A parent learning that his or her child is lead poisoned is facing a new experience. You may feel that you do not know what is going to happen to your child or your family and be afraid that you will have no idea how to handle the situation.

Parents are afraid their children will have to undergo painful treatment or that the treatment will not work. They are afraid they are inadequate as parents. Sometimes they try to overcompensate for what they feel must have been a lack of good care for their children and drive themselves crazy constantly washing their children's hands and toys. A more moderate, reasonable approach is healthier overall for the family.

Some parents of lead-poisoned children are afraid they will be seen as bad parents, or even have their children taken away by the state. This fear is especially common in cases where state officials intervene on behalf of the child. However, it is a very rare eventuality—only where there is other significant neglect on the part of the parents—that the state takes any action to protect the child from negligence or abuse. Lead poisoning in and of itself is not grounds for neglect, and cannot be used to take your children away.

Shame

There is sometimes a sense of shame combined with this fear. A middle-class parent might have thought that only families of lower socioeconomic status could get lead poisoning and feel that they have failed to keep up a level of care for their children that is expected of a middle-class family. The idea that only poor inner-city children can be lead poisoned is a myth. Families of all social classes fall victim to the disease.

Conflict

Some parents of lead-poisoned children are afraid they will lose the DREAM HOUSE they worked so long to buy. They feel pushed into a position of having to choose between the health and safety of their children and holding on to this dream of building a better life. In the case of rental property, the financial burden imposed on the property owner may be difficult to handle. This can cause conflict between a tenant and a landlord who is unable or unwilling to spend the money to do the job right.

Frustration

In some cases of lead poisoning, the family is legally forced to have the lead paint in the home removed. The experience of dealing with contractors and public health officials can be very stressful. Even if a home owner wants to do the right thing, he or she may be unable to do so because of financial limitations. Even if money is not a major issue, it might be very difficult to get the work you want done completed in a timely and competent manner, in spite of all of the efforts you may make.

A homeowner having property abated may feel pushed by public officials, stretched financially, and overcharged and disappointed by contractors. Work is not finished when it is supposed to be, or in the manner agreed on. The estimates seem exorbitant. And the health department treats you like a criminal.

Anger

Anger can be a healthy response if it leads to action. There is a lot that a parent can do in response to lead poisoning. Measures that you can take to help your child are described throughout this book. Actions you can take to reach beyond your personal situation and work toward protecting others from lead poisoning are discussed in Chapter 18.

HOW TO GET HELP

A variety of services are available both to assist with concrete tasks and to support you through the PSYCHOSOCIAL impacts of lead poisoning, that is, the stress, guilt, frustration, and anger that can result from this kind of crisis. Parents and professionals who have experience with lead poisoning can help by listening sympathetically and can often provide helpful advice. Do not be afraid to ask for help.

Public Agencies

Some parents have found that when state authorities are difficult to deal with, the local health department may be the source of needed support. In other cases, if the local agency is unable to help, parents may find the necessary expertise and assistance from the state lead program. In one case, when a family was having a hard time getting local authorities to come to their aid, a journalist intervened and advocated for them, and got a response at the state level. Some parents have even found individuals at federal agencies, such as the CDC, or the lead hot line run by the National Safety Council to be very helpful.

Lead poisoning laws may seem inflexible and impossible to comply with in some circumstances. The amount of work that is required or the time frame within which it must be completed may seem so unrealistic that a parent might not know how to respond and end up feeling frustrated.

As a parent, your interests are ultimately the same as those of the state (or municipality)— to protect your children. Even if you are unable to meet the letter of the law, you can work with the agency enforcing the law and negotiate a way to accomplish your shared goal in a reasonable way. Show them that you are making good faith efforts to comply. Let them know what you are going through and how difficult the situation is. If the inspector who visits your

---

Ellen and Carl Goodman conscientiously brought their daughter, Natalie, for a checkup and lead screening at eight months of age rather than waiting until the recommended one year, concerned that renovation work they were doing in their home might put her at risk of lead poisoning. Little did they know how dramatic an impact this move would have on their life.

The Goodmans' first shock was learning Natalie had an elevated level of lead in her blood. Their second shock followed shortly thereafter when a City Board of Health inspector showed up with no prior notice at their home, pointed a strange-looking machine all over the walls, doors, and windows of their brownstone, and cited them for 44 violations of the lead poisoning law, with a warning that these hazards must be remedied within FIVE DAYS. If not, the City would send in their own contractors and, if the Goodmans couldn't pay the bill, a lien would be put on their property.

The Goodmans looked desperately for a contractor to do the work. When the first estimate came in they had their third shock. It would cost them between $30,000 and $55,000. The contractor insisted that in order for Natalie to be safe, not only the cited violations had to be corrected but all of the potential lead hazards in the entire house had to be remedied. Carl was unemployed at the time. How could they possibly afford this? It all seemed totally impossible.

They spoke to the health department, who didn't seem to understand how financially demanding the requested work really was. Once Carl showed them the estimates they had received, they showed a little more understanding. He found that the key word to negotiating was HARDSHIP. Using that particular terminology seemed to get a sympathetic response. Supported by paperwork documenting both the fact that concrete efforts were being undertaken and the high costs involved, they were able to get some flexibility.

The process continued to be the source of great stress and frustration. The contractors seemed not to understand the subtleties of working with mid-19th century woodwork. Twice a month, various inspectors showed up with no previous knowledge of their case and with inconsistent opinions and declarations. When local legal requirements changed to provide more flexibility, no one bothered to inform the Goodmans of that fact.

The Goodmans learned to deal with the system. They feared that if they antagonized an inspector, he or she might strike back by testing more surfaces, which could then be added to the list of violations. They found that while more experienced inspectors seemed more reasonable, when a "rookie" was on their case the letter of the law ruled and their pleas for flexibility were best addressed to supervisors back at the office. A helpful Board of Health official advised them to take an attitude of "don't ask, don't tell." If an inspector remarked that a certain violation seemed to be remedied and marked it off as such, they would let it be.[4]

house does not seem willing or able to accommodate you, contact his or her supervisor. Always get everything in writing—communications with the public agency as well as with contractors.

Parent Support Groups

In many locations, groups have been organized by parents of lead-poisoned children specifically to help other parents of lead-poisoned children. They provide various forms of support and information. If there is a group in your area, contact them. If not, you might want to consider organizing one. Contact an existing group to get advice. *For listings of support groups in your state, see Appendix A. For a discussion of organizing, see Chapter 18.*

Social Workers

Hospitals and state lead programs may have social workers to help lead-poisoned families deal with some of the repercussions of lead poisoning.

Social workers try to offer any type of support that will help strengthen the family so that they can deal with the disease. They help parents with medical insurance. They provide support administering medication, if a chelating drug is prescribed. If transportation is a problem, social workers will help work out an arrangement to enable the family to get to the hospital or doctor's office when they need to.

Social workers serve as resource coordinators. They are knowledgeable about various support services that are available and will empower parents by putting them into contact with needed resources. If there is a possible learning disability resulting from the lead poisoning, social workers can refer parents to early intervention programs, Head Start, or preschool screening programs. *For more information on early intervention, Head Start, and services available through public schools, see Chapter 8.*

In some cases parents are reluctant to take advantage of this type of resource, because they don't want their child labeled. The social worker will encourage the parents by pointing out the positives, namely, the long-term benefit that the child and the family may get from such a program.

Social workers are familiar with the lead poisoning law in the state and can advise parents on how to comply.

Perhaps most importantly, social workers give parents an often much-needed opportunity to talk it out. They reassure parents that their exaggerated fears and conflicts are normal, and that they will not lose their home or their child. They give positive reinforcement to parents who are oppressed with guilt, informing them that many parents feel the same way, but that the problem is not their fault.

Social workers listen sympathetically to what a parent is going through and make suggestions on how to deal with the situation in a reasonable way. A parent might feel overwhelmed with guilt or anger. The social worker will support the parent through the crisis.

A parent may become obsessed with cleanliness in an effort to compensate for what he or she might perceive as past carelessness. A social worker will try to work out with the parent a responsible but still livable way of caring for the child.[5]

Family Counseling

If a sympathetic social worker is not available, a parent may want to seek the services of a family counselor. In some cases, social workers will refer families who are having a hard time coping to counseling.

PART FIVE

Controlling Lead Paint Hazards

Living in a house with lead paint is like having a lion sleeping in your living room. You've got a dangerous situation. The difficulty lies in how to cage it without awakening it—lest it devour your children. And the saddest part of it all is that when it pounces you won't even hear its silent roar.
Jonathan Bader, parent of lead-poisoned child, Wisconsin

CHAPTER TEN

Lead in Paint and Dust

Lead-based paint is responsible for most lead poisonings of children in this country. Twelve million children a year are exposed to lead paint, more children than are exposed to any other source of lead in the environment.[1] And, when they are exposed to lead paint that is peeling or chipping, the quantities of lead children ingest can be very high. According to one medical center that treats lead-poisoned patients, 99.9% of severe cases of lead poisoning in children are caused by ingesting lead-based paint or dust containing lead from paint.[2]

Although lead-based paint was banned from use in homes in the United States in 1978, 3 million tons of old lead-based paint still line the walls and fixtures of 64 million homes. About two-thirds of our homes have lead-based paint.[3]

In older homes (those constructed early in this century and before), not only were the walls, trim, and other wood components painted with lead-based paint, but almost all metals were primed with red lead or painted with lead-based paint. Lead may be present in milk-based (casein) and water-based paints (distemper and calcimines). It may also be contained in varnishes, which used lead acetate as a drying agent, as well as in window glazing putty.[4]

In addition, lead-based paint is still permitted for commercial and industrial uses. Because lead helps paint stand up to sun and harsh weather, it is often used for painting the exteriors of automobiles, boats, buildings, and bridges. Children's playground equipment may

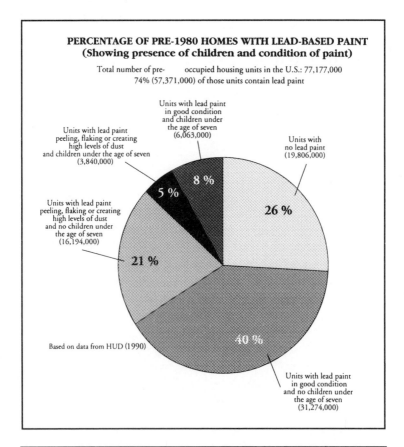

PERCENTAGE OF PRE-1980 HOMES WITH LEAD-BASED PAINT
(Showing presence of children and condition of paint)

Total number of pre-   occupied housing units in the U.S.: 77,177,000
74% (57,371,000) of those units contain lead paint

Units with lead paint
in good condition
and children under
the age of seven
(6,063,000)

Units with lead paint
peeling, flaking or creating
high levels of dust
and children under the age of seven
(3,840,000)

Units with
no lead paint
(19,806,000)

Units with lead paint
peeling, flaking or creating
high levels of dust
and no children under
the age of seven
(16,194,000)

8 %

5 %

26 %

21 %

40 %

Based on data from HUD (1990)

Units with lead paint
in good condition
and no children under
the age of seven
(31,274,000)

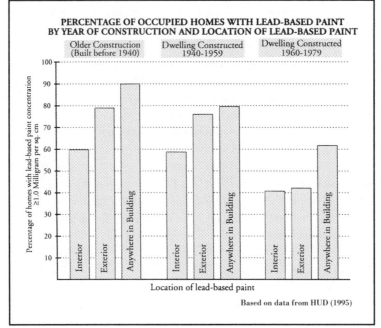

PERCENTAGE OF OCCUPIED HOMES WITH LEAD-BASED PAINT
BY YEAR OF CONSTRUCTION AND LOCATION OF LEAD-BASED PAINT

| Older Construction (Built before 1940) | Dwelling Constructed 1940-1959 | Dwelling Constructed 1960-1979 |

Percentage of homes with lead-based paint concentration ≥1.0 Milligram per sq. cm

Location of lead-based paint

Based on data from HUD (1995)

be painted with lead-based paint. The white and yellow lines on our roads contain large amounts of lead, which contaminates the environment as they wear away.

Children may also be exposed to lead paint on toys and furniture purchased before 1976, after which time it was prohibited for that purpose. Old baby cribs and bassinets, which might be gnawed by teething infants, present one of the greatest hazards in this category.

HOW LEAD FROM PAINT ENTERS OUR BODIES

It is commonly known that children can be poisoned by chewing on windowsills or eating paint chips containing lead. However, even a child who does not put paint into his or her mouth may be threatened by lead paint. There are several other ways that children, as well as adults, ingest lead from paint.

Lead-paint and lead-contaminated dust can be threats to children not only in their homes but in any environment where they spend a lot of time. This includes day-care centers and schools as well as the homes of friends, relatives, or baby sitters.

Deterioration of Lead-Painted Surfaces Causes a Lead Hazard

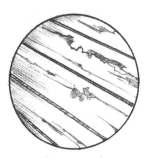

Lead-based paint becomes a hazard when it becomes accessible to small children. This happens when paint deteriorates. Paint deterioration can take the more obvious form of chipping, peeling, or chalking, or the more subtle form of wearing away to a fine dust. Both the level of maintenance of the home and the initial preparation of the surface before it was painted affect how well paint will hold up over the years. Paint deterioration is generally caused by either moisture or poor bonding due to inadequate preparation of the surface before it was painted.

Lead from Paint Can Reach Us through House Dust

Not only do the small pieces created by chipping, peeling, or flaking paint present a danger when they are eaten by small children, but these lead-laden chips can be ground into dust that can be spread over hard surfaces where they can be picked up inadvertently and ingested by children.

Through Friction and Abrasion of Interior Paint

Lead-based paint in the interior of your home can contaminate household dust even if the paint on the walls is not flaking and peeling and the home appears to be in good condition. When painted surfaces are rubbed against or bumped into, minute particles of lead paint are released into the household dust which covers our floors, windowsills, shelves, furnishings, and belongings. The frequent opening and closing of windows is one of the leading causes of

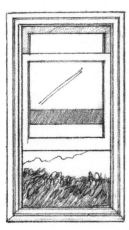

lead dust. The friction between the painted surfaces of the window and the track sends invisible particles of lead into the air.

This fine dust settles on objects and flat surfaces, especially windowsills and floors. Children crawling and playing on the floor can get this lead dust on their hands and playthings. They ingest the lead-contaminated dust when they touch their mouths or food. They can get lead dust in their mouths by putting toys that have been on the floor into their mouths. The lead dust can also be tracked around the house.

Through the Air Outside

Lead dust can also be created when minute particles in the air outside enter through open doors and windows and settle down inside our homes. Peeling or chipping lead paint from the exterior of our homes, for example, can find its way into household dust this way. If your home is near an industry that emits lead into the air, this also can contaminate your household dust.

The repairing of large painted structures, particularly bridges, can pose an especially pronounced threat if adequate precautions are not taken. During any activity that disrupts the paint on such structures, as in the sandblasting of a bridge, the air in the adjacent area can have extremely elevated concentrations of lead. The consequence of this type of work can be large quantities of lead being deposited on the soil in nearby neighborhoods, where it can threaten the safety of children in their yards, parks, and playgrounds.

Through Dirt

The dirt from outside our homes is a major source of house dust. Lead that contaminates our soil also can end up in the dust in our home. This includes sources such as deteriorated house paint, paint that has fallen off of old playground equipment, cars, boats, or agricultural machinery, industrial emissions, pesticides, or years of exposure to leaded gas exhaust from passing cars and trucks.

Home Renovation and Poorly Done Paint Removal Are Significant Sources of Lead Paint Poisoning

Renovating old houses can cause very dangerous levels of lead exposure. Any type of work that disrupts lead-painted surfaces carries this threat if not done with the proper safeguards. This includes demolition, remodeling, repainting, weatherization, or rehabilitation. The danger is greatest when the family remains in the home while the work is being done. However, even if they vacate the home during the work, the dust that remains after the work is completed can be dangerous. There have been many cases of upper-middle income families who were shocked to find their preschoolers severely lead poisoned after renovating their home.

Although the lead is invisible and the amount of dust that is produced may seem insignificant, lead is so toxic that the amounts released during remodeling activities pose substantial dangers to children and workers. For example, if only 1 square foot of painted surface is sanded and the paint on that square foot contains 1 milligram of lead per square centimeter (which is the lowest level covered by HUD regulations) and even if the dust is diluted by being spread out over 100 square feet, there will still be 9300 micrograms per square foot of lead dust. That is nearly 100 times greater than the level found safe to be left on floors by HUD regulations.[6]

Whenever you disrupt lead paint—that is, whenever you sand, scrape, or strip a surface that has been painted with lead-based paint (even if it is covered with other paint or wallpaper)—you may be releasing lead into the environment. Unless you take adequate safeguards, you are putting lead dust into the air to be breathed and spreading it as a dust throughout your home, where it can easily be ingested by your children when they touch their hands to their mouths or food. The same type of precautions need to be taken in protecting the home and cleaning up after home renovation work as is recommended for lead paint removal work.

Areas where lead will be disturbed must be separated from the rest of the house to avoid contaminating other areas with lead dust. Protective clothing and properly fitting respirators must be used. Dry scraping is particularly hazardous. But wet scraping should not be done near electric circuits, even if they have been deenergized.

Waste must be placed on 6-millimeter-thick plastic sheets, rather than directly on the ground, and stored in a secured area if kept overnight. For demolition, debris should be handled in a way to minimize lead dust. The normal drop chute method, for example, where debris is simply dumped down a tube onto the ground or a dumpster, creates unacceptable hazards.

Even bare wood, after all of the lead paint has been removed, can still be dangerous, because leaded particles can be embedded in the pores of the wood and be absorbed by children if they touch, chew, or mouth the wood.

Removing windows disrupts the lead-based paint coated surfaces of the window frame and the wall, so it must be done using precautions. However, once the window is removed, installing the new window can be done without these precautions. The same applies to removing and replacing other components, such as moldings and cabinets.

The Mahoneys lived in a two-story 19th century Victorian farmhouse with ten rooms. Most of the wooden floors, moldings, walls, ceilings, and door frames had been painted with lead-based paint.

When they had the home renovated, surfaces were restored by removing the paint down to the bare surface on floors and woodwork and recoating with new varnish. Ceilings were repaired, and wallpaper and paint were removed from a number of walls. Two workers used rotary power sanders, hand sanders, scrapers, heat guns, and chemical paint strippers. The family left the house during most of the renovation work, but returned after it was only partially completed. There was dust throughout the house.

After one of the family's dogs started to have seizures, a veterinarian determined that the dog was lead poisoned. Linda and her two children were then tested. The children had blood lead levels of 104 µg/dl and 67 µg/dl. These are five to ten times above the level of concern established by the federal government. Linda had a blood lead level of 56 µg/dl. All three were admitted to a local hospital where they were treated for severe lead poisoning. Linda was 8 weeks pregnant. Aware of the serious damage that lead can have on an unborn child, she decided to have a therapeutic abortion. Even the babysitter's two children, who spent a lot of time in the home, were affected. They were tested and found to have blood lead levels of 80 µg/dl and 68 µg/dl, and so were hospitalized and treated for severe lead poisoning.[5]

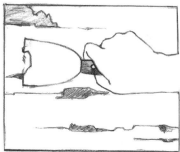

Unless you know that the paint in your home is not lead-based, you need to take these precautions for protecting yourself and your family from lead dust when remodeling, just as you would for lead paint removal or other hazards control work. *For more information on precautions for protecting against hazards from work that disrupts lead-painted surfaces, see Chapter 12. For more information on renovating homes with lead paint, call the National Lead Information Clearinghouse at 800-424-LEAD and ask for the EPA's brochure,* Reducing Lead Hazards When Remodeling Your Home, *or call your state lead program, listed in Appendix A.*

Note for landlords: If you do any kind of renovation in a unit where there is or may be lead paint, you or your contractor need to take measures to protect both the living space and your tenants' property from lead contamination. It is also your responsibility to educate tenants about the dangers of lead, the importance of keeping away from work areas, and the importance of their belongings being removed or covered.

Lead from Paint Can Reach Us through Soil

Lead can get into our soil from paint flakes or chips from homes, garages, playground equipment, or other structures. Children get this dirt on their hands when they play outdoors. They ingest the lead when they touch their hands to their mouths or their food. Pets can bring contaminated soil into the house on their feet and fur. This dirt is spread around the house and gets on children's hands when they touch their pet. Small children may also put pacifiers, toys, and other objects into their mouths after having touched the dirt and picked up lead.

HOW LEAD IN PAINT IS REGULATED

Federal Law Regulates Lead in Paint

Lead-Based Paint Ban

In 1976 lead paint was prohibited for use on eating, drinking, and cooking utensils, and in 1978 it was banned from toys and furniture.

In 1973 the U.S. Consumer Product Safety Commission set a limit of 0.5% lead for any paint manufactured for use in or on housing. In 1978 the current, much more protective standard of 0.06% maximum lead content was set. This had the effect of banning the use of paint with dangerous levels of lead in apartments and houses.

Title X

The most important federal law regarding lead paint poisoning is the Residential Lead-Based Paint Hazard Reduction Act of 1992, referred to as Title X. Although much of the law affects only publicly owned or assisted housing, there are also important provisions regarding licensing of contractors and information disclosure, which apply to private housing also.

Disclosure Requirements

Federal law requires that anyone selling or renting housing built before 1978 give the buyer or tenant a pamphlet about lead paint hazards, as well as any information the owner has about lead paint in the house. A landlord who has tested and found no lead-based paint is exempted from this requirement. A potential purchaser has 10 days after signing a purchase and sale agreement to have a lead paint inspection or risk assessment before being committed to buying the house. Contracts for purchase and sale must have special warnings about lead paint hazards. Sellers, lessors, and real estate agents are required to ensure that these requirements are fulfilled.

Contractors renovating housing built before 1978 must also give property owners a special pamphlet about lead.

Licensing Contractors

States must require contractors to be trained, certified, and licensed according to certain standards in order to abate (remove or otherwise control) lead paint. Specific types of contractors who do renovation and remodeling will also have to be trained and certified. If any state does not yet have a training and certification program in place by September 1998, the EPA will set up a program for that state by September 1999, out of its regional office.

Federally Owned or Assisted Housing

According to federal law, where paint has more than 0.5% lead content by weight, or where there is more than 1 milligram of lead for each square centimeter, hazards must be controlled or removed from TARGETED publicly owned or assisted housing (where young children are likely to live). *For a brief summary of these laws, along with legal citations, see Appendix H. For a brochure explaining this law in more detail, contact the Alliance To End Childhood Lead Poisoning, listed in Appendix B, under* Advocacy.

Some State and Local Laws Regulate Lead-Based Paint in Housing

Most states in the Northeast, where lead poisoning from lead-based paint is the most serious in the country, a few states elsewhere in the country, and some cities and counties have laws to protect the public from lead paint poisoning. Some of these only prohibit the use of lead-based paint in locations where young children might be exposed to it. A few states and localities require property owners to remove the lead paint in a home, usually only when there has been a case of lead poisoning. *To find out if your state has any laws regarding lead paint poisoning prevention, contact your state lead poisoning prevention program, listed in Appendix A.*

CHAPTER ELEVEN

Identifying Lead Paint Hazards

Any house built before 1980 and containing any paint, varnish, or plaster could present a hazard to your family. There are certain factors that make your home more likely to be contaminated with lead-based paint.

RISK FACTORS

Age of Home

Older homes are more likely to have lead-based paint. A house built before 1940 has a 90% chance of containing lead paint. One built between 1940 and 1959 has an 80% chance, and a home built between 1960 and 1979 has a 62% chance of containing lead-based paint.[1]

Not only are older homes more likely to have lead-based paint, but the concentration of lead in the paint also tends to be higher the older the home is. Before 1950, paint often contained as much as 50% lead. In the mid-1950s, manufacturers decreased the concentration of lead in their paints. In 1955, many paint manufacturers adopted a voluntary standard of 1% maximum lead content. In the mid-1960s that level was changed to 0.5%.[2] However, it was not until 1978 that the strict limit of 0.06% lead was imposed on house paint. Unless your home was built after 1978, you cannot be sure you are free of the threat of lead paint. Even some houses built a short time after the ban on lead paint could have been painted with supplies left over from the previous year. At least 74% of all private housing built before 1980 in this country contain some lead paint.[3] In addition, older homes tend to have more surface area painted with lead-based paint. The average home built before 1940, for example, has nearly 2000 square feet of lead-based painted surface, including exterior and interior walls and other building components, whereas the average home built between 1960 and 1979 has under 500 square feet.[4]

Condition of Paint

Lead paint is more dangerous to your family if it is in bad condition. Chipping, peeling, and flaking paint is easily converted into invisible dust contaminating floors, windowsills, shelves, furnishings, and belongings. About 10 million homes with lead paint have children under 7 years old living in them. Of these homes, about 4 million contain lead paint in dangerous condition.[5]

Recent Renovation

If there has been remodeling or major repairs in your home recently, you might be at increased risk for having high levels of lead dust. Any work that disrupts lead-painted surfaces will generate lead dust that spreads around onto floors and other hard surfaces unless measures are taken to minimize and contain it. Ordinary house cleaning is not effective in removing this fine dust.

TESTING FOR LEAD HAZARDS IN YOUR PAINT OR DUST

If your child is lead poisoned, you will need to know immediately if your paint contains lead. However, even if you do not have a lead-poisoned child, you might want to know anyway, in order to prevent any future harm from lead paint or dust.

Just before you are about to rent or buy a home is an ideal time to check out the lead, so that you know what you are getting into before you make a commitment. A federal law, referred to as Title X, now requires that a buyer be given 10 days to inspect a house for lead before being legally bound to go through with the purchase. If at this time you assess the lead hazards, as well as how expensive it might be to remedy them, you will be in a better position

to either choose a more affordable house, if the cost is prohibitive, or bargain down the price of the house, so that you will have enough funds available to abate the lead paint. *For more information on Title X, see Chapter 10 or Appendix H.*

There are 3 different approaches for checking out the lead paint hazards in your home—a screen risk assessment, a risk assessment, and a lead-based paint inspection—depending on your situation.

Screen Risk Assessment

If your home is in good condition and you do not think there is much risk of lead exposure, you can get an abbreviated type of assessment, referred to as a screen risk assessment, just to be sure. It is much simpler and less expensive than a standard risk assessment or a paint inspection. A screen risk assessment consists of a visual inspection of the condition of the paint and the analysis of only a few dust samples. If lead hazards are found, however, a full risk assessment should be done.

Risk Assessment

For an evaluation of the potential hazards in your home related to lead-based paint and dust, as well as advice on controlling those hazards to make your home safe, you can use the services of a professional risk assessor.

The risk assessor will ask you questions about your use patterns, most notably regarding where the children spend time, lead-related occupations of household members, how cleaning is done, the history of renovations, and the use of windows and entrances. He or she will visually examine the home, looking for deteriorating paint. The risk assessor will note any chalking, mildew, worn spots, blistering, scaling, peeling, cracking, flaking, or patterns of cracks or scales (that form from lack of elasticity or poor bonding). He or she will look for visible dust buildup, bare soil, painted surfaces that are worn from rubbing against each other, and any that show signs of having been chewed. Any water leakage or other form of moisture will be noted.

Sampling and Testing

The risk assessor may take dust and/or paint samples, generally from window areas and floors where children would be likely to play. He or she will usually not take water samples unless you so request. If a paint inspection has been done, then the results will be reviewed. Otherwise, any deteriorating paint would be analyzed by XRF or laboratory analysis. Any bare soil in outdoor play areas or sandboxes, vegetable gardens, or pathways should also be analyzed.

Dust testing is done by wiping a commercial wipe over a measured hard surface in a prescribed manner, and sending it to a laboratory for analysis. The risk assessor should send in a SPIKE or QC (quality control) sample, that is, one with a predetermined amount of lead dust, to test the accuracy of the laboratory analysis. He or she should also send in a wipe that has not been used to collect a sample. This is known as a FIELD BLANK or BLIND BLANK. Analyzing this unused wipe will determine whether the wipes are being contaminated by handling.[6] Specific wipes have been found to work well for these tests, including: Little Ones Baby Wash Cloths, Little Ones Diaper Wipes, (KMart) Pure and Gentle Baby Wipes, Walgreen's Wet Wipes, and Fame Baby Wipes.[7]

Dust Testing

Dust Wipe Sampling

A homeowner or tenant can also do dust wipe sampling to assess the safety of his or her home. This gives a good indication of how much lead dust is collecting around the home from friction and abrasion or deteriorating paint.

Vacuum Cleaner Bag Sampling

Dust from a vacuum cleaner bag can also be tested by a laboratory. This is a useful method because it provides a good sample of the dust throughout the home, without needing to test many individual surfaces.

The vacuum cleaner bag can be sent whole, in a large plastic Ziploc-type bag. Or you may cut off a portion of the bag and send that in. Simply cut straight through the bag and enclose one-quarter of it in a plastic Ziploc-type bag. Alternatively, you can send a sample (about a cup) of the dust collected in the vacuum cleaner by working it through a #20 sieve to remove large clumps of dirt, hair, and the like, leaving the finer dust, which is more likely to be picked up by a child touching hard surfaces, and is also more likely to contain lead. Be careful to contain any dust that spills so that it does not get back into the living environment.[8]

Laboratory Analysis

An analytical laboratory can analyze the dust from either a wipe or a vacuum cleaner bag using ICP (inductively coupled plasma) spectroscopy for about $25. Other methods that are used are FLAME or GRAPHITE FURNACE ATOMIC ABSORPTION SPECTROPHOTOMETRY (FAAS or GFAAS) and ENERGY-DISPERSIVE X-RAY FLUORESCENCE (XRF).[9]

If a dust wipe from a floor shows a concentration of over 100 μg per square foot, it is considered to indicate a lead hazard. For wipes taken on windowsills, the level suggesting concern is 500 μg per square foot, and for a window trough, 800 μg per square foot.

If the dust from a vacuum cleaner has a lead concentration above 200 mg/kg, there may be a problem and you might want to do more tests. A concentration below 200 mg/kg means you probably do not have hazardous levels of lead dust in your home. Concentrations over

1000 mg/kg are signs of serious potential danger. The results are considered reliable enough to be used in a court of law as evidence of the presence of dangerous levels of lead dust in a home.[10]

Whether your sample is collected with a wipe or a vacuum, it should be sent to a laboratory certified by either the NLLAP or ELPAT. *To be sure the laboratory is certified to analyze for lead in dust, call the National Safety Council's National Lead Information Clearinghouse (NLIC) hotline at 800-424-LEAD or one of the agencies that run the accreditation programs, listed in Appendix B, under* Testing/Laboratory Analysis.

Paint Testing

There are a number of ways of testing paint for lead. There are also a number of reasons you might want to test your paint. Depending on the situation, you might want your whole home inspected or you might want to test only certain areas. For example, you may want to test a particular room that you are considering remodeling or a specific spot where the paint is deteriorating and might present a hazard if it contains lead. A curved or ornate surface may need to be tested separately because the x-ray fluorescence method used by inspectors is not effective in these cases.

Home Test Kits (Chemical Spot Tests)

There are several simple and fairly inexpensive products on the market for do-it-yourself testing of painted surfaces. The paint spot is analyzed by using a chemical (either sodium sulfide or a rhodozinate) that changes color in the presence of lead.

Some involve applying a product to a patch of paint in your home and observing whether there is a color. This can make it difficult to read the results for a dark-colored paint. Others require removing a small chip of paint, containing all layers down to the substrate (the wood or metal surface that was painted). This should be done in a way that creates as little lead dust as possible.

Some home test kits instruct the tester to sand the surface to be tested in order to expose covered layers of paint. This is not advisable because it creates fine dust that can be inhaled by the person doing the sanding. It is much safer to take samples with a special blade that cuts down through multiple layers of paint to remove a small amount of each paint layer. A linoleum block cutting tool, available at art supply stores for about $5, can be used in this way. Some test kits have limited shelf lives. Be sure to purchase only as many as you will use within the time indicated in the instructions, and use them within that time frame.

Spot test kits should be used only as a screen, or an indication of whether your paint has lead. The results are not definitive. These test kits offer qualitative, not quantitative, information. That is, they show whether lead is present, but not the concentration of lead. Testing your home with a lead test kit is not a substitute for a lead paint inspection. However, it can provide some information at a much lower cost, and in many cases may be the only affordable means of knowing whether paint has lead.

Depending on the particular kit you use and, in some cases, how carefully you conduct the tests, some percentage of the results are likely to be incorrect. A recent report published by the EPA showed varying degrees of inaccurate results for a number of commercially marketed test kits.[11] A number of different spots should always be tested to get a general picture of the presence of lead in your home. *For a listing of test kits available commercially, see Appendix G.*

Laboratory Analysis of Paint Chips

Analytical laboratory testing is the most precise way to measure the amount of lead in a particular sample of paint. To test paint, a small piece of paint must be removed, placed in a container, labeled, and brought to a laboratory where it is tested using a scientific method such as atomic absorption spectroscopy (AAS) or inductively coupled plasma (ICP) spectroscopy. The latter is the more accurate method, as AAS tends to underestimate the concentration of lead at higher levels.[12] The spot where the chip was removed must be repaired afterwards to prevent further chipping and dust generation.

This method is rarely used for testing an entire house, the expense being too high to test enough samples to get a true picture of the dwelling. If there is a particular surface that you are concerned about, either because you are thinking of scraping it or because it can be reached and chewed by a young child, this service might be of interest to you.

Although laboratory analysis is considered the most reliable method of testing paint for lead, some professionals find that it can occasionally yield incorrect results, because of poor sampling. If the sample contains only the top layers of paint, the result will be lower than it should be. Also, if part of the substrate (the wood or other underlying surface) is included in the sample collected, a lower concentration of lead will show up in the analysis. *For more specific information on paint chip sample collection and preparation, call the ASTM, listed in Appendix B, under* Testing/Laboratory Analysis. *To be sure the laboratory is certified to analyze for lead in paint, call the National Lead Information Clearinghouse at 800-424-LEAD for a list of accredited laboratories. You can also get a list from the specific agencies that run the accreditation programs, listed in Appendix B, under* Testing/Laboratory Analysis.

Lead-Based Paint Inspection

A lead paint inspection identifies all of the lead paint in your home but doesn't assess potential hazards or recommend ways to remedy them. This information is useful for someone who plans to do renovation or major repair work where special precautions might be involved if the surfaces disrupted have lead paint. A lead paint inspection using x-ray fluorescence (XRF) is the method most commonly used by public agencies to test a home for lead-based paint. An inspection can determine which surfaces have lead paint. This type of inspection is also useful for confirming the absence of lead paint in various situations involving transferring property, meeting specific legal requirements, or applying for insurance or financing.

Sampling

The paint in a number of different spots in your home should be tested to provide an indication of whether lead paint presents a hazard to you. A home often contains several different types, ages, and thicknesses of paint. Certain areas might have been repainted more recently than others. Different qualities of paint might have been used on different surfaces. Certain spots might have been repaired after others. Some spots might have been given several layers either to cover a darker color or to compensate for uneven absorption of a porous surface. The percentage of lead also might vary with the quality of the paint. Higher-quality paints usually contain more lead. Paint that was applied to exteriors tends to contain more lead, especially in colder climates. Woodwork, cabinets, doors, and metal surfaces were often painted with higher concentrations of lead.

You therefore should test spots on each of the different components in each room, from each different type of surface and from each color of paint. If all of the walls appear to be the same in a given room, then sampling one should be adequate. But if it is apparent that they are not the same, you should sample each one that is different. The same applies to windows and other types of surfaces.

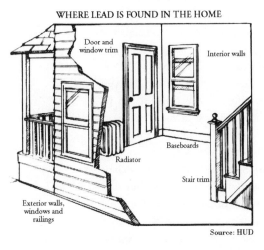

WHERE LEAD IS FOUND IN THE HOME

Door and window trim

Interior walls

Baseboards

Radiator

Stair trim

Exterior walls, windows and railings

Source: HUD

Each type of component should be sampled in each room, including:

- Window sash, casing, and sills
- Columns, railings
- Trim, moldings, and baseboards
- Stairs, risers, treads, posts, railings
- Radiators, vents
- Walls—upper, lower, and chair rail if any
- Floors, ceilings
- Cabinets, shelves, and shelf supports

Porches and decks should be sampled. Stained and varnished surfaces, as well as plaster, could contain lead and should be tested using the same methods.

XRF

Lead paint inspectors generally use portable X-ray fluorescence (XRF) detectors to measure the lead in paint; the method is quick and cost efficient, and does not remove or disturb the paint in any way. It is not a do-it-yourself method. The equipment is very expensive and its operation requires special training, both for safety and for accuracy. XRF is neither safe nor effective for testing curved or ornate surfaces.

Although the initial cost of having an inspector come to your home is high, the cost of each additional XRF test is small. The results are not quite as accurate as a laboratory analysis would be. However, XRF testing can be a reasonably accurate and efficient way of testing for lead paint hazards in your home, as long as it is done by an inspector who is not only well trained but also careful and conscientious.

The procedures listed below should be followed by the inspector:

- First the instrument must be warmed up and quality control procedures followed.
- Next it must be calibrated with three check readings. This is repeated every 4 hours.
- For some machines, it may be necessary to correct for the effect the underlying surface might have on the reading by placing special test paint films on scraped surfaces.[13]
- Three readings should be taken for each type of component, type of surface, and color of paint in each room (or equivalent, such as hallway, or exterior area of the home). Although the standard practice has been to do the same tests at the exact same spot, recent EPA tests conclude that it is better to take the three readings at different spots on the same component (at the top, side, and bottom of a window frame, for example).[14]

If you have a choice, you might want the inspector to use a K-shell instrument rather than an L-shell instrument. The same EPA report suggested that of the types of XRF instruments in use for lead paint inspection, K-shell instruments are more accurate.[15]

Results of XRF testing will generally indicate whether the paint tested is safe (below a certain cutoff) or hazardous (above a certain cutoff). Some XRF results, however, may fall between the two cutoffs and be inconclusive. In that case, a paint chip will be sent to a laboratory to be analyzed, as described above. *For detailed information on specific XRF instruments, call the National Lead Information Clearinghouse, listed in Appendix B, under* Testing/Laboratory Analysis. *The NLAC, listed in Appendix B, under* Inspectors/Risk Assessors, *is compiling a list of proficient XRF operators.*

If you do not have either a risk assessment or lead-based paint inspection, you must assume that all surfaces have lead-based paint and take precautions accordingly if you are doing any work that disrupts painted surfaces. Also, once the controls are completed, you will need to have a licensed assessor inspect for any other hazards before your home can be officially declared safe.[16]

HOW TO CHOOSE A LEAD PAINT INSPECTOR OR RISK ASSESSOR

In some locations, your state lead poisoning prevention agency will send an inspector or risk assessor to your home if your child's blood lead is above a certain level. Otherwise, you can get a referral for a licensed lead paint inspector or risk assessor by contacting your state lead poisoning prevention program or one of the organizations listed in Appendix B.

A trained professional should conduct the assessment or inspection. If your state has a certification program for inspectors and risk assessors, check that the one you hire is certified. If not, finding one who is certified in another state is recommended, if possible. Ask to see his or her credentials. You can expect to spend a couple of hundred dollars. If you are offered an inspection for under $50, you can guess it is not legitimate (though such a low cost would be reasonable for a screen risk assessment described earlier in this chapter). Unfortunately, the fact that an inspector is trained and certified does not ensure that he or she is conscientious. You should do some careful screening to find the best person for the job.

Look for the following when choosing a risk assessor/lead paint inspector:

☐ At least three references of parents or property owners for whom the contractor has done work similar to that you need done. In the case of an investigation into the source of lead exposure for a child with an elevated blood lead level, find one with that specific experience.

☐ State lead inspector or risk assessor certification or license. (Ask to see the certification papers.)

☐ Insurance for both comprehensive liability and errors and omissions. (Ask to see the certificate.)

☐ Use of an NLLAP (National Lead Laboratory Accreditation Program)-approved laboratory.

☐ Whether the individual or firm has a relationship with the laboratory or gets a percentage for each lab analysis.

☐ Conformance with all federal, state, and local laws and regulations as well as the federal HUD guidelines for evaluation and control of lead-based paint hazards.

☐ A record free of any complaints with the local Better Business Bureau.

☐ A record free of any complaints or violations with the state agency that regulates asbestos inspectors. Many people who have recently begun doing lead inspections previously did asbestos inspections, and this will give you an idea of how responsible the individual has been in past work.

Once you have hired an inspector, watch how he or she works to ensure you are getting an accurate inspection.

☐ Does he or she take three measurements of each surface inspected?

☐ Are spiked samples (prepared samples to assess the accuracy of the laboratory) and blind blanks (wipes with no dust sample taken, to check for any contamination in their handling) included in the dust sampling?[12]

It is also a good idea to use someone who will allow you to pay the laboratory fee directly. If the inspector turns a profit on each analysis, he or she might want to do more testing than necessary to make more money, at your expense.[17]

CHAPTER TWELVE

Preparing for Lead Paint Hazard Control

CHOOSING A CONTROL STRATEGY

Generally, you can choose any one of a number of methods to control lead paint hazards, except for those that are prohibited, as long as the property is found to be safe when it is inspected and tested after the work and cleanup are completed. In a few states and localities, the law requires certain measures for rental property. Less stringent standards may be set for owner-occupied housing. *Check your state lead program and local board of health to see if there are any specific requirements in your area.*

Your choice of lead hazard control method depends on a number of factors, including the condition and age of the home and the complexity of its components, your financial resources, and whether the work can be done when the home is empty.

Cost

Although well worth it in health benefits IF done properly, controlling lead hazards in your home can be expensive. Estimates for removing the lead paint from a medium-sized house range from $2500 to as much as $60,000, or even higher, for example in the case of a historic building.[1]

If lead work is incorporated into repair or renovation work, it can be done more cost effectively. In the case of rental property, it is more efficient to do lead work when the property is turned over and routine maintenance is being done. If the job is done according to building code, the additional cost of lead hazard reduction and safe work practices will usually add no more than 30% to the cost of the job.[2]

Market Factors

The local wage rate is a significant factor, as from one- to two-thirds of the cost is labor. In areas where there is a higher demand for lead abatement, there often is a greater supply of certified contractors, so that there is more competition and the price is driven down. Unfortunately, this can drive contractors to cut corners in order to save money. Be careful not to hire a contractor who is willing to sacrifice safety precautions for low prices.

Where the competition is not yet so keen, you may find contractors taking advantage of the situation and grossly overpricing their services. Contractors in some instances double the prices they would charge for the same type of job if it were done in a home without lead-based paint, using the extra precautions they will need to take as an excuse, when in actuality their added costs might be much less.

Nature of Work

Structural problems and water infiltration may have to be taken care of before lead hazard control work begins. So the whole project becomes more expensive if the home is in need of such repairs. Older houses may be more expensive to deal with because they tend not only to have more layers of paint to contend with, but also to have more decorative elements which are difficult to work with, as well as painted kitchen cabinets, radiators, and porches.

Obvious other factors affecting the price are the size of the home and the number of surfaces to be abated.

Financial Assistance

The federal government gives grants to states and local governments for programs to reduce lead-based paint hazards in affordable housing.[3] It also encourages HUD Community Development grants to be used for lead paint hazard reduction.[4]

If a child living in the home has been diagnosed as lead poisoned, you can take advantage of a federal tax break. The IRS allows the costs of removal of lead paint to be deducted from your income taxes as medical expenses. The provision only applies when the expense is greater than 7.5% of your income.[5]

In some states, a variety of government-funded loans and grants are offered for lead abatement work. In addition, some states offer tax credits for expenses for abating lead paint. Financial assistance varies greatly from state to state. *To learn about financial assistance programs in your area, contact your state lead program, listed in Appendix A.*

Note: You might be able to reduce your costs by doing part of the work yourself, once all of the lead is removed and cleanup is completed. You are not required to use a certified lead abatement contractor for tasks that do not involve any contact with lead. Removing old moldings or windows, for example, is a potentially hazardous activity, but installing replacement windows or moldings does not involve disrupting lead-painted surfaces and need not be done by a licensed deleader.

Note for landlords: Liability insurance policies may cover the costs of abatement as loss-mitigation expenses. *Contact your insurance agent for more information.*

Timing

Coordination with Other Construction

If you are planning any type of remodeling or major repairs on your home, you can save a lot of expense and effort by scheduling the lead hazard control work for the same time frame. If renovation is done before lead work begins, construction will be subject to the same precautions (worker protections and containment to protect residents) as lead work. So it is better to do the lead work first, or at the same time as the other renovation work.

Before You or Your Tenants Move In

If the home you are planning to do lead hazard control work on is one you are just purchasing, or one that you are renting out, and it is possible to do the work before it is occupied, the job will not only be much more convenient, but also more efficient and less expensive. In an unoccupied house, you won't have to worry about protecting personal belongings or cleaning up every day in preparation for residents to reenter the area.

Note for landlords: Some states and localities require that lead hazard control measures be completed before property is turned over to a new tenant. *For specific requirements for abatement of rental property where you live, contact your state lead program, listed in Appendix A.*

CHOOSING A CONTRACTOR

If your state has a certification program for lead abatement contractors, be sure to hire a contractor who is fully certified. If your state does not have a certification program, hire someone who is certified in another state, if possible. This ensures that he or she has undergone training and demonstrated competence. *Ask your state health or labor department for a list of contractors who have lead abatement licenses or consult the National Lead Abatement Council's Lead Listing service, included in Appendix B.*

It is required by the law that a licensed contractor be hired for abatement work, and strongly recommended for any work where a lead-painted surface is disrupted, including interim controls and remodeling. You must be able to show that you used a certified lead abatement contractor in order to qualify for some state financial assistance programs, tax credits, or utility company rebates.

Certification demonstrates that the contractor has taken special courses and passed a test, but not that he is reliable, skilled, thorough, or courteous. It is critical to the health and safety of your family that lead abatement, or any other work that generates lead dust, be done using proper precautions. Some contractors are more conscientious than others in following measures for containing lead dust during their work and cleaning up after it is done. It is not unusual for corners to be cut to keep costs down.

The timing of your lead hazard control work can also be important. If you (or your tenants) have moved out of the home while the work is being done, you cannot move back in until the job is completed and checked out to the satisfaction of an inspector or risk assessor. If it is not done right the first time, it may have to be repeated. This could mean not only inconvenience but added expense for alternate living quarters. If you (or your tenants) are staying in the home pending completion of the work, this can mean prolonging the threat of exposure to lead dust. The fact that a contract gives a deadline for the work to be completed does not guarantee it will. Some contractors are more dependable than others, with or without a contract.

It can be difficult to find a contractor who will do the job right. The precautions needed to protect your family and home are complicated and the supply of well-trained, competent

---

To avoid being disappointed by your contractor, take the following precautions:

☐ As you would when you select any contractor, ask for a list of references and check at least three to see that other people have been satisfied with the contractor's work. Ask each reference how careful the contractor was to keep the area contained, to clean up well, and so forth.

☐ Ask the contractor if he or she has ever left a lead abatement job unfinished, and if so, why. Also ask if any penalties were ever paid on a contract and why.

☐ Make sure that liability insurance is covered if this is a concern.

☐ Ask the contractor if there have ever been any legal challenges regarding her or his lead abatement work. If so, find out the details and how they were resolved.

☐ Check whether any complaints have been filed with your local Better Business Bureau or state attorney general's office.

☐ Many lead abatement contractors formerly did asbestos removal work. Ask the contractor if he or she does or has done asbestos work and, if so, whether it was under a different business name. Check with the state or local agency regulating asbestos contractors to see if there are any violations on record.

☐ Make sure he or she is familiar with HUD's guidelines on lead paint hazard control.

☐ Discuss safety measures that the contractor uses to protect his or her workers. If the contractor does not seem to take seriously the danger to the workers, he or she may also be lax about precautions to protect your family and home from lead contamination during the abatement work.

☐ Ask specifically how your home and belongings will be protected from being contaminated during the work. Make sure the contractor intends to take the types of precautions described later in this chapter to isolate work areas and securely seal your belongings. (See that belongings are in fact protected, once work begins.)

☐ Make sure the contractor plans to clean up carefully and dispose of waste according to legal requirements. The owner of the property is legally responsible for the waste, wherever it may go.

contractors is not adequate to meet the demand. It is worth making the effort to carefully search for and screen a reliable contractor.

The whole experience can be very frustrating for a well-intentioned homeowner. In spite of your best efforts, you may find that a competent job is not being done.

A good-willed landlord—and there are some—may have more pressures still. If you are having rental property abated, you may also have to deal with impatient tenants eager to get back into their apartments. Between the tenant, the health department, and the contractor, it may seem like EVERYONE is against you. *See case history (boxed text) on pages 110–111.*

THE CONTRACT

You should clarify exactly what is to be done before work is begun. Get everything in writing, and in language that is clear to you as well as to the contractor, so there will be no misunderstandings.

Your contract should contain the following:

☐ Description of all work that is to be done. Everything should be spelled out in detail. Make clear what kind of windows will be installed if you are having them replaced, how floors are to be sealed (whether with paint or polyurethane), and any other details important to you. You might want to reserve the right to specifically sign off on all choices of brand, model, or color of any finished items.

☐ Warranties. You should be given copies of any warranties on items that are purchased for you by the contractor.

☐ Schedule for the work. Clarify when the work will begin and when it will be finished. Specify what work is to be done right away, if some tasks are more urgent than others.

☐ Payment schedule. Normally you will be expected to pay one-third before the work begins and make payments as work is completed. Be sure to keep one-tenth to one-third of the payment for after the job is completed and approved by a certified inspector or risk assessor.

☐ Precautions. Make sure the contractor will take all necessary precautions to protect your home, your belongings, and the workers. Also there should be a guarantee to clean up correctly so that the house will pass final inspection and testing when the work is done.

☐ Right to cancel. Any major contract should reserve the right to cancel within 3 days so that you have a chance to think things over and decide if this is really what you want.[6]

REPAIRS BEFORE YOU BEGIN

Structural Repairs

Any structural defects should be taken care of before abatement work begins. This includes any dry rot or insect damage that would affect the structural soundness of the home. Any windows that don't work should be repaired.

Water Leaks

It is critical that all sources of water or moisture leakage be repaired. This includes any plumbing leaks, including those from radiators, as well as roof, soffit, or gutter leaks. In many cases, paint deterioration may result from such moisture infiltration. Unrepaired moisture leaks can prevent new paint or encapsulant from drying properly and staying in place. The most common sources of moisture and water leakage are shown in the drawing below.

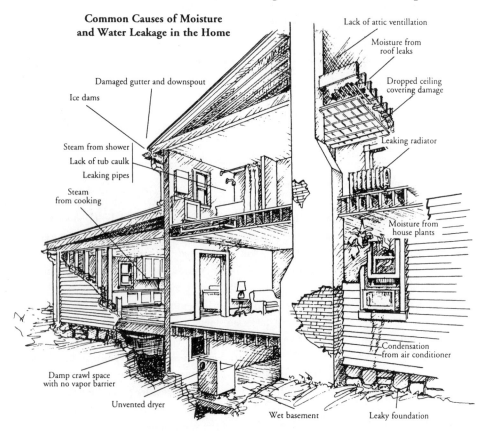

Common Causes of Moisture and Water Leakage in the Home

Lack of attic ventillation

Moisture from roof leaks

Damaged gutter and downspout

Ice dams

Dropped ceiling covering damage

Steam from shower

Lack of tub caulk

Leaking pipes

Leaking radiator

Steam from cooking

Moisture from house plants

Condensation from air conditioner

Damp crawl space with no vapor barrier

Unvented dryer

Wet basement

Leaky foundation

Source: Dennis Livingston, Community Resources *(See listing in Appendix B)*

Utilities

Heat

When deleading work is in progress, forced air systems must be shut down so that lead dust doesn't spread. Unpainted radiators need to be covered to protect them from lead dust, although it is important to have adequate heat, both for the comfort of the workers, and for new paint, encapsulants, or chemical strippers to work properly. You may need to provide electric space heaters if work is done during cold weather. If you use flame heaters, be sure to ventilate well and keep volatile chemicals a safe distance away.

Electricity

It is important to have proper lighting for work to be done well, so be sure that electricity is functioning and adequate lights are provided.

Running Water

Water must be available for cleaning up both the workers and the work area after work is done, as well as for some chemical paint removal methods.

PREPARING THE WORK SITE FOR DELEADING

Unless extreme care is used, removing lead paint can be much more dangerous than leaving it alone. Any time a lead-based painted surface is disrupted, toxic lead dust is released into the environment. In addition to hazards from the lead itself, some methods of removing lead utilize toxic chemicals. This is important not only for the persons doing the work, but also for household members who might enter the area where the work is being done.

Protecting Your Family

Restricting Access to Work Area

Only properly protected workers should be allowed to enter any area where lead-painted surfaces are disrupted until it is thoroughly cleaned up. Pregnant women, children, and pets should not be present in the home during lead hazard control work. Entry should be allowed only if dust samples are taken and come back showing the home is safe.

Relocation

It is safest, more efficient, and more convenient to work on a home when no one is living in it.

In certain circumstances, it might be all right to live in parts of the house where no lead work is being done. You must have access to bathrooms, as well as to at least one living area and ways of entering and exiting the house without entering the work area. This may mean that front and rear porches cannot be worked on at the same time. If any special hazard exists, such as exposed electric wires, your family should not be present in the house.

If you do remain in the house during the work, a dust sample should be taken at the end of each workday, before the area is cleaned up, from a spot that is likely to be the most contaminated from the work. If the dust level is above the level considered safe by federal or local authorities, you must relocate until final clearance is received.

For exterior lead work, it is considered safe to remain in the home when less than 10 square feet is being worked on, the proper precautions are taken, and you stay away from the areas being worked on and can get in and out without going near the work area. For medium-

Maggie Miller owned a triple-decker in a working-class suburb of Boston, where she raised her 11-year-old son. She rented two of the three units to young families.

One of her tenants, who was having a hard time keeping up with rent payments, asked the local health inspector to come out to the property. He had heard that when health code violations are found, a tenant cannot be evicted for a number of months, even if the rent is not paid. No violations of the health code were found, but the inspector offered to do an inspection for lead paint. The tenant agreed. Lead paint was found, and Maggie was informed she had to eliminate the lead paint from the unit.

Since tenants on the top floor had a small child, she felt she should take care of their unit as well.

She phoned several contractors and found one who was very personable and helpful. He advised her on obtaining a HUD-sponsored loan for the work. After a lot of running around, interviewing, filling out forms, and waiting, Maggie was able to get a loan for the amount of the abatement work.

She arranged for alternative housing for her upstairs tenants for the period of time when the work was being done. The contract specified that the unit would be ready to reoccupy after 5 days. When the work was completed, she had it tested by an inspector, but it was not clean enough for a certificate of occupancy to be issued, which would have authorized her to allow tenants in again.

Although all that was necessary was to wipe down the windowsills, it would have been illegal for Maggie to clean up herself. Massachusetts law requires that any work that puts a person in contact with lead dust must be done by a licensed professional. She phoned the contractor, but wasn't able to reach him. Several days later, after a number of desperate messages were ignored, she called a second contractor. He did come in and clean up satisfactorily. Although a week after originally planned, her tenants moved back in.

The second unit was also to be done in 5 days. This time she hired the second contractor. Delay after delay added up to 3 weeks before the work was done. The windows didn't come in on time. When they finally

(continued)

sized jobs, where from 10 to 50 square feet is involved, it is suggested that you stay away from the home during the day. For larger jobs, covering over 50 square feet of deleading, it is recommended that you relocate for the entire period of the work.

Protecting the Inside of Your Home: Containment

CONTAINMENT means keeping the dust and debris from a work area away from the rest of the house. Putting down plastic sheeting is enough in some cases, while in others, an area has to be sealed with plastic sheeting covering the doorways. (Note: When a contractor uses the same drop cloth on different jobs, the cloth itself can be a source of contamination. Only use disposable plastic sheeting.)

If paint chips and flakes are present, they should be removed with a high-efficiency (HEPA) vacuum so that they are not ground into dust by the workers and tracked into other areas of the house.

did come in, they were not the windows she had asked for, but she didn't want to delay the work any further so she accepted them.

The unit was inspected but failed. The levels of dust on the windowsills were higher than the allowable limit. The window units were newly installed and completely lead free, but dust that had been generated during the work had settled onto them in high concentrations, and was not adequately cleaned up.

The contractor came back and cleaned again. Maggie paid another $200 for dust testing, which was not covered by the loan. The unit failed a second clearance testing. A third time the contractor cleaned the apartment. It was inspected again.

The time pressure and financial stress were getting oppressive by this point. She had to have the apartment safe and get the tenants back in. She was doing all she possibly could, but it wasn't working. This time Maggie drove the dust wipes over an hour to the analytical laboratory that the inspector used, to help expedite the matter. The results were supposed to come back the next day. She waited and waited for word from the inspector. Finally she was told that the laboratory lost the results. She drove out to the lab and spoke to a less-than-friendly receptionist who came across as secretive and suspicious, refusing to release the results to anyone but the inspector. Maggie began to wonder if the whole thing was legitimate, or if they were faking failing results so the inspector would earn additional fees, at her expense, both financial and emotional.

The unit failed final clearance for a third time.

This was about all she could take. Maggie went to the drugstore, bought some TSP, put on rubber gloves and protective eyeglasses, and scrubbed the windowsills. She called the inspector, who finally gave the OK for her tenants to move back in. She wonders how the contractor was charging her $2000, as she had done a better job than him.

This was something she felt was thrust on her. It took its toll emotionally. Her work even suffered. In addition to having to take time off to deal with all of this, she found she had trouble concentrating because of the stress.[7]

Small Jobs

If a very small area is being deleaded (under 2 square feet), a single layer of plastic can be laid out at least 5 feet around the work area to catch the debris and dust. A warning sign should be placed outside the entrance to the room, and the doorway should be blocked with furniture or a piece of wood, to make sure that no one inadvertently comes in.

The ventilation system should be turned off, and any vents within 5 feet of the area being deleaded should be covered with plastic. Any furniture that cannot be moved farther than 5 feet from the work area should also be covered with plastic sheeting.

Large Jobs

For any job larger than 2 square feet, two layers of plastic sheeting should be spread over the entire floor. If any part of the home is not being worked on, you need to isolate the work area from the rest of the house by taping two layers plastic sheeting over the doorways in such a way as to create an air lock.

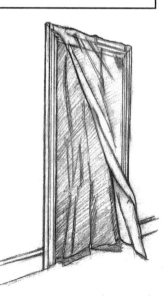

Windows should be kept closed. An alternative form of ventilation should be provided if volatile chemicals (strippers) are used.

Warning signs should be posted on the exterior of the building and at all entrances, instructing people not to enter. Heating and air conditioning vents should be sealed with plastic sheeting. Furniture should be removed from the work area if possible. Any furniture that remains in the rooms being worked on should be sealed with a single layer of plastic sheeting.

Protecting Your Belongings

Before you begin deleading you should remove all bedding, curtains, food, cooking and eating utensils, small appliances, toys, and personal items from the work area. Also remove any furniture and floor coverings you are able to. If you have nowhere to store them, put them in tightly sealed 6-millimeter-thick (or double) plastic bags, or cover them with 6-millimeter-thick polyethylene plastic sheeting and seal the edges with duct tape. If deleading is done in the kitchen, seal the door of the refrigerator to protect your food.

Protecting the Outside of Your Home

If you are deleading the outside of your home, the ground, shrubs, and trees should be covered. Six-millimeter-thick polyethylene plastic sheeting should be secured to the wall with tape and spread on the ground extending 10 feet beyond the surfaces being worked on, or 5 feet from the base of the house, and 3 more feet for each additional story. If the job takes more than 2 days, vacuum the sheeting and roll it up at the end of the day to avoid loss of shrubs and lawn. The sheeting should be weighted down with bricks or rocks to keep it in place and raised at the edges, with two-by-fours, so that any contaminated runoff created by unexpected rain will be retained by the plastic. HUD recommends that holes be made in the sheeting so that the feet of the ladder are lodged on the ground and not the plastic. A more protective alternative is using footings to prevent the ladder from slipping on the plastic. Other areas of the plastic should be protected from being punctured from falling debris by placing boards on it.

Deleading should not be done if winds are higher than 15 or 20 miles per hour. Work should be stopped before any rain begins. If paint chips and dust do land on the ground, they should be removed so they do not deteriorate into dust and contaminate the soil.

Windows and vents near the work area should be sealed so that the lead dust cannot get into the house. Any windows within 20 feet of work areas should be closed. Doors within 10 feet should not be used. Any movable items, such as lawn furniture and children's play sets, should be removed from within 20 feet of the area being worked on. Those that cannot be moved should be sealed with taped plastic sheeting.

Temporary fencing or barrier tape, as well as warning signs advising no one to enter the area, should be placed at a 20-foot perimeter around the work area, or less if a building or sidewalk is closer than that.

Windows

If windows are being removed, in addition to the precautions described above, two layers of plastic sheeting should be taped to the side of the wall opposite the side where the work is being done. If the window is being removed from the inside, take the normal precautions for inside work (for small jobs) and also attach plastic to the exterior of the house, and if the window is being removed from the outside, take the normal precautions for exterior work and also attach plastic sheeting to the interior wall.

Protecting Workers

For any work where lead-painted surfaces are disrupted and lead dust is created and dispersed, workers should be protected from exposure.

Clothing

Workers should wear protective hair covering, goggles, work clothes, gloves, and special shoes or shoe coverings that will not be worn outside the work area. Street clothes should be kept out of the work area. Work clothes should not be stored or washed together with street clothes.

Respirator

Workers should wear a NIOSH-approved respirator appropriate for the type of removal that will be done. The respirator should be equipped with a purple coded HEPA filter cartridge. Respirators should be checked to see that they fit properly and are in good working order. The mouthpiece should be cleaned according to instructions at the end of each workday.

Food

There should be no eating, drinking, smoking, or chewing gum or tobacco in the work area. Any food or drink should be kept outside of the work area. Before eating, workers should wash their hands, arms, and face with soap and water and rinse their mouth well.

Particular methods require additional precautions; these are mentioned in the sections describing each method, in the next chapter.[8]

CHAPTER THIRTEEN

Lead Paint Hazard Control Measures

INTERIM CONTROLS

Interim controls are measures that can be taken on an interim basis, until full-scale abatement can be done, permitting you to live safely with lead-based paint, temporarily, by preventing it from generating any additional dust and removing the dust that it has generated. The major advantage of interim controls over abatement (removal or permanent coverage of lead paint) is that they can be significantly less expensive and done relatively quickly. The disadvantage is that they require you to monitor the situation on an ongoing basis and possibly do minor repair work over the years in order to remain effective. Some advocates point out that interim controls have never been proven scientifically to be effective in reducing lead exposure, but others agree that it is only common sense that reducing the environmental availability of lead dust will reduce the amount of lead a child ingests.

Repair of Painted Surfaces

Lead-based paint that is blistering, flaking, peeling, or chalking can be repaired (technically referred to as being STABILIZED) to prevent the hazard from continuing. Once deteriorating paint surfaces are repaired, lead will not get into the environment and pose a threat to your family.

The most common reason that paint deteriorates is water leakage and the trapping of moisture in the painted surface. When water or water vapor gets onto a painted surface, changes in temperature produce expansion and contraction, which causes paint to deteriorate. Before paint is stabilized, any moisture or leakage problems must be repaired. *For a discussion and illustration of sources of potential moisture in a home, see Chapter 12.*

The surface that is being worked on must also be structurally sound. Any dry-rotted or rusty siding or rails, or loose siding, trim, plaster, or wallpaper should be repaired, and missing door hardware should be replaced.

The surface to be stabilized must be prepared by removing scraps and debris by wet scraping and wet sanding. Spraying the surface with a mister before working on it will minimize the lead dust that is created. Dry sanding is recommended only in small areas close to electrical circuits. Contaminants that might interfere with the new paint staying in place should be removed by cleaning. Additional measures may need to be taken to degloss the surface and to make it more adhesive, or to adjust the pH to an appropriate level.

Paint should be applied according to the manufacturer's instructions. It's best to use a high-quality primer and top coat from the same manufacturer that are intended to be used together. (Note: Be sure not to block weep holes in the bottom of storm windows; these are needed for ventilation and drainage to control moisture.)

Abrasion and Impact Surface Correction

Surfaces that rub together or get bumped into can generate dangerous levels of dust. Such surfaces can often be repaired to minimize the abrasion and impact. Repairs that accomplish this include:

- Rehanging doors to eliminate wood-to-wood contact except against the stop on the side with the knob
- Repairing cabinets, drawers, etc. to eliminate rubbing of painted surfaces
- Replacing lead-based painted molding, jambs, and stop beads
- Covering window channels with plastic or metal
- Covering stair treads with rubber
- Putting felt bumpers on drawers, and wooden or plastic corner beads on outside corners of walls painted with lead paint

Surfaces that actually rub against each other should not be painted.

Dust Removal and Control

Dust can be removed to minimize the health threat it presents in your home. There are specific methods of cleaning, requiring specialized equipment, skills, and protective clothing, which are more effective than the type of cleaning you could do on a routine basis. The method focuses on areas in your home that are the most likely to accumulate large amounts of dust: rugs and upholstered furniture; floors, stairs, porches, and windows; and grates, radiators, and heating vents.

- First, wash cleanable toys and nonupholstered furniture and remove your belongings from the area to be cleaned.
- Take down drapes and wash them, as well as any washable area rugs.
- Change the filters in heating and air conditioning units.
- Clean your home, always working from top to bottom, from dirtiest to cleanest, and from the back of the house to the front entry.
- Vacuum with a HEPA-vac with crevice and brush tools. Filters as well as prefilters should be changed according to the manufacturer's instructions, preferably off site. If the exhaust of the vacuum is on the bottom, it should be placed on a hard surface or plastic sheet so as not to blow around dust.
- Wash hard horizontal surfaces with water and detergent or a lead-specific cleaning product. (If you use a solution of phosphate-containing dishwasher detergent or TSP, gloves and protective glasses must be worn.) The product should always be tested on a small area of each type of surface you want cleaned to determine if it will damage it. Two buckets should be used, one with the cleaning solution and the other with clean rinse water. Some advocates recommend using 3 buckets, one being used for squeezing out the lead-contaminated wash water from the mop. Wash water should be replaced regularly, as well as sponges and cloths.
- Carpets are particularly difficult to clean. If you have an old or worn carpet, or one you are not particularly attached to, you might consider removing it to make it simpler to keep your home clean and lead-safe.
- If rugs are removed for off-site cleaning, they should be misted first to reduce the amount of dust that is released from them when they are moved, and the floor underneath should be cleaned well. Rugs that are cleaned on-site should be slowly, carefully HEPA vacuumed using a beater bar or agitator attachment. The underside of area rugs should also be vacuumed as well as the floor underneath them. A final steam cleaning may remove additional dust.
- Upholstery should be HEPA vacuumed and covered with throw, slip, or vinyl covers.
- Forced air heating and air conditioning system registers and vents should be vacuumed and washed, as well as the ducts as far as possible.

Note for landlords: This type of cleaning should be done when the unit is vacant if possible. Otherwise, the resident should be warned and, in some places, must give authorization.

ABATEMENT

ABATEMENT refers to measures that get rid of lead-based paint hazards for at least 20 years. Some abatement methods are permanent, such as removing a window or removing the lead paint on a wall. Others involve covering up lead paint, such as by enclosing a wall with paneling or encapsulating a surface with a liquid coating. Although some of these measures are not permanent, they are fairly long-term remedies and do not require as much monitoring and maintenance as the interim measures discussed in the last section.

IT IS IMPORTANT THAT ABATEMENT BE DONE CORRECTLY, OR IT CAN ACTUALLY MAKE THE PROBLEM WORSE.

Because abatement is so dangerous, it must be done by individuals who have been trained and certified according to criteria established by the EPA. Do not try to do this yourself.

Replacement

Removing and replacing the entire architectural component contaminated with lead paint is often the simplest, safest, and least costly method for reducing lead hazards. Doors, windows, posts, moldings, etc. lend themselves to this approach. Any loose putty that is made with lead should also be removed and replaced with unleaded putty.

Once the lead-paint-bearing component is removed in a safe manner by a licensed contractor, you can complete the task of installing the replacement component yourself, or have someone else do it—a licensed lead abater is not required.

Although this method creates a large amount of waste and can be costly in some cases, it also can add value to the home and improve both its appearance and energy efficiency. The net result may be money savings, not only from lower heating bills, but in some cases from rebates that local utilities give for energy-saving improvements. *Check with the oil, gas, or electric company that provides your heat to see if it offers any such rebates.*

Enclosure

Protecting against hazards of lead paint on wall surfaces with intact (not peeling or chipping) lead paint by ENCLOSURE or covering and sealing it up, has a number of advantages. Since it does not involve disrupting existing lead-painted surfaces, it does not create the type of danger from lead dust and debris that other abatement methods do. It is also often the simplest and least costly method of eliminating lead hazards in a home.

It is critical, however, that the enclosure be well sealed around all edges, especially the bottom. When an area of paint is walled in, it will deteriorate more quickly, because moisture will be trapped behind the enclosure. Lead dust will be generated and will escape through cracks or fall to the floor. If the seal is not complete, with spackle and tape or back caulking, the dust can escape into the living environment. Since dust is most likely to escape at the bottom of the wall, it is important to seal the bottom edge, baseboard, and/or shoe molding with caulk.

Plasterboard, wood paneling, fabric-covered paneling, or wallboard can be used effectively to cover up areas of wall with lead paint inside a home. Aluminum siding can be used to cover exterior walls. Check local fire laws to see if any particular wall covering materials are prohibited where you live. These materials should be permanently attached by cementing, gluing, or nailing so that they cannot be easily removed by wear and tear or young curious hands. Moldings should be attached at floors, ceilings, and corners to keep the covering material on tight. Some protruding surfaces, like doorjambs and windowsills, might be covered with metal or plastic L- or J-shaped moldings.

Simply painting over lead paint with another layer of paint is not effective. As the new layer peels, flakes, or wears away, the lead paint will be exposed again. Covering with a layer of ordinary wallpaper is also unacceptable as it is not durable or permanent.

If the material enclosing the lead-painted surface is punctured or not sealed well, lead dust can escape. This system of hazard control must be monitored, and if any defect appears it must be repaired.

Keep a record of any locations where lead hazards are covered in your home. Some authorities also recommend writing "LEAD PAINT," or stamping such lettering, on the wall, under the new plasterboard or paneling. Be sure that extra caution is used if anyone ever removes the covering material to remodel or in any way disrupts lead-containing surfaces.

Encapsulation

ENCAPSULANTS generally refer to specially designed coatings that are painted over a lead-based painted surface to cover up the paint and make it inaccessible. There are also encapsulant products that can be bonded to lead-painted surfaces with an adhesive to accomplish the same thing.

The main advantage of encapsulation is that it is easier and less expensive than other means of abatement. However, encapsulation is only effective if the coating sticks well to the paint, and the layers of paint already there stick well to each other and to the surface they are painted on.

Special types of encapsulating coatings have been developed that are more effective than ordinary paint in keeping a contaminated area covered. These products must be flexible, abrasion resistant, chemical and water resistant, temperature resistant, and in conformance with fire code requirements. They are more expensive and more difficult to apply than ordinary paint, but are more difficult to dislodge and more effective at keeping the old paint covered up. Some states have certified specific products for covering lead paint. *To find out if encapsulants have been certified in your state for lead abatement, call your state lead program, listed in Appendix A.*

Encapsulants are to be used only on surfaces where the paint is in good condition. There must be no paint deterioration (blistering, flaking, chalking, mildewing, peeling, or cracking). In order for encapsulation to work, the following steps have to be taken:

Before an encapsulant is used, the surface you are thinking of encapsulating must be tested to make sure it is in good enough condition to be encapsulated effectively. This can be done by means of patch tests, where the tester cuts an X, tries to peel or chip the paint off, and presses a piece of tape onto the paint to see if any of it comes off. If there is very limited deterioration, it may be possible to employ a product that uses cloth, mat, or fiber as a reinforcement.

Make sure that the proper product is chosen for the surface and conditions, and that it is tested on small patches of the type of surface involved before being used on larger areas. Factors to be considered are the type of surface to be covered, the kind of paint present on the surface, health and safety issues, and the conditions the surface will have to endure (abrasion, temperature change, etc.).

Because encapsulation is only effective on clean, stable, solid, dry, dust-free surfaces, proper preparation and application are critical. The manufacturer's instructions should be followed carefully, including any directions for cleaning or deglossing the surface. Depending on the condition of the surface, preparation might involve repairs that generate lead dust, which should be done with the necessary precautions and protective equipment, by trained certified contractors.

Application of encapsulants may be done by the homeowner. Follow the directions carefully, including those regarding safety precautions and protective equipment to be used. *For a videotape demonstrating the encapsulation process, contact the Massachusetts state lead program, listed in Appendix A.*

Paint Removal Methods Requiring Extra Precautions

Wet Scraping

Keeping the painted surface wet will reduce the dust generated by scraping. The area to be scraped should be sprayed with a mister as it is scraped. The person doing the scraping should use a NIOSH (National Institute of Occupational Safety and Health)-approved respirator for toxic dusts, equipped with a high-efficiency filter (HEPA). The respirator should fit properly and be kept clean and in proper working order.

After the flaking paint has been taken care of, any spots where there is a problem should be checked to make sure there isn't any new flaking in subsequent days or weeks.

HEPA Sanding

Sanding should also be wet, to minimize the dust generated, except for work near electrical circuits. Electric sanders should not be used without HEPA vacuum filter attachments to catch and filter the dust that is created. Respirators are recommended.

Heat Guns

Infrared lamps and electric heat guns can be used to soften lead paint so that it can be scraped more easily. However, extremely dangerous organic fumes may be created. These devices should not be used at temperatures over 1100 degrees Fahrenheit. Care must be taken to keep them away from flammable materials, such as wallpaper or insulation. Fire extinguishing equipment must be kept at hand. Heat guns should be used only by persons experienced in using such equipment, and only with the proper NIOSH-approved respirator equipped with a yellow cartridge to protect from toxic (organic) fumes as well as the purple coded filter for lead dust. Infrared units require protective eyeglasses and clothing.

Chemical Paint Removers/Strippers

Some gels and nontoxic caustic paint removers can be useful in removing lead paint, but also require extra precautions. Solvents may be toxic, flammable, or both. Lye gel, a caustic, can burn the skin. Chemical paint removers contain volatile substances and pose the risk of inhalation of these toxic chemicals, as well as of their absorption through the skin. A NIOSH-approved respirator should be used, equipped with a yellow cartridge to protect from toxic (organic) fumes as well as the purple coded filter for lead dust, along with good ventilation. Skin should be protected with impermeable gloves and the floor should be protected from spills with an impermeable drop cloth or plastic sheet. Lots of water should be available for flushing the chemical from skin or eyes.

Noncaustic strippers may not be effective if there are a number of layers of paint to be removed, so they should be tested on a small spot before being used on a larger area. Caustic strippers are best for metal surfaces because they may leave leaded residues on porous surfaces, such as wood. Careful attention should be paid to neutralizing the chemical and removing any residue so that you are not removing one toxic substance and replacing it with another potential hazard.

Off-Site Paint Removal (Dip Tank)

Individual pieces of woodwork, spindles, molding, etc., can be removed and dipped into a dip tank of paint remover for thorough removal. The pieces should be neutralized, according to the directions for the particular stripper, and immediately repainted or otherwise sealed. A COLD TANK is preferable to a HOT TANK, which uses lye and can be more destructive to old and dried pieces that are stripped. Lead may remain in the grain of the wood. The use of particularly caustic strippers tends to leave potentially hazardous levels of lead on the surface of stripped wood.

This is an expensive process and results are inconsistent. Dipping can ruin wood pieces because the porous wood soaks the chemicals up like a sponge. It can also dissolve glue that may hold together doors or furniture. It is therefore usually used only in the case of especially valuable pieces of woodwork, such as in historical restorations.

Dangerous Paint Removal Methods
(Prohibited in some areas)

Blasting

Abrasive blasting and sandblasting are prohibited because they generate highly contaminated lead dust. This applies to all methods that use small particles under pressure to remove paint, including GRIT BLASTING, BEAD PACK, and BLACK BEAUTY.

Hydroblasting and high-pressure washing spread lead-contaminated waste water in the environment. These methods should be used only in very exceptional cases, in which elaborate measures are taken to contain the dust and waste generated.

Sanding (without HEPA Filter)

Sanding is the greatest source of lead dust. Electric sanders, grinders, or planes are sometimes used after scraping to remove any paint that scraping did not get off. Although this method is simple and inexpensive, it is not recommended because it creates large amounts of toxic lead dust, unless a vacuum attachment connected to a HEPA-vac is used with the sander.

Even when sanding is done WITH the recommended attachment, lead dust can escape if the sander is not kept perfectly flush with the surface at all times. Sanding should only be done on totally flat surfaces.

Gas Torches

The use of gas torches with open flames is very dangerous and therefore not recommended. They create a risk of fire on the surface where the paint is being removed. Also, heating lead-based paint to over 1100 degrees Fahrenheit creates lead fumes.

Chemical Paint Removers

Methylene chloride paint removal products are prohibited in some localities because they can cause liver and kidney damage, carbon monoxide poisoning, and possibly cancer. *For a comparison of the advantages and disadvantages of the various methods of lead paint abatement, see Appendix F.*

LEAD PAINT HAZARD CONTROL IN HISTORIC BUILDINGS

If you want to preserve the historic value of an older home, another layer of complexity is added to lead paint hazard control work. There are a number of ways in which lead paint can be removed or covered while preserving the historic character of a building. Rather than full-scale abatement, you could choose a combination of paint removal (by wet sanding, chemical stripping, and/or low-level heat stripping) and removal of such elements as doors, shutters, and moldings for off-site stripping or replacement. In some cases encapsulation is also appropriate.

Each method has its disadvantages. Paint removal sacrifices information about the history of the building. Scraping can result in gouging painted surfaces irreparably. Sanding can be very time-consuming, and in some cases can damage surfaces, especially carved and ornate ones. Dip-tank stripping can dissolve the glue that holds pieces such as doors together and even damage the wood itself. When components such as windows and trim are removed for replacement, identical pieces may be hard to find and sometimes must be custom made at great expense.

There are certain features that will have a higher priority in terms of preserving their historic value. In some cases, leaving all layers of paint intact is important to preserve the paint history. Paint chronology is important in historic buildings to date alterations and to document decorative period colors. If your home has special decorative finishes such as graining, stenciling, or murals, you can have them evaluated by a painting conservator who can advise you on proper treatment to preserve these features. If you do remove components for stripping or replacement, you might also want to save any nails by carefully cutting them from behind with side cutters, as they are sometimes used for dating purposes.

The U.S. Department of the Interior's Cultural Resources Office recommends that the historical significance, integrity, and architectural character of a historic building be assessed before work is undertaken. Your State Historic Preservation Office (SHPO) can provide names of preservation professionals to do this type of evaluation.[1] *For a directory of State Historic Preservation Offices, contact the Advisory Council on Historic Preservation, listed in Appendix B, under* Historic Restoration. *For sources of more specific information on lead paint hazard control and historic buildings, see the resources listed in Appendix B, under* Historic Restoration.

CLEANUP AND CLEARANCE

Daily Cleanup

A thorough cleanup should be conducted at the end of each workday, before anyone is allowed to enter the work area, and before children, pregnant women, or pets are allowed to enter the home. For small jobs, the cleanup procedure should be done in the area up to 5 feet from the spot being deleaded. Any adjacent hallways or other areas where workers might have passed during the workday should also be cleaned thoroughly.

Daily cleanup consists of the following steps:

- The work area should be vacuumed with a HEPA-vac. An ordinary vacuum should not be used, because it will blow fine dust, including lead dust, back into the air.
- Hard horizontal surfaces should be damp mopped or sponged with a solution of water and household detergent or a lead-specific detergent. [If TSP (trisodium phosphate) or a phosphate-containing automatic dishwashing detergent is used, precautions should be taken, as described in Chapter 3.]
- Debris should be sealed in double 4-millimeter-thick or single 6-millimeter-thick plastic bags, or plastic sheeting sealed with duct tape, and put in a secure locked area. Consult your state environmental agency on disposal methods allowed in your state for lead-contaminated waste. Never burn lead-contaminated trash. Plastic sheeting should be repaired and removed.
- The bottom layer of plastic sheeting should be repaired with 6-millimeter-thick plastic and duct tape. The top layer may be removed and discarded.
- Protective clothing should be vacuumed (with HEPA) and removed by rolling it off.
- HEPA-vac attachments and respirators (but not the cartridges) should be washed with soap and water and stored in plastic bags.
- All workers should shower and wash their hair before entering a living space or coming into contact with young children or pregnant women.

Final cleanup for the project should be delayed at least 1 hour after the work is completed so that dust has had time to settle.

- Plastic sheeting should be misted, cleaned, and removed from containment areas.
- All rooms should be thoroughly cleaned. Even rooms that had no lead paint will probably be contaminated.
- Porches, sidewalks, and driveways should be cleaned if there was work done outside, or if debris was dropped or stored outside.
- Cleaning should proceed from top to bottom and from the back of the house to the front entry. HEPA vacuum, wet wash, then HEPA vacuum again.
- The HEPA-vac filter should be changed according to the manufacturer's instructions, debris removed in a containment area or off site, and the waste disposed of properly.
- Hard surfaces should be washed with water and detergent or a lead-specific cleaning product. Two buckets should be used, one with the cleaning solution and the other with clean rinse water. Wash water should be replaced regularly, as should sponges and cloths. Workers' clothing, tools (including HEPA-vac attachments), supplies, and protective equipment should be washed.
- All floors must have a smooth, nonporous surface that is intact and cleanable. Wood floors can be coated with paint or polyurethane, or covered with tile or linoleum. Vinyl and linoleum can be waxed. This should be done after cleaning and visual examination but before final clearance.
- All work materials, debris, and contaminated clothing should be wrapped up and removed to a location that is out of reach of children.
- Consult your state environmental agency on disposal methods allowed in your state for lead-contaminated waste. Never burn lead-contaminated trash.

Clearance

CLEARANCE is the evaluation undertaken to make sure that the intended work was actually done, and that the area is now safe for you and your family. It is similar to a punch list for a construction job, but in addition to looking at the specific work that was done, environmental testing is conducted to ensure that there are no lead hazards remaining. It should not be started until at least an hour has passed since the work was completed, to allow for most lead dust in the air to settle onto the floor and other surfaces. During this hour, no one should enter the work area, so that the dust will not be stirred up again.

Clearance should be assigned to a certified risk assessor or inspector. To ensure that the evaluation is objective, it should not be done by anyone who is paid or employed by the contractor who did the abatement work. HUD recommends that if no risk assessment was done initially, one be done at this point, in case there are additional hazards that have not been identified.

Visual Inspection

A VISUAL INSPECTION (also referred to as VISUAL EXAMINATION or VISUAL CLEARANCE) should be done on each room separately, making sure that:

- Each component so specified was actually removed and replaced. No surface that was supposed to have paint removed was overlooked, such as the underside of windowsills, or the back side of radiators.
- If new drywall, paneling, etc. was used to enclose lead surfaces, the fastening system is "dust-tight."
- Encapsulants are present on surfaces where they were supposed to be applied.
- For interim controls, lead-based paint was stabilized (sealed, intact, smooth, and cleanable) and friction and impact surfaces were treated properly.

If surfaces are to be repainted, visual clearance should be done before the painting is begun, so that the bare deleaded surfaces can be examined. If there is any dust visible, further cleaning is required before the clearance procedure can proceed. Dust sampling should be done after surfaces have been repainted or otherwise sealed.

For exterior work, the area around the house should be checked to make sure that no paint chips are visible.

- If soil is involved, was all bare soil covered as intended?
- Waste and debris should not be visible on the grounds.

Dust Sampling

Three types of surfaces should be tested for lead dust. Samples of dust are taken using a wet wipe (similar to one used for babies) according to a very specific procedure, and these are analyzed in an EPA-approved laboratory according to specified methods. Dust samples from floors should not have more than 100 μg of lead per square foot. Samples from interior windowsills should not have more than 500 μg per square foot, and those from window troughs and exterior concrete or other rough surfaces, not more than 800 μg per square foot.

If any element fails the test, it has to be recleaned and tested again along with other similar elements. (If one windowsill in a room fails, for example, all the windowsills in the room have to be cleaned and tested again.) If it fails twice, then you may have to do more abatement or at least sealing of surfaces to get the levels down.

Soil Sampling

Before sampling soil, any paint chips from the paint removal work should be removed with a HEPA-vac as part of the cleanup. Soil samples should be taken both directly around the house and in play areas. One composite sample should be taken for each area. Any bare soil should be sampled. If there is none, the ground covering, such as wood chips or mulch, should be sampled. Any paint chips that remain on the soil should be tested right along with the soil that is picked up for the sample. There should not be any soil with lead over 2000 ppm (parts per million) or any soil in play areas with over 400 ppm.

Records

Records of all abatement, interim controls, inspection, and clearance results should be kept by the property owner as well as by the contractor and the clearance examiner.[2]

For more information on lead paint abatement, see the sources listed in Appendix B, under Lead Paint Hazard Control.

PART SIX

Controlling Other Sources of Lead

A child lives in a lead world.
J. Ruddoch, *The Journal of the American Medical Association* (1924)

CHAPTER FOURTEEN

Lead in Soil

Soil and young children are no strangers. This is especially true when children play outdoors a lot, and even more so when they play in areas with open soil rather than a well-cared-for lawn. If that soil is contaminated with lead, children will carry lead-bearing soil with them on their clothes and on their skin. It will be tracked into their homes on their shoes and on the paws and fur of pets. Their toys will be dirtied with it, and it will get under their fingernails. When they touch their hands to their food or mouths, they will end up ingesting lead.

HOW LEAD GETS INTO OUR SOIL

Lead gets into our soil primarily via lead paint that chips and peels from the exteriors of buildings, and from the exhaust of cars and trucks during the decades of leaded gasoline use.

Paint from old playground equipment can fall into the soil and contaminate it. Old farm equipment or vehicles that are left to deteriorate on land can leave high concentrations of lead in soil. Specific areas of soil can also become heavily contaminated from lead paint on rain gutters and the leads that drain the water from the roof away from the house.

When bridges are sandblasted without adequate precautions to contain the lead dust, highly toxic fallout can contaminate soil in surrounding neighborhoods.

In some areas, soil can also be contaminated by emissions from industries such as lead smelters, lead reclamation plants, etc., or from the accumulation of lead arsenate, used as a pesticide in orchards before 1988.[1]

Even if contaminated soil is removed from a particular area, the area may become recontaminated. When lead-contaminated dirt is exposed, with no grass or other ground covering to hold it in place, it spreads easily. People track it into their homes on their shoes. Dirt is tracked onto streets, sidewalks, and other locations by people walking as well as by natural erosion.

Unfortunately, although a lot has been done to keep lead out of soil, the soil we will be living with for the foreseeable future still bears the contamination from years and years of accumulation. Lead does not degrade. Unless it is covered by new silt deposits or washed away by erosion, the lead deposited in our soil presents a permanent health hazard to those who may come in contact with it.[2] So we had better learn to protect ourselves from it.

HOW LEAD IN SOIL IS REGULATED

Federal guidelines set specific limits on concentrations of lead in the soil that are considered safe.[3] These are newly developed and have not yet had an impact in reducing the amount of lead in our soil. *For a summary of these limits and recommendations for treatment, see Appendix F.*

In addition, by prohibiting some sources of lead, federal laws have been effective in reducing the amount of lead that gets into our soil. The phaseout of leaded gasoline, for example, has had a major impact on reducing the lead content of agricultural soil. The banning of lead in house paint will eventually also reduce the lead added from peeling exterior paint. But the benefits of this will be seen only slowly over the years, because there are still millions of homes with lead-based paint that is peeling, or may peel in the future, to decay into the ground. The EPA's refusal to reauthorize the pesticide lead arsenate after 1988 has eliminated yet another source of soil contamination.

There are few state laws regarding allowable limits for lead in soil. Minnesota has legislation that is viewed as a model. That law has guidelines to protect children from contaminated soil, involving covering the dirt up with sand or wood chips or growing grass.[4]

HOW TO KNOW IF YOUR SOIL HAS DANGEROUS LEVELS OF LEAD

Soil is most likely to have elevated lead levels in sites near highly traveled roads and in cities or older densely populated towns, where lead has accumulated from automobile exhaust and peeling house paint.

Specific areas of soil might be contaminated if they are, or ever were, close to any structure that was painted with lead-based paint. Soil near lead smelters accumulates large amounts of lead from emissions. Areas formerly used as orchards might also have lead-contaminated soil from the application of lead arsenate, used as a pesticide until 1988 (most commonly before the 1940s). A spot where old farm equipment has sat or a park where playground equipment has aged and peeled might also be contaminated.

The only way to be sure whether your soil presents a lead hazard is to have it tested.

Taking Samples

Lead concentration in soil can vary from one location to another, even a foot or so away, so you should test several spots. Lead levels are usually highest in areas close to buildings that have had lead paint, next to roads, and near trees in old orchards that were sprayed with lead arsenate. Take samples from the areas that are of concern to you, either where your children play or where you are considering planting a vegetable garden.

The depth of the soil you should test depends on the purpose for which you are testing. If you are testing the contamination level of dirt that might enter your home, either in the form of airborne dust or by being tracked in on shoes or by pets, test the top three-fifths of an inch of soil in a variety of spots outside your home. If you want to test the soil in the children's play area, take samples from the top inch of soil, since this is primarily the soil your children will come into contact with. If you are testing soil for gardening, sample the top 6 or 7 inches, as this will be the soil that the roots of your plants will come into contact with.

Use a clean spoon or scoop to collect about one cup of soil from several spots and put it in a plastic bag. Leave the roots of any plants that are in the dirt, but cut off any stems and leaves. If there are any paint chips, leave them in the soil to be analyzed.[5]

Laboratory Analysis

Contact a laboratory that is approved by the National Lead Laboratory Accreditation Program (NLLAP) or Environmental Lead Proficiency Analytical Testing (ELPAT) Program. *To find out if the laboratory is certified to analyze for lead in soil, call your state lead program, listed in Appendix A, the National Lead Information Clearinghouse at 800-424-LEAD, or one of the agencies that run the accreditation programs, listed in Appendix B, under* Testing/ Laboratory Analysis.

Some laboratories don't always explain the results. Test results are sometimes phrased in specific scientific terminology not readily understood by the nonscientist. The types of measurements given may vary from one laboratory to the next, so that you cannot always know exactly what is meant by the numbers you get. Ask for a full explanation of the results so that you are satisfied you understand them.

PROTECTING YOUR FAMILY FROM LEAD IN SOIL

If you are at risk for soil contamination either because you live near a busy street or industrial source of lead or because you have had lead paint deteriorating on your property or a history of lead arsenate pesticide spraying, you should take precautions, unless and until you have had your soil tested and are told that it is safe. Limit your children's exposure to the soil, and exercise caution regarding any vegetable gardening.

Permanent solutions involve either paving over the soil with concrete, or removing the top 6 inches or so of soil and disposing of it in an approved landfill. A core sample should be taken to confirm that the contamination does not go farther than this. Before putting in replacement soil, have that tested, and do not accept anything with over 200 ppm lead content. Contact your state environmental agency regarding how and where to dispose of the contaminated soil. This solution can be very costly compared to other ways to limit a child's exposure to lead.[6] And even if you go to the trouble of having contaminated soil replaced, it can easily be recontaminated afterwards.[7]

Protect Children from Lead in Soil in Play Areas

Unless you have tested your soil and are told it has under 400 ppm lead (400 parts of lead for every million parts of soil), it might present a danger for young children. You should take the following precautions:

- □ Be sure that everyone entering the house wipes their shoes well on a heavy-duty mat. Even better, establish the practice of removing shoes at the entrance to your home.
- □ Wash your children's hands well when they come inside from playing outdoors.
- □ Encourage your children to play in grassy areas or a sandbox, rather than in the dirt. Use clean, uncontaminated sand and keep it covered when not in use so that it does not become contaminated with lead dust.
- □ Keep your children away from the soil closest to your house by planting shrubs there. The most contaminated soil is usually within 3 feet of the house, so encourage children to play farther out in the yard.
- □ Plant grass or other ground cover, or spread gravel, sand, or wood chips over the dirt in your yard.Covering contaminated soil with grass, bark, artificial turf, or gravel will keep children away from it. If bark or gravel is used, 6 inches is recommended to be effective. *For specific information on ground covers, see the resources listed in Appendix B under* Soil.
- □ Remove play equipment from areas with exposed soil and provide children an alternative area to play.
- □ Ensure that no additional lead is added to the dirt by having peeling leaded paint removed from the exterior of your home and other buildings on your property (garage, shed, etc.).
- □ As a temporary measure, the soil can be turned or sodded. This dilutes but does not remove the hazard.[8]

Take Precautions Regarding Planting Vegetables in Soil with Lead

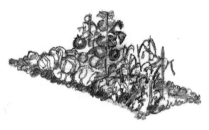

Unless you have tested your soil and know that it is safe, you should take precautions to protect your plants, and those who eat them, from lead contamination. There is no specific level proven to be safe and a strong difference of opinion exists as to the concentration of lead above which planting should be avoided. The USDA Extension Service considers any level under 200 ppm lead in soil to be safe. The standard set by the State of New York is 250 ppm.[9] An organic farming publication advocates taking extreme precautions against lead contamination. It advises that levels over 100 ppm can be toxic to plants, and that you should not plant root or leaf crops in soil with over 10 ppm if the pH is under 7, or in soil with over 20 ppm lead if the pH is 7 or above.[10] This would eliminate over 90% of soil for gardening use.

The best way to protect your household from lead in the soil is to avoid planting where there is the most lead:

☐ Plant as far as possible from the road and from any buildings with lead paint.

☐ Find out about prior uses of the land to learn whether lead arsenate was ever sprayed (as an insecticide for fruit trees), and whether there has ever been demolition work to remove any buildings that might have stood on the property.

To reduce the amount of lead your family will ingest from food grown in soil with lead, take the following precautions:

☐ Use at least 25% organic compost by volume, the more decayed and the less fibrous the better.

☐ For plants that are not especially sensitive to pH, use lime to get your soil to a pH of 6.5 or 7. Lead is less soluble at these levels.

☐ Keep the soil moist and use mulch, to minimize dust.

☐ Plant fruiting crops (including tomatoes, beans, squash, etc., plants where neither leaves nor roots are eaten) rather than leafy crops (lettuce, spinach, etc.) or root crops (beets, potatoes, etc.), which absorb more lead from the soil.

☐ If you do grow leafy crops, remove the outer leaves. These can contain as much as five times more lead than inner leaves.

☐ If you do grow root crops, peel them before eating.

☐ Wash all produce thoroughly with water and a small amount of vinegar (1%) or a nontoxic liquid dishwashing detergent that specifically states on the label that it is safe for washing food, such as can be found in a health food store. Rinse well before eating.[11]

The USDA Extension Service recommends that if your soil tests between 300 and 500 ppm lead, it is safe for growing produce for adults to eat. But for children, who are more vulnerable to lead poisoning, the above precautions are a must.

If your soil has over 500 ppm lead and you have a child with high blood lead levels, avoid growing root and leaf crops.

If soil lead levels exceed 1000 ppm, avoid leafy and root crops, and either dilute the top 6 inches of soil with new uncontaminated soil or plant in containers, or raised beds lined with plastic, with the top 6 inches of soil replaced with clean topsoil. If the soil has over 3000 ppm lead, no planting of edible crops should be considered.[12]

The higher the level of lead in the soil, the more will be absorbed by the plant, and the greater hazard it presents. There is no specific level that is absolutely safe. Whether you plant in lead-contaminated soil depends on your needs and the risk you are willing to accept.

Maintain Walks, Parking Areas, and Lawns

Worn dirt paths and loss of grass in lawn areas create dust that can spread and threaten your family's health. Take the following precautions unless you know that your soil is not contaminated with lead:

☐ Have walkways paved or covered with concrete, stone, wood chips, or gravel.

☐ Park on a paved area rather than on grass, or cover an area with crushed stones or gravel to use for parking to save the grass.

☐ Maintain your lawn and fill in worn corners with gravel or stones to keep soil covered.[13]

CHAPTER FIFTEEN

Lead in Food

The amount of lead in our food has decreased drastically in recent years. The levels of lead that an infant or child was exposed to in food in the early 1990s were only about 10% of those seen just 10 years earlier.[1]

Today crops are grown in soil and air containing less lead because leaded gasoline is no longer commonly used as an automotive fuel. Less lead gets into canned foods because U. S. food processors have stopped using lead solder to seal the seams of cans.[2]

Even though lead from food is responsible for only a small percentage of today's lead poisoning cases, it is still of concern because it is one more factor adding to an individual's total lead exposure. And there have been isolated cases, even in recent years, of severe lead poisoning caused by specific food sources.

HOW LEAD GETS INTO OUR FOOD

Lead may enter the food supply when crops are grown in contaminated soil, water, or air, or when food is stored or served in containers that release lead.

Lead Gets into Crops as They Grow

Contaminated soil passes lead along with nutrients to the crops that are planted in it. Plants take up the lead mostly in their roots and green leafy parts. Fruits and grains are affected very little. However, root crops, such as beets and carrots, and leafy vegetables, such as lettuce and spinach, grown in lead-contaminated soil could have dangerously high levels of lead.

If crops are watered by irrigation systems containing lead, the lead can LEACH, or be drawn from the pipes and dissolved into the water. This lead will also enter the plant, being stored primarily in the roots and leaves. Water contaminated by industrial lead emissions will likewise contaminate crops.

The use of sewage sludge on agricultural fields is another source of lead in crops. Because of increased awareness, this practice has decreased in the last dozen years.[3]

Although crop contamination from air pollution has declined greatly since the phaseout of leaded gasoline, in some cases lead that enters the air from other sources, such as smelters or sandblasting of buildings and bridges, may contaminate crops.

Lead Gets into Food When It Is Stored or Served

The most severe lead contamination of food in recent years has been from cans soldered with lead or from ceramics or leaded crystal used to store or serve food.

Ceramics

Improperly glazed or fired ceramic containers can leach large amounts of lead, especially if they are used to hold acidic foods. This is particularly true for earthenware. Ceramic cups used for orange juice every morning, or mugs used several times a day for coffee or tea, can be responsible for cases of severe lead poisoning.

We may be using ceramic pieces made before 1971 when these regulations were passed. Also, foreign-made ceramics brought into this country by tourists and immigrants have been responsible for numerous cases of severe lead poisoning in children and adults alike.

Ceramics manufactured in the United States or imported commercially into this country are now regulated by the federal government; however, because of budget constraints, not all china is tested.

Do not assume that expensive china is necessarily safe. Although such instances are rare, even the finest china from prestigious manufacturers has been found to contain hazardous levels of lead.

Cans

As of June 1993, up to 10% of imported foods (230 million pounds a year) still used lead to seal the side seam of the can, according to the FDA.[4] This can create extremely high lead levels, especially in acidic products, such as fruit juice. An incident in 1991, where a young child was poisoned by imported canned fruit juice, brought this danger to public attention. On examination, some of these juices were found to contain over 1000 parts per billion of lead, over 12 times higher than the level considered safe by FDA standards.[5]

Wine Bottles and Crystal

Federal studies in 1991 found that up to 4% of the wine in the United States contains dangerous levels of lead.[6] This is largely due to the leaching of the lead from the foil that is wrapped around the cork and neck of many wine bottles to keep out insects and oxygen. These CAPSULES used to be made from tin but manufacturers switched to lead because it was less expensive. Although this use of lead is now prohibited, many imported wines that were bottled before 1996 still have lead capsules.

Leaded glass crystal contains from 24 to 32% lead oxide, which can leach out into its contents. It can be particularly dangerous for storing alcoholic beverages. The more acidic the liquid, the more lead it absorbs. Recent studies of numerous brands of crystal decanters found unsafe levels of lead, leading to moderate to extremely high contamination of wines and other alcoholic beverages they contained.[7]

Folk Remedies and Cosmetics

Various traditional ethnic remedies and cosmetics have been found to cause lead poisoning.

SURMA, used by some Asians (Muslim communities from the Indian subcontinent) as an eyeliner, has produced cases of lead poisoning in children in this country. Its importation has been banned, but it is brought here by individuals. KAJAL and CERUSE (ALKOHL, KOHL) are also used as eye cosmetics and contain lead

Lead has been used in hair dyes since ancient times. In the United States the concentration of lead is restricted to 0.6%, and warning labels are required on the product.[8]

Some traditional Asian herbal medicines contain lead, as do popular home remedies used in Hispanic communities. The most common of these in use in this country are AZARCON or GRETA, two remedies for stomach ailments used by Mexican Americans. These have been found responsible for a number of serious lead poisoning cases in California.[9] A Chinese medicine called PAY-LOO-AH has also been frequently associated with lead poisoning.

The remedies that present a lead hazard include[10]:

AZARCON (RUEDA, CORAL, MARIA LUISA, LIGA, ALARCON)
GHASARD   KOHL (ALKOHL, CERUSE)
KANDU   KAJAL
PAY-LOO-AH

Calcium Supplements

Dietary calcium supplements have been found to contain lead. Natural source and bone meal supplements tend to have higher amounts of lead than dolomite supplements. Since

bone is used to store lead in the body, if the animal whose bone is used to make the supplement has been exposed to lead, or has eaten food contaminated with lead, the bone could contain hazardous levels of lead. The variation from brand to brand is huge. Some are perfectly safe, and others are dangerously contaminated. Although calcium chelates and refined calcium carbonates generally have less lead, again, brands vary greatly.[11]

Miscellaneous

Bread wrappers may contaminate food when they are used inside out to store food in, and the lead paint from the lettering and designs gets onto the food that is stored. Pewter used to be made with lead. Although lead is rarely found in newer pewter, there was a recent case of pewter baby cups being recalled because of lead content.[12] There have also been cases of lead poisoning from such unexpected sources as moonshine distilled in an old radiator with lead solder, juice drunk from a glass having decorative decals close to the rim, coffee that picked up lead from the urns, and draft beer, contaminated from bronze and brass equipment that contained lead.[13]

HOW LEAD IN FOOD IS REGULATED

The Food and Drug Administration (FDA) of the U. S. Department of Health and Human Services is the federal agency that sets standards for the safety of the public food supply.

Ceramics

Today ceramics sold in this country are required by the FDA to contain the proper proportions of lead silicate and lead oxide in the glaze and to be fired at a temperature higher than 1200 degrees Celsius. That temperature converts any lead into lead silicates, which cannot easily be dissolved.

Limits on how much lead could leach into food were first set in 1971, and have been made stricter over the years. The most protective standards apply only to those ceramics manufactured or imported after the most recent regulations, in 1992. Stricter standards are set for cups, mugs, and pitchers, because they are considered the most dangerous, relating to their frequent use for acidic drinks (which absorb more lead).[14]

Decorative ceramics are not held to the same standards, but are required either to bear both stick-on labels and permanent statements that they are for decorative use only and could poison food, or to have a hole bored through the part that would be used to serve or store food.[15] Unfortunately, however, these warnings are sometimes painted over, so that some imported items are ultimately sold without any way for the consumer to know that they are unsafe.

In the past, cans used for storing foods had seams sealed with lead solder. Because of the health hazard of lead from solder migrating into the food inside the cans, in 1982 U. S. manufacturers voluntarily stopped using lead solder in baby formula cans. By November 1991, they stopped the practice for all food products.[16]

In response to extremely high lead levels found in some imported fruit juices, the FDA has begun the process to prohibit the use of lead solder in domestic or imported food cans.[17] Until this prohibition is in effect, the agency has set emergency limits on how much lead is permitted in imported canned goods. Stricter limits were set for fruit juice because it is more likely that a young child would consume large quantities of fruit juice on a daily basis than other foods.[18]

Lead Foil on Wine

The FDA has prohibited the use of lead foil capsules on wine.[19] Most U. S. manufacturers stopped using them years ago.

PROTECTING YOUR FAMILY FROM LEAD IN FOOD

If you grow your own food, Chapter 14 gives advice on how to protect your produce from lead-contaminated soil. Otherwise, be careful about food coming into contact with any ceramics or leaded crystal. These precautions are especially important for young children and pregnant women, whose exposure to lead affects the extremely vulnerable fetus.

Ceramics

If you have any doubt about whether your ceramics may leach lead, test them. A number of the spot test kits on the market can be used for testing ceramics. *For information on products available commercially, see Appendix G.*

The Environmental Defense Fund (EDF) has published a list of makes of china that are safe. *For a copy of their brochure on lead in china, contact the Environmental Defense Fund, listed in Appendix B, under* Ceramics.

Unless and until you have tested any old, homemade, or imported ceramics for lead, do not use them for storing or serving food.

The FDA recommends that you:

☐ Avoid using any ceramics for regularly storing or serving fruits or fruit juices, coffee, tea, tomato juice, soup, or sauce. Even well-made ceramics can leach some lead into acidic foods.

□ Do not use any ceramic items that show a chalky gray residue after washing, or any items that bear the warning "Not For Food Use—Plate May Poison Food. For Decorative Purposes Only." These mean the glaze may leach lead into your food.

□ If you are pregnant, do not use ceramics on a daily basis for hot drinks.[20]

For more specific information about lead in ceramics, check the resource list in Appendix B, under Ceramics.

Cans

□ Restrict consumption of imported canned goods unless you are sure lead solder has not been used.

Wine

□ If your wine is sealed with a foil capsule and was bottled before 1996, wipe the rim with lemon juice or vinegar before removing the cork and again before pouring the wine.

Leaded Crystal

□ Do not use leaded crystal regularly for drinking.

□ Do not use leaded crystal for drinking if you are pregnant.

□ Do not let young children use leaded crystal.

□ Do not feed babies from leaded crystal bottles.

□ Do not store beverages in leaded crystal containers.

CHAPTER SIXTEEN

Lead in Drinking Water

In most cases of lead poisoning, drinking water is not the primary cause, but only a contributing factor. Drinking water contributes about 20% of the lead exposure for an average 2-year-old, and from 5 to 50% for children generally. However, in some homes with corrosive water and lead pipes or fairly new lead solder, water could be the primary exposure route for lead. The most alarming occurrence of drinking water causing severe lead poisoning is that of an infant fed formula made with lead-contaminated tap water, in which case the water can account for 85% of the lead exposure, and can result in quite severe lead poisoning.[1]

HOW LEAD GETS INTO OUR DRINKING WATER

Lead usually gets into our drinking water when the water absorbs the toxic element from our household plumbing systems or our water distribution systems.

Aggressiveness of Water

Drinking water will wear away at more of the lead it is exposed to if the water has certain characteristics. Water is referred to as AGGRESSIVE or CORROSIVE if it tends to eat away at the lead in the pipes (and solder, etc.). Chemical measures such as pH, acidity, and total alkalinity, as well as carbonate and other forms of hardness contribute to how corrosive the water is.[2] Other things being equal, more acidic water will contain more lead than less acidic water.

Approximately 34,000 water systems, comprising 58% of the nation's water supply systems, serving 42 million people, have at least moderately aggressive water.[3]

The quality of the water affects how much lead it picks up not only from the water distribution system, but also from our home's plumbing system.

Water Supplies Are Contaminated in a Very Small Percentage of Cases

It is rare that lead contaminates our water supplies themselves, whether they are groundwater (underground aquifers) or surface water (lakes and reservoirs). Only about 3% of our population's water supplies at their sources have levels of lead that are considered high.[4] In these cases the lead may get into the water from industrial sources such as smelters or from sources such as batteries disposed of in landfills.

Water Distribution Systems Often Account for Lead in Drinking Water

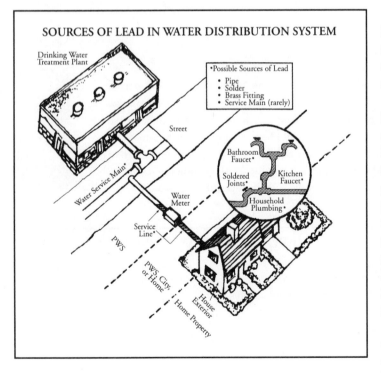

SOURCES OF LEAD IN WATER DISTRIBUTION SYSTEM

Drinking Water Treatment Plant

•Possible Sources of Lead
• Pipe
• Solder
• Brass Fitting
• Service Main (rarely)

Street

Bathroom Faucet•

Soldered Joints•   Kitchen Faucet•

Household Plumbing•

Water Service Main•

Water Meter

Service Line•

PWS

PWS City or Home

House Exterior

Home Property

Certain communities are more likely to have lead-contaminated water than others because of the composition of the water distribution system as well as the nature of the water itself.

Lead can come from service lines that bring water from the water main to your house. About 20% of large- and medium-size water systems in the country either have lead pipes or lead was used to connect the pipes together.[5] Most lead pipes were installed before 1920 but they are generally used for over 50 years. Approximately 10 million lead service lines and connections are currently in place in the United States, in our public water systems.[6]

Some cities have banned the use of lead in water distribution systems or have even begun removing existing lead water lines.

Household Plumbing Is a Common Source of Lead Contamination of Drinking Water

Pipes

Lead pipes pose a danger primarily in houses that were built prior to 1920, when such pipes were commonly used.[7] No matter how old these pipes are, they may continue to leach lead into your drinking water depending on the specific characteristics of the water (that is, lead from the pipes will be dissolved by the water) until they are replaced. Water that sits in them over a period of hours picks up much higher amounts of lead than water that just runs through them on the way to the faucet. However, if your water is hard, your pipes become coated over the years with minerals that protect the water from dissolving lead.[8]

Solder

After 1930, lead pipes became too expensive, so copper pipes were used instead. But the copper pipes were soldered together with lead. Lead solder was commonly used until 1986, when it was outlawed. However, it continues to be used illegally, and is still manufactured and on the market. Only its use in household plumbing installation and repair is prohibited.

The solder leaches less and less each year, so that levels of lead leaching into the water decline over time. The greatest loss of lead into drinking water occurs during the first 2 years of use. Even after 5 years, however, significant amounts of lead can still end up in the water, depending on its corrosiveness.[9]

Fixtures

Fixtures containing lead can also be a source of contamination, both in our water distribution systems and in our homes themselves. Brass fixtures, such as faucets, can contain up to 8% lead, some of which can leach into drinking water, especially when it has been sitting in contact with the brass for several hours or overnight.

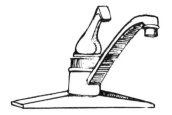

Submersible Water Pumps May Contaminate Drinking Water

An estimated 30 million Americans drink water from private wells that use pumps made of lead alloys such as brass or bronze. These pumps are usually located under water, which they can contaminate with hundreds or even thousands of parts per billion (ppb) of lead. The maximum safe level according to the Environmental Protection Agency is 15 ppb.

The danger is the greatest when the pumps are new. The EPA has advised households with recently installed pumps to use bottled water until lead contamination tests are done. Those with older pumps should also test for lead, although the risk may not be great enough to merit switching to bottled water immediately.[10]

School Drinking Fountains May Contaminate Water with Lead

In 1988 the EPA found that the water from some drinking fountains had lead levels up to 20,000 ppb, 400 times the then-existing maximum level considered safe. Since 15 ppb is now the acceptable level, the levels found in these fountains would be over 1000 times the limit. About 1 million drinking fountains contain lead solder.[11] *For a list of drinking fountains that contain lead, contact the EPA Safe Drinking Water Hotline, listed in Appendix B, under Drinking Water.*

In our schools, water sits for long periods of time in the fountains—overnight, over weekends, and even weeks or months of vacation time—so the lead that is in contact with the water has ample time to leach out. Federal law mandates states to correct the situation, but some states have done better than others. If you have children in school, check to see if your town has tested for lead in the drinking fountains. If not, you might want to encourage your school district to have them tested.

Kettles and Samovars May Leach Lead into Water

Antique kettles may have lead solder which will leach into the water during boiling. Samovars, used for making tea by some Middle Eastern and Russian immigrants, can also have lead solder, likewise contaminating the water boiled in them.

Baby Formula Mixed from a Powder May Become Contaminated

Lead-contaminated water mixed with powdered formula for feeding infants is of special concern. Water is often taken from the tap first thing in the morning to mix the day's bottles. This first-drawn water is the heaviest in lead content. The directions for powdered formula are to boil the water before mixing the formula. The intention is to kill any microbes in the water. However, this has the effect of concentrating any lead already in the water. Since formula might be the sole source of nourishment during the first few months of a baby's life, and since lead in liquids is more readily absorbed than lead in solids, this source of lead is particularly dangerous. In a number of cases, infants have been severely poisoned by lead in mixed baby formula.[12]

HOW LEAD IN DRINKING WATER IS REGULATED

Solder

The federal government prohibited the use of lead solder for installation and repair of residential plumbing in 1986.

Brass Faucets

Federal law restricts the amount of lead in brass faucets and fixtures to 8%.

The Lead and Copper Rule Sets Limits on How Much Lead Can Be in Drinking Water

In 1991 the federal government responded to the new information about the dangers of lead exposure with a program for monitoring and reducing lead in drinking water. The Lead and Copper Rule[13] reduced the ACTION LEVEL for lead in drinking water from 50 to 15 ppb. This means that if drinking water in a certain percentage of selected HIGH-RISK homes in a community has more than 15 ppb lead, the water supplier must take steps to reduce it. High-risk homes are those most likely to have high levels of lead in drinking water on the basis of their age and the type of plumbing materials they have.

Monitoring

All water suppliers are required to test the drinking water at the taps of a number of HIGH-RISK households. The accuracy of the results of this monitoring has been criticized. Only a small number of households are tested, and the choice of the households tested is left to the water supplier and not reviewed by the EPA.

If 10% of these have more than 15 ppb lead, the water suppliers are required to take action to reduce the lead level. That action could consist of either controlling the aggressiveness of the water so that it dissolves less lead, or controlling the lead in the water distribution system so that less of it is dissolved.

Since replacing plumbing in homes, or municipal water distribution pipes, is very expensive, it makes sense to control the problem of high concentrations of lead in drinking water by controlling the water's aggressiveness. This is referred to as corrosion control.

Corrosion Control

Aggressive water will leach more lead. Lead levels in aggressive drinking water may be high even when only a small amount of lead exists in the plumbing system. Lead levels in nonaggressive drinking water may be low even when more lead is present in the plumbing.

If a water supplier finds that its water is above the action level, it must choose a manner of reducing the corrosiveness, or aggressiveness, of the water so that the tap water meets the federal standard. Corrosion control methods involve adding a substance at the filtration plant that will make the water dissolve less lead.

The water supplier must choose a method that is appropriate for its specific water characteristics through a rigorous testing program. Permissible methods involve adding an alkaline chemical to adjust the pH, adding minerals to increase the hardness, or adding corrosion-inhibiting mineral compounds.

Problems with Corrosion Control.   Each of these methods has its potential problems. For example, adding orthophosphates or silicates does not work if the water is too acidic. Phosphates, although they can effectively coat pipes so that lead doesn't leach into the water, contain metals that could be damaging to aquatic ecosystems coming in contact with waste water. They can also cause growth of algae (EUTROPHICATION) and problems with cloudiness (TURBIDITY), taste, and odor.[14]

When they choose a corrosion control method, water systems are required to study all of the potential complications and ensure that their actions do not cause the water supply to violate any of the other federal drinking water standards. *For technical information on corrosion control, contact your regional EPA office, listed in Appendix A, and the organizations listed in Appendix B under* Drinking Water.

Source Treatment

If the above corrosion control technologies do not adequately reduce the lead levels in the drinking water, the water supplier might have to install equipment to treat the water at its source.

Service Line Replacement

If the lead levels at the tap are still too high after the corrosion control and source treatment have been completed, the water supplier must replace its lead service lines. This is considered only a last resort because of the inconvenience and expense involved.

Generally, the EPA is encouraging the smaller water systems to use mechanical methods to control lead in the water, such as replacing the pipes that carry the water, or simpler methods, such as limestone softening. Although these may be expensive at the outset, they require low maintenance. Chemical methods demand more expertise than many small users may have, and if they are not properly implemented, they could pose a public health hazard.

Public Awareness

In systems where action levels are exceeded, the Lead and Copper Rule has requirements for educating the public in addition to more monitoring and corrosion control. Notices are to be included in water bills, and more extensive written materials have to be provided directly to facilities such as schools, pediatricians, and the health department.

Information has to be provided to the general community in newspapers and on the radio, alerting residents to the fact that the water has been found to be high in lead and that this may present a health risk.

Technical Assistance

Technical assistance is available through the EPA regional offices and the National Technical Information Service. The EPA holds workshops in coordination with the Association of Metropolitan Water Agencies, the American Water Works Association, and the

National Rural Water Association. Also, the American Water Works Association offers publications on controlling lead in drinking water.[15] *For technical information in this area, contact the EPA, NTIS, or AWWA, listed in Appendix B, under* Drinking Water.

DETECTING LEAD IN YOUR DRINKING WATER

Water's Appearance Gives No Clues about Lead

Lead in water is invisible at the concentrations found in drinking water. Lead-contaminated water does not look dirty or cloudy.

You cannot tell from the way your water smells or tastes if it has lead.

Soft Water Dissolves More Lead

If your water leaves a residue when allowed to evaporate from pots and pans, you have hard water (water containing certain types of minerals). Soft water does not have these minerals and does not leave a residue. In general, soft water is more desirable because it is better for creating suds with soap or detergent and is therefore better for washing. Unfortunately, soft water tends to be more aggressive in dissolving lead from pipes, solder, and faucets. The minerals in hard water coat the pipes and prevent the lead from leaching into the water.[16]

Grounding of Electrical Systems onto Plumbing Increases Lead Contamination

Electrical systems are often connected in some way to the ground so that any potentially dangerous electrical power from the malfunctioning of appliances is routed into the ground where it does no damage, rather than being conducted through the casing of the appliance, where it could harm anyone touching it. Since water pipes go into the ground, electrical systems are often connected to the pipes for grounding.

If your electrical system is grounded in this way, it could increase the rate at which lead is dissolved by the water in your pipes and consequently your chances of lead contamination.[17] Interpretation of the national electrical code varies from locality to locality in terms of the legal requirement for grounding electrical systems onto plumbing systems.[18] In no case should you attempt to make any changes in your electrical system's grounding yourself; any work related to this should be done only by a licensed electrician.

The Age of Your Home Can Affect Your Risk of Lead-Contaminated Water

Certain houses are considered to have a HIGH RISK of having lead-contaminated water. This means that some homes are MORE LIKELY than others to have lead in drinking water. It does not mean that all houses in these categories have high lead levels, or that you are safe if your home is not in the high-risk categories. The following are high-risk homes:

- Houses built between 1910 and 1940, when lead pipes were common
- Houses built less than 5 years ago, but with lead solder. Although lead solder was outlawed in 1986, it is possible that it could have been used after that date.

Even if your home is not high risk, you may want to have your water tested to be sure. Your water could already be contaminated by lead service lines when it reaches your home. Plumbing fixtures, such as brass faucets, could also leach lead.

The Only Way to Know If Your Water Contains Lead Is to Have It Tested by an Analytical Laboratory

Two or three samples should be taken.

One is called a FIRST-DRAW sample. This should be taken in the morning before any water has been run in the house, even for flushing the toilet. This will tell you how much lead is in water that has been sitting in the plumbing in your home for several hours, and has had a chance to dissolve lead from the pipes, solder, and fixtures it has come into contact with.

A first-draw sample should be taken from any faucet that is commonly used for drinking water. First-draw samples can vary drastically within the same house because of the lead contained in the brass faucet itself.

A FLUSH sample (also referred to as PURGED-LINE or SECOND-DRAW) should be taken after letting the water run 5 minutes, until there is a noticeable change in its temperature. This will tell you whether the town water is contaminated before it even gets into your home.

This procedure will tell you not only how much lead is in your drinking water, but also whether the lead is coming from your own plumbing or from the water distribution system, and how effective letting the water run for a couple or a few minutes is in controlling the amount of lead it contains.

Some laboratories suggest taking an additional sample after the water has run from the faucet for a shorter time, to test the water as it flows through the plumbing in your house and has not been stagnant.

The laboratory that tests the water will provide specific instructions on drawing samples. They will also provide containers for the samples and the packaging to mail them, or they will advise you on how to prepare these yourself. Contact the laboratory directly. *For names of analytical laboratories that test water for lead, contact the EPA Safe Drinking Water Hotline, listed in Appendix B, under* Drinking Water.

Note: Even if you have not received notice from your water supplier that your community's water has been found to have high lead levels, you cannot be sure about the water in your home without testing. Only a few homes in the community are tested in the EPA monitoring program, and the amount of lead in a particular house depends on the characteristics of that home's plumbing system.

PROTECTING YOUR FAMILY FROM LEAD IN DRINKING WATER

Let the Water Run

If the main source of lead is within the house, water that has been sitting overnight or for several hours during the day has had a chance to dissolve more lead than water that has run for a couple minutes and been flushed through the system. Therefore, many water suppliers simply advise running the water in the morning until there is a noticeable temperature change before using it. The water that you run can be saved in containers and used for purposes other than cooking and drinking, such as cleaning or watering house plants.

Whether this system works for you depends on a number of factors such as:

- Will children forget to let the water run when they want a drink first thing in the morning?
- Might the adults be in a hurry and grab hot water from the faucet to make a quick breakfast?

You might also want to consider whether you could get into a routine of saving those first few gallons you run so you won't be wasting water.

Based on the lead level in your water, you may or may not want to depend on this system. Whether this alone is enough to protect you against lead exposure depends on whether the source of the lead is in your house or in the water distribution system and on how high a level of contamination you have. Testing the cold water after it has run for a while will give you an indication.

Use Cold Water

Use cold water for drinking, cooking, and preparing baby formula, because hot water dissolves more lead from the pipes.

Check for Lead Solder

Check your pipes for lead solder. If it is dark gray and looks shiny when it is scratched with a key, it may be lead. You could test it with a spot test kit to be sure.

If you find that lead solder has been used after 1986, when it was made illegal, have the person who installed it replace it and notify your state environmental agency.

Remove loose lead solder and debris from plumbing after any remodeling involving the plumbing and every year or so thereafter by removing the faucet strainer from all taps and letting water run for 3–5 minutes.

Check for Lead in Your Water System

Ask your water supplier if you are serviced by lead pipes.

Use a Water Filter to Remove the Lead

The surest way of getting the lead out of your drinking water if you do have dangerous levels is to use a good drinking water treatment device. Be sure to buy a model that states that it removes a high percentage, at least 90%, of the lead from the water it filters.

There are a number of technologies available for removing lead from drinking water. The most common are distillers, reverse osmosis, carbon, and alumina filters.

Reverse Osmosis

Reverse osmosis is a process that acts like a sieve to remove organic and inorganic contaminants from water. This includes heavy metals such as lead, as well as nitrates and fluoride. The device is attached to the plumbing under the sink. It is an effective process but tends to be slow. Once the storage tanks are depleted, it typically takes 2 to 4 hours to clean another gallon of water. Reverse osmosis units tend to waste 15 to 30 gallons of water daily. They are expensive, with costs ranging upwards from $400.

Distillers

Distillers boil water and collect the steam, which condenses into water WITHOUT minerals and heavy metals, such as lead. They do a good job of removing all such dissolved inorganic solids, although they do not necessarily remove volatile organic chemicals (such as benzene and chloroform). They are extremely slow, taking several hours to distill a gallon of drinking water. Although the cost of the unit (around $100) may not be prohibitive, they use a lot of electricity, so that the cost of distilling the water adds up to around 25 cents a gallon.

Carbon Filters

Activated carbon filters have been the most popular, mostly because they are fairly inexpensive and effective for a variety of contaminants. However, carbon filters without alumina are not designed for lead removal.

The surface of the carbon attracts and removes a number of contaminants from the water as they come into contact. The more carbon that comes into contact with the water, the better the job it does. It is especially good for organic contaminants and pesticides, as well as chlorine and radon, but not always effective in removing heavy metals.

Activated Alumina

Activated alumina's role in a water filter is similar to that of carbon. When water comes into contact with it, it attracts and removes certain contaminants, notably arsenic, fluoride, selenium, and LEAD. When activated carbon and alumina are used together, the filter can be highly effective in removing lead, as well as a number of other contaminants. Success of lead removal varies from brand to brand.

Filter Styles

Some types of filters are more affordable, and others more convenient. Those attached to the plumbing offer the advantage of convenient use, but more effort (or even the expense of hiring a plumber) to install. Some clean all of the water that enters the home, so filters have to be replaced more often. Others require installation of a separate faucet for the filtered water. Carafe-style filters require no installation. Rather than receiving the water directly from the plumbing system, the user pours tap water through the filter into a pitcher which stores the clean drinking water.

Replacing Filters

The filters on all of these devices have to be replaced regularly. If an old filter is left in too long, the unit not only fails to purify the water but can actually put contaminants back into the water and breed bacteria. This could make the water more dangerous than it was before being filtered.

Water Softeners

Water softeners DO NOT remove lead. Instead they could have the effect of increasing the lead in your drinking water.

Water softeners are used generally to remove minerals from water as it enters a household, so that it will clean better and leave less mineral residues (spotting on dishes, scaling on sinks and tubs). They use a chemical process called ion exchange to remove calcium and magnesium. They can also remove some toxic chemicals and radiological contaminants. They do not remove lead. The softer water actually is better able to dissolve the lead from pipes and plumbing fixtures. When the water has less minerals, and thus coats the pipes less, the lead more easily leaches into the water. (It also becomes richer in sodium, which might pose a particular problem for persons who must restrict their sodium intake.)

How to Select a Water Filter

In choosing a water filtering device to purchase, consider the following factors:

- How much lead does it remove? Look for a statement that it removes at least 90%.
- How quick and convenient is it? Consider both installation and how long it takes to filter a gallon of water.
- How expensive is it? You will pay not only the original purchase price but also the price of replacement filters and, in the case of the distiller, electricity costs.[19]

Use Bottled Water

Bottled water is an option, but is much more expensive than using a water filter. If you do buy bottled water, you might want to choose a brand that is a member of the International

Bottled Water Association, which sets strict requirements for testing for lead content. Although federal regulations call for bottled water to contain less than 5 ppb lead, these standards are not well enforced. *For a list of bottled water manufacturers that adhere to strict limitations on lead content, contact the International Bottled Water Association, listed in Appendix B under* Drinking Water.

Follow Other Precautions

In addition to these precautions regarding protection from lead in water, remember that lead poisoning is cumulative. Be aware of other sources of lead exposure which could add up to danger. Also, follow other preventive steps advised throughout this book and summarized in Appendix I.

PART SEVEN

Fighting Lead Poisoning

Turn your anger into action.
Slogan of Oxfam America Activist

*Never doubt that a small group of thoughtful committed citizens
can change the world; indeed, it's the only thing that ever does.*
Margaret Mead

CHAPTER SEVENTEEN

Suing for Personal Injury

If your child was clearly damaged by lead poisoning from exposure to lead in poorly maintained rental property (or in any situation caused by a specific person outside your family), you may be able to bring a lawsuit for personal injury. Whether your case will be taken on by an attorney will depend largely on how likely it is to succeed. This is determined by how clear the damage and the exposure are, as well as the specific laws in your state and how courts have decided similar cases.

DECIDING WHETHER TO SUE FOR PERSONAL INJURY

Reasons to Sue

Lawsuits for lead poisoning are brought to provide money to compensate for the damage suffered by children as well as to encourage property owners to be more vigilant about preventing lead poisoning.

Money Damages

In a personal injury lawsuit, you will ask for money (DAMAGES) to compensate not only for the actual costs you have incurred to treat your child for lead poisoning but often also for LOST INCOME. Lost income is the amount of money that your child would have been able to earn in his or her life but cannot because of the injury from lead poisoning.

The amount of these damages will depend on the family's particular situation as well as the severity of the injury. A child who has better-educated parents will usually be given more money, because that child would probably have also been better educated and had a better-paying job but for the lead poisoning. A child who is only slightly injured will receive less than one who is so severely injured that he or she might never hold a job.

For example, if the parents have no college education, an expert would assume that the child would have had a job earning about $16,000 at age 19, and that amount would have increased slightly each year until age 67. In the case of an individual with a 30% disability, that would amount to about $300,000. In a family where the parents have undergraduate degrees, a higher income would be assumed. And in the case of a more severe disability, a higher amount of lost earnings would result.

Damages are usually under $500,000. There are cases, however, of severely injured children receiving damages of millions in lost income and in schooling costs.

Other factors that might affect the amount of damages to expect from a lawsuit are:

- How many assets the defendant has (if he or she doesn't have insurance)
- The specific insurance company involved
- Who the defense counsel is

The vast majority (over 90%) of cases are settled out of court. If a case goes to trial, the amount of damages may vary more, because it depends on the feelings of the 12 individuals of the jury, which is less predictable. Damages can be anywhere from thousands to millions of dollars.

Some lawyers recommend establishing a trust to retain the money damages, ensuring they are used for their intended purpose of helping the child throughout his or her life.

Deterrent Effect

Trial attorneys point out that in spite of everything you may be put through in a lead poisoning case, by enduring this ordeal you may not only receive compensation for your injuries, but also serve a greater good. By raising consciousness about the issue, lawsuits serve to discourage neglectful behavior. Winning the lawsuit means that those responsible for the poisoning will pay. This should encourage the people who are responsible for protecting others from lead poisoning to take their obligation more seriously.

Reasons Not to Sue

Suing for lead poisoning can be a long, drawn-out process involving anxiety, humiliation, invasion of your privacy, and restrictions on your free speech.

Stress and Anxiety

The entire experience can be emotionally draining. According to many parents who have gone through the experience, the most devastating part is being blamed for injuring their child. Some parents choose not to pursue a lawsuit even though they believe they have a right to recover, seeking instead just to avoid the ordeal. Others do sue, but are shocked at the painful test they are put through. They assume that because they have been damaged by a landlord's negligence, they have the right to receive compensation, as simple as that. But it might not be so simple.

Depositions may be taken of anyone with any connection or knowledge of the case. These may drag on for many hours and contain questions that are personal, difficult to answer, or intimidating. Plaintiff's attorneys point out that "I don't know" or "I don't understand" is an acceptable answer if it is true. However, it may be difficult to simply answer this way. It can be stressful being questioned in this type of a formal situation by an experienced attorney trying to get compromising information.

The defendant's attorneys may subject your child to neuropsychological examinations, trying to show that no damage has been done, so that the landlord has no liability. Plaintiffs' attorneys recommend keeping a close eye on any such testing sessions to make sure they give the child enough time to answer questions that are posed and do nothing to slant the results.

A certain amount of anxiety is inevitable as a result of pursuing a lawsuit, simply from the fact that you are not getting closure for a number of years. States vary from months to years in how long cases take to get to trial. However, simply to determine the amount of damages you are asking for, you may have to wait several years before the neurological damage to your child can be assessed. The typical case in Massachusetts drags on for 3 or 4 years. Although this entire time period does not require your active involvement, the waiting can be difficult.

Invasion of Privacy and Humiliation

A parent suing for personal injury for lead poisoning will inevitably be accused of failing to raise his or her child properly. The opposing attorney's job is to try to show that the lead poisoning could have been the fault of someone other than the property owner (or whoever is being sued in the case). Expect to be told that you did not supervise your child carefully, that you should have seen the child eating the paint chips, chewing on the windowsill, etc., and that therefore you are an irresponsible parent.

Your privacy may disappear. The defendant's attorney will probably try to investigate medical records not only of your child but also of other members of your family, trying to show some tendency to mental illness or emotional problems that could be the cause of the child's symptoms. He or she may go into your school records to see if there was any suggestion of a learning disability that the child might have inherited. If there is an alternative explanation for the injury that you claim has resulted from lead poisoning, the landlord may not be held responsible.

You may want to do your own testing and come forward with records if you are pretty sure you can show that members of the family have high IQs and good academic records. If not, you may be able to stop this type of invasion of privacy if your attorney files the correct papers asking the judge to not allow this kind of investigation (referred to as DISCOVERY).

Restriction on Freedom of Speech

An attorney may advise against freely discussing the facts surrounding the lead poisoning so as not to adversely affect the case. If facts, and possibly exaggerated or slightly inaccurate statements, are made publicly, the defendant might be able to use them to weaken the case for the lead-poisoned child. When facts are related under the supervision of an attorney, care is taken that as little as possible is presented in such a way as to be detrimental to the case.

A lead poisoning parent may feel it is very important to be able to speak freely about lead poisoning and his or her personal experience, so as to warn others of the danger, and advocate for solutions to the problem. The potential benefits of a lawsuit might not be worth the price of being restricted from talking openly.

CHOOSING AN ATTORNEY

Get a referral for a lawyer who is competent and experienced in lead poisoning cases. The verdict in your case depends to a very great extent on how competent your attorney is. Lead poisoning cases require a very specific kind of expertise as well as long, hard work.

Ideally seek a local attorney with a thorough understanding of lead poisoning and the laws related to it, who has a proven record with such cases. Many of these attorneys have a landlord–tenant background. Others have a background in medical malpractice, product liability, or some other type of personal injury lawsuits. A good personal injury lawyer who has no experience with lead poisoning but who will quickly get up to speed on the subject by contacting the experts can also represent you competently.

Although it is simpler to work with a local attorney, if you are not able to find one who has your confidence, you might consider selecting an experienced attorney from another area. Lawyers who specialize in lead poisoning cases are often willing to take a case in another state, or to work along with and assist a local attorney with less expertise.

If you want to receive the amount of money damages you believe you are entitled to, avoid hiring a lawyer who is in a hurry to bring the case quickly and expects to get only a few thousand dollars. There are some lawyers who will try to get the case decided before the child's blood lead level goes down and routinely accept small awards, for example $25,000 for a case. This is typical of a number of "mills" that have sprung up in inner-city neighborhoods and sacrifice quality for quantity. They take on a large volume of lead poisoning cases but sell their clients short.

The best way to get a referral is by word of mouth from someone who has had a good experience with a similar case. Any number of professionals or organizations may be able to provide you this type of referral: a social worker, a pediatrician, doctor, or nurse at a lead poisoning clinic, Legal Services, parent support groups, etc.

A second way to get the name of a lawyer is to ask the local, county, or state trial lawyers association or bar association or the Association of Trial Lawyers of America (ATLA). *For ATLA's address, see Appendix B, under* Legal, *and for the addresses of state trial lawyers organizations, see Appendix A.*

Although Legal Services offices are available to help low-income people with legal problems, they do not handle cases for damages, so would not be the place to go for a personal injury case for lead poisoning, although they might be helpful with other legal matters that might be involved in lead poisoning situations, such as landlord–tenant actions.

Assessing the Lawyer's Qualifications

A referral, particularly from a lawyers association, is not a recommendation. Even if you have received the name of a lawyer from someone who has had a good experience with him or her, you should make sure that this is the right choice for you.

Ask for and check references. Contact the local bar association to see if there have been any complaints or disciplinary actions against the lawyer, just as you would check with the Better Business Bureau regarding a business. Finally, interview several candidates until you are satisfied that one will represent you competently.

If a corporate landlord is involved, look in the Martindale–Hubble directory to see if the law firm has a conflict of interest by virtue of representing any other client related to the person or corporation you are suing.

Make sure the attorney is experienced about lead, or knows how to get access to the kind of expertise that will be needed. Ask about the specific experience the attorney has had with lead poisoning cases and how many have been won, settled, and lost. You can expect the vast majority to have been settled, but will want to know the amounts of the settlements. The larger the number of cases, the better, but you don't want a lawyer who has a record of losing or settling for a fraction of the actual damages.

Discuss how he or she would build a case. The attorney should have a good idea about how to find out about the child's exposure to lead as well as how that exposure will impact the child's life. He or she must understand the types of damage that can result from lead poisoning, long term as well as short term. You only recover once for past, present, and future damage. At a minimum, be sure the attorney plans to:

- Talk to the child's treating physician, and obtain all medical records
- Evaluate the child's prenatal and pediatric history
- Examine inspection records thoroughly
- Ascertain how much of the child's time was actually spent on the inspected premises (versus relatives' homes, day care, previous residence, etc.)
- Evaluate how severe the poisoning was and if the treatment was reasonable and necessary
- If the child is 6 or older, get an evaluation by a psychologist or neuropsychologist, and the child's teacher

- Understand landlord–tenant, negligence, and personal injury law
- Have a rehabilitation or vocational counselor and/or neuropsychologist explain to the jury the impact of the injury on the development and the potential of the child as an adolescent, an adult, and throughout his or her life

Since expenses are generally covered, at least temporarily, by the lawyer, make sure the firm has the resources to pay for top-notch experts.

You may need the services of an attorney in other areas in addition to suing for personal injury. Ideally, your lawyer will represent you in landlord–tenant issues and help you to get the lead hazard in your home controlled so that your child and others will not be poisoned again.

Paying the Lawyer

Cases for damages are generally brought on what is called a CONTINGENCY basis. This means that you pay nothing for the services of an attorney unless and until you win the case.

The standard arrangement is that the lawyer (or law firm) gets one-third of whatever amount is paid for the injury, in addition to being reimbursed for any expenses incurred. The contract with the lawyer might also specify that if the case is appealed (obviously requiring additional work by the lawyer), a higher percentage will go to the lawyer. Some states have certain legal requirements regarding how much can be charged. Sometimes the contract also states that if you lose the case (or drop it), you must still pay the expenses. Most lawyers, however, will not enforce this provision, even if its inclusion in the contract is required by state law. Make sure you clarify any such clause in your contract.

Expenses

Strictly speaking, any expenses that are incurred in bringing a case have to be paid for by the client, not the lawyer. However, as a practical matter, the expenses are covered by the law firm until the case is settled or won, and only then is money taken out of the damages to pay for expenses.

Lead poisoning lawsuits are very expensive. Expenses may run between $10,000 and $50,000 for a full-fledged court trial. A number of experts have to be compensated for developing the case, for depositions, and for testifying at trial. Expert testimony is required not only regarding the medical aspects of the damage to the child but also regarding the economic impact of the damage as well as the extent of the contamination that caused the child to be exposed to lead. The experts may include:

- Neuropsychologist
- Pediatrician
- Toxicologist
- Economist
- Vocational expert
- Lead inspector
- Chemical engineer

MAKING THE CASE

If you can show that the illegal activity of the landlord has caused lead poisoning and consequent injury to your child, the landlord will have to pay to compensate for the injury. The lawyer representing the child has to prove two things: that the child was actually injured by lead and that the landlord had a legal responsibility to prevent the condition that led to the injury.

Establishing Liability

There are a number of theories on which to base the legal responsibility, or LIABILITY, of a property owner for an injury from lead poisoning.

Common Law

Common law is the law that is made when courts decide specific cases and come up with legal doctrines, or principles, on the basis of which other similar cases can be decided. There are two areas of common law that can apply to lead poisoning cases: the law of negligence, also known as torts, and contract law.

Negligence.   A negligence case is one that alleges that a particular injury was caused by someone's failure to be as careful as they should have been. Generally speaking, in order for an injured person to win a negligence case and receive damages, or money compensation, for the injuries suffered, it has to be shown not only that the defendant (the person blamed for the injury) caused a hazardous situation to exist or persist, but that he or she knew or should have known that the specific condition existed and that people in the position of the plaintiff (the injured person bringing the lawsuit) could be harmed by it.

In the case of lead paint poisoning, it would have to be shown that the landlord could have reasonably foreseen that a child might be injured by the condition of the house or apartment that caused the harm. The major issues that are brought up to show negligence are:

- Whether the landlord was in a position that he or she should have known about the hazardous condition
- Whether he or she should have known there were children who could be harmed by the condition

Different courts in different states interpret this differently. A number of factors are looked at in determining if the landlord was negligent, including:

- Whether the paint was in a defective condition, chipping, peeling, flaking, etc.
- Whether the landlord knew of the defective condition of the paint when the unit was rented out
- Whether the landlord knew that the paint was lead based
- Whether the landlord kept the information of the defective condition from the tenant

- Whether the landlord knew of the defective condition before the time of injury
- Whether the tenant knew of the defective condition before the injury
- Whether the eating of paint chips by children is an abnormal behavior or one that could reasonably be expected
- Whether the landlord had CONTROL of the premises, that is, whether he or she had the right to enter and inspect (in contrast to a situation where the tenant was the one who made repairs and the landlord never entered the house or apartment)
- Whether the landlord knew that there was a child on the premises
- Whether the landlord could have expected that a child would be in the particular area where the unsafe condition existed, such as a common hallway

Contract.   Contract claims are based on the grounds that a landlord promised to make repairs of deteriorating lead paint, and either didn't make the repairs or made them in a negligent manner. To be a contract, such a promise has to have been made in exchange for some action or promise from the tenant, called CONSIDERATION, such as a promise by the tenant to continue renting the apartment if the landlord makes the repairs. The promise must also be specific enough to necessarily cover repairs of lead-based paint. A promise simply to fix the place up without mentioning the paint may not be enough.

Once a landlord has a contractual obligation to remove lead from the premises, then any damage resulting from failure to do so, or from doing so in an unsafe manner, makes him or her responsible, or liable, for damages.

Specific State Statutes

Housing Codes and Habitability Requirements.   Some states have laws that can be applied to cases regarding deteriorating lead-based paint, such as housing code provisions requiring rental property to be maintained in good repair, or in a habitable condition. If such a statute is not obeyed by a landlord, he or she can be found automatically liable for injuries, without having to go through the steps of proving negligence. A number of factors affect whether the landlord may be held liable depending on the law in the specific state and how it has been interpreted by the courts.

- Whether a landlord had NOTICE, or knew that there was lead-based paint
- Whether the parent was being responsible in watching the child
- Whether the specific statute was intended to protect a class of persons that included the person injured
- Whether eating paint is a use of the property that is considered normal
- Whether the statute is intended to make landlords responsible to pay not only costs of repairs but also costs of injury resulting from the poor conditions

Unfair and Deceptive Acts and Practices.   There have been cases where landlords have been held responsible for damage from lead paint because it was an UNFAIR OR DECEPTIVE ACT OR PRACTICE, prohibited under state law, to rent out property in hazardous condition without informing the tenant of this important fact. Other courts have said that the landlord was not responsible, because he or she either did not know of the hazard or had no way of knowing the tenants were going to have children, without which fact the condition did not present a hazard about which a tenant should be informed.

State Lead Poisoning Laws.   When state law requires a landlord to remove any lead paint before renting to a tenant with young children, then he or she is generally STRICTLY LIABLE for damage from lead paint—that is, the landlord is automatically liable, without regard to whether he or she did know or even could have known about the lead paint or whether he or she was negligent in removing it. In some states, however, statutes that prohibit the presence of lead paint in residential units have been interpreted not as creating strict liability but as requiring a showing of negligence.

Federal Statutes

If you live in housing that is owned by or associated with the federal government, you are protected by laws requiring lead paint inspection and hazard control. *These are cited in Appendix H.*

Showing Causation

Once you prove liability, you need to prove causation, that is, that the child's ingestion of lead is the reason he or she is injured. This is where the expert witnesses come in. Generally, both a physician who is knowledgeable about lead poisoning and a neuropsychologist who is experienced with child and developmental neuropsychology will present their observations and assessments. They will educate the jury regarding lead poisoning, underlining the severity of the disease and the fact that it causes brain damage. They will describe the damage that was done to the child and explain why they believe that the lead was a SUBSTANTIAL CONTRIBUTING FACTOR, if not the sole cause, of the injury. *For a discussion of the role of the neuropsychologist in analyzing neuropsychological injury, see Chapter 8.*

Lead poisoning is hard to pin down in terms of specific symptoms that distinguish it. However, the experts will try to convince the jury that the injury to the child was indeed caused by lead poisoning, First they will evaluate and describe the damage to the child. Next, they will explain that the damage to the child is consistent with lead poisoning, that is, that it is one of the kinds of injuries that is known to be caused by lead poisoning. Finally, they will explain why they believe that the child would not have had the problems he or she is having in the normal course of events, and that it is therefore reasonable to conclude that the lead poisoning caused them.

It is best to have any clinical practitioner see the child. This way, although the expert may not be the professional who has actually treated the child, he or she will be able to testify that his or her observations of the child's behavior are consistent with the conclusions reached by other witnesses. A teacher may also be asked to testify to confirm that his or her observations of the child are consistent with the injury that you are claiming.

Statute of Limitations—When You Can Recover

State laws set limits on how long after an injury you can bring a lawsuit. These are referred to as STATUTES OF LIMITATIONS. They vary greatly from state to state both in terms of how many years after an injury you may sue and in terms of when they consider the injury to have taken place, whether at the time the child was exposed to the lead or at the time the damage can be measured.

The extent of the damages from lead cannot be assessed until the child reaches the age of 6 or 7, at which time the development of the brain has reached a certain stage. In some states, any action must be brought within a certain number of years of the date of the diagnosis. Also, in some states, individuals may bring a lawsuit until or within a certain number of years from when they reach adulthood. Certain defects may show up on initial diagnosis at age 6 or 7, but others may not become apparent until annual or semiannual follow-up examinations are performed in ensuing years.[1]

CHAPTER EIGHTEEN

Community Organizing

Some parents of lead-poisoned children, as well as individuals who are aware of the issue through professional experience or otherwise, feel strongly enough about lead poisoning as to take action beyond their own homes, into their communities, or in state or national policy addressing lead poisoning prevention.

You can reach out to others in a variety of ways. These can range from discussing the issue with friends and clients you come into contact with in the course of your work and social life, to going out into the neighborhood and knocking on doors to warn people about the hazards you have learned about, to conducting community outreach with an organized group.

You can work toward long-term solutions to lead poisoning as a public health and social justice issue by addressing it at the public policy level, pushing for stronger laws and programs addressing lead poisoning in your state or on the federal level.

ORGANIZING

You will be better able to make real changes in your community if you work together with others who have like concerns. The key is organizing. Organizing is people working together toward the goal of determining their own future and improving the quality of life, not only for the members of that organization but also for the general public.

There are dozens of organizations in the country that are fighting lead poisoning. *To learn if there is a lead poisoning organization in your state, see Appendix A.*

If there is no organization in your area specifically working on lead poisoning, you might introduce the issue to an organization that addresses environmental and/or public health policy. Or bring the issue up in any meeting dealing with related local issues, such as housing, social justice, or children's rights.

If you are not able to find a group interested in taking lead poisoning on as an issue, start your own group.

When Maurci Jackson found that her daughter was lead poisoned because of an ignorant contractor scraping and sanding lead paint from her home and her own lack of knowledge of the dangers of uncontained paint removal, she was angry.

Maurci was determined that if she could help it, others would not suffer as she had. She spoke to everyone she knew with small children. She printed up fliers, handed them out, and posted them around Chicago. She met parents who were also concerned about lead poisoning, and organized a group called Parents Against Lead (PAL). *They committed themselves to the work of getting information out to parents on how to prevent lead poisoning, as well as supporting poisoned families by helping them find resources to cope with the problem.*

When the Alliance to End Childhood Lead Poisoning held its national conference in Washington in the spring of 1994, Maurci met other parents who had also formed groups to fight lead poisoning. A number of these joined together to form a national parents support organization called UPAL, United Parents Against Lead. *Maurci served as president of this group during its first years. The organization has grown, and now has 18 affiliated groups around the country. Parents can become informed by calling the hot line or attending workshops.*

Maurci has also testified before lawmaking bodies, both state and national, and helped to get provisions enacted to require preschool screening of all children in the state and certification for abatement contractors. Lead paint abaters now have to be trained in the precautions necessary to protect children from lead dust, preventing tragic experiences like Maurci's from occurring to others.[1]

Getting Educated

The first step is to learn all you can about lead poisoning. Read up on the specific aspect of lead poisoning prevention that interests you. Study the appropriate sections of this book as well as materials listed as resources.

Learn how the issue affects people in your community:

- How much lead poisoning occurs?
- Is there a need for alternative living facilities for families while their homes are being abated?
- What populations are the most affected?
- What percentage of children are screened?

Request information from local, state, and federal agencies as well as private organizations. *For names, addresses, and phone numbers of these organizations, see Appendixes A and B.*

Get Information about Lead Paint in Your Community

Check out the age and condition of housing in different parts of town, through public records or your own observation, to pinpoint the neighborhoods of greatest concern.

Learn about lead in the water in your community. The law gives the water supplier a great deal of responsibility for protecting you from lead in your drinking water. The federal government cannot keep an eye on every water supplier to make sure they are doing what they should. You can help protect your community's water supply by getting involved in the process as a citizen activist. Some steps you can take are:

- Find out how much lead is in the water that is actually delivered in the distribution system. If it is more than 15 ppb, the legal limit, ask what is being done to improve it.
- If your water supplier needs to choose a corrosion control technology to reduce lead levels, find out what options they are considering and what the pros and cons are of each.
- Find out from your school department or state department of education whether the water from drinking fountains in your public schools has been tested and whether any lead contamination has been eliminated. Demand that any problem be taken care of.

Get to Know the Players in Agencies and Community Groups

Find out who the players in your community are, both in public agencies and in private organizations. Develop relationships with them. Introduce yourself and listen to them to find out where they are coming from. Study the personalities and roles within agencies you might want to influence so that you know the appropriate person to make your demands to. Search out local pediatricians, social workers, or other service providers who might be supportive of your goals.

Find out about the Laws in Your State and Locality Concerning Lead Poisoning from Your State Lead Program

The Conservation Law Foundation (CLF), in Boston, has established a data base to provide information to advocacy groups around the country about various state laws pertaining to lead poisoning. *For the phone number of your state lead program contact, see Appendix A. For information on CLF's lead poisoning data base, see the listing in Appendix B, under Advocacy.*

Building an Organization

Get Others Involved

Start by talking with friends. Reach people through existing networks such as where you work, your church, or any other group you may belong to. Knock on doors in your neighborhood and explain your concerns and what you are trying to do.

When people show interest, give them concrete tasks relating to organizing a meeting, such as:

- Finding a convenient, preferably public, meeting location
- Designing a flier
- Distributing the flier
- Arranging for babysitting
- Bringing refreshments

This not only lightens the work load for you as leader and gets things done, but also increases the chances of the interested individual becoming involved and committed in the effort.

Check in with those helping to organize the meeting and make sure that the tasks are being completed. Reassign a task or pitch in where you see problems.

Hold an Organizational Meeting

In your first meeting you will want to agree on a name for the organization and define your goals. Specific organizing goals are discussed later in this chapter. The meeting should be run by a FACILITATOR who is a good listener and can keep the conversation on track. Someone should keep notes of the meeting to remind those who attended as well as to fill in those who were unable to attend or who join the effort later.

Meetings should be short enough so that people can stay focused for the duration, and also so that people can fit them into their schedules without giving up their whole evening. But you might want to allow socializing time before or after the business session for those interested who have the time available.

To open the meeting, give people the opportunity to introduce themselves and say something about their concerns, interests, ideas, and what they can contribute to the effort in terms of skills, contacts, access to office equipment, etc. Before adjourning, schedule the next meeting and assign specific tasks to be accomplished by that time. It is usually most effective to assign a task to the person who contributed the idea, when possible. Specific tasks include:

- Get names of persons at the local radio station, TV station, and newspapers, who deal with public health, environmental protection, and children's issues, to use as a contact list.
- Raise public awareness and involvement. Issue press releases and call press conferences when any significant report is issued or decision is made that you can comment on.
- Inform more residents and encourage them to join the effort, through contacts at their workplace, community organization, or church, or in your neighborhood or circle of friends.
- If not enough attention is being paid to the process, write letters to public officials.
- Circulate petitions.
- Call public meetings with officials involved with the issue.

Hold Skills Workshops

You may have members who are willing to work but do not have experience in the specific skills necessary. Set up sessions where individuals who have strong research, public speaking, or door-knocking skills, either from among your own ranks or from other, sympathetic organizations, can share these skills with others. Not only the organization will benefit from the increased effectiveness of trained members; members can also benefit from this personally.

Setting a Mission and Goals

You want to set an overall mission, or purpose, for the organization, as well as specific goals that are compelling and exciting enough to get people involved, but that are accomplishable with the people and financial resources you have available. Goals should have a sense of both urgency and hope.

Specific types of goals might include:

Conducting Education and Outreach

Arming parents with information on how to minimize the risk of lead poisoning to their children, or to cope with a lead poisoning crisis, is a common goal of lead poisoning organizations.

Organizations reach parents in a variety of ways. They may print up and distribute informational brochures either to parents individually or through other organizations. Some hold workshops or set up information hot lines for parents who have questions. Specific ways to conduct outreach are discussed in a later section.

Providing Services Such as Screening or Hazard Control Training

Some groups provide specific services to help reduce the threat of lead poisoning. An organization might screen young children in the area. This serves not only to inform the individual parent as to whether his or her child is at risk but also to raise the community's consciousness regarding lead poisoning as a public health issue.

Some organizations set up training programs for property owners to learn how to control lead hazards in a safe manner. This not only increases the chances of work being done responsibly but also facilitates measures being taken in cases where funds are not available to hire a contractor.

Prodding Responsive Action from a Public Agency

Public agencies will often be more responsive on an issue if a community group is actively involved. The fact that a law or policy exists does not always mean that it is complied

Community Resources in Baltimore uses government funds and strategies managed by grass-roots organizations to turn environmental problems into economic development opportunities.

Directed by Dennis Livingston, Community Resources has designed and implemented a youth training program that prepares young people in low-income neighborhoods to do outreach, education, sampling, paint stabilization, and clearance testing. Livingston helps community-based organizations (CBOs) set these programs up and continues to consult with them once they are operating.

The program consists of a 10-week training session. After the first 4 days, students become EPA-certified as lead abatement supervisors. The remaining weeks provide in-depth training in areas including site supervision and set up, health and safety, project management, spec writing, and estimating. Six weeks of in-the-field instruction conclude the program.

Community Resource's approach to training is an integrated one, incorporating sound home maintenance and renovation techniques with a sophisticated understanding of the residential hazards created by lead paint, as well as by other environmental contaminants (including mold and mildew, insect infestation, and urea formaldehyde).

The key to the program's success is the quality of the instructors—top-notch tradespeople who are also skillful at working with young people. In the 3 years the program has been operating, over a hundred young people have been given a strong competitive edge, with a level of training far beyond the basic EPA requirements.

Community Resources also works with both municipalities and contractors to help individuals from low-income communities gain entrepreneurial, organizational, and craft skills needed to effectively do environmental remediation work. Finally, Community Resources trains property owners in a dozen states to protect themselves from liability, as well as protect their tenants, by maintaining property in a way that minimizes lead hazards and by keeping the needed documenting evidence.

By supporting community organizations in applying for grants and setting up these kinds of programs, Community Resources is helping the groups realize their own potential to effect positive change in their communities. They have found that the CBOs' awareness of their ability to solve their own environmental problems is opening up development opportunities in many other areas.[2]

with. Medicaid patients are not always screened despite a law that says they must be. School departments do not always test the water in the drinking fountains used by young children.

Public agencies might also need to be watched to make sure they are careful when doing renovation work that involves disrupting lead-painted surfaces. The renovation of public buildings, whether owned by a school district, recreation or parks department, or any other local governmental body, can be a threat to the safety of children who play in or near those facilities, if the work is not done using proper precautions.

If there is a need for alternative housing for families while their homes are being abated, you might want to push your health department to set up a SAFE HOUSE program.

Pushing for State Legislation

Many lead poisoning organizations have been working to get lead poisoning prevention laws enacted in their states. The real estate and insurance industries are not remiss at making their views known to lawmakers. In order for legislatures to enact laws that take due consideration of all sides of the issue, it is necessary that they also hear the public health perspective on the subject.

Serving on advisory boards, talking with legislators, and running letter-writing campaigns can all be effective tactics for getting legislation passed.

A number of organizations have been successful in getting programs set up in their states to train and certify lead abatement contractors. Others have gotten screening programs established.

The Alliance to End Childhood Lead Poisoning and the Conservation Law Foundation have drafted a model state lead poisoning law for advocates to use in legislative work, as has the National Conference of State Legislators. *For a copy of this model legislation, contact the Alliance to End Childhood Lead Poisoning or the Conservation Law Foundation and the National Conference of State Legislators, listed in Appendix B, under* Advocacy.

Forcing the Lead Pigment Industry to Take Responsible Action

Legislation can be advocated that would put the burden of abating lead paint on the industries who originally marketed it. Also, legislation can help lawsuits against corporations succeed, by supporting the market share theory of liability, so that industries could be held liable for injuries done by products even though it was not possible to identify the manufacturer of the specific product involved in the particular case.

Corporations that manufactured lead paint can be sued for damages for personal injury from lead poisoning, or for the costs of abating lead paint from housing.

Action can also be taken toward specific corporations by boycotts and stockholder resolutions.

Outreach

Reaching people to teach them about lead poisoning is often one of the primary goals of an organizational effort. In any event, an organization, no matter what its goals, needs to do outreach in order to be effective. Reaching people takes a lot of effort. You want to both solicit new active members to the organization and establish rapport with sympathetic people who will pass along the word about what you are doing throughout the community.

Hold House Meetings

Invite people to an informal gathering where you, or an aspiring new leader from your group, explain the issue, the organization, and the solution as you see it. Five to fifteen is recommended as a good number of people for a productive meeting. Have different interested individuals host meetings at their homes and bring new people in from their circles of friends.

Offer Educational Presentations

Offer interested organizations a short educational session on lead poisoning. Present information in a simple and organized form. Enlarged reproductions of diagrams, charts, and graphs can help people follow and understand the material. Try churches, community or civic organizations, ESL (English as a Second Language), Head Start, and other parent groups. This can serve the purpose of reaching potential new members as well as developing into a coalition with the other organization. Or offer presentations to the general public in public meeting places like the town hall or library.

Community Forums

One of the reasons there has not been more success in lead poisoning prevention efforts is that there is very little coordination among the many agencies, businesses, and individuals involved in dealing with the problem. These players all need to be educated and brought together to support one another's efforts. Some groups you might want to hold forums for are:

- Real estate agents
- Educators
- Parents and daycare providers
- Healthcare workers and public health officials
- Social workers
- City or state officials and lawmakers
- Landlord or tenant organizations
- Clergy and church groups

Approach People One on One through Knocking on Doors

Especially in areas where there is a high rate of lead poisoning, going door to door and talking to individual residents can be an effective way of reaching people. Introduce yourself and the organization. Ask what they know about lead poisoning, and if they have any concerns or questions. Then describe the goals envisioned by the organization. The persons knocking on doors should be prepared with written material on the issue and the organization as well as a clipboard. It is helpful to distribute some kind of written materials that they can keep and refer to or pass along to others. These visits can include some type of health survey, or collecting samples for testing for lead in paint or dust. Invite the people you meet to help your effort by joining the organization. Try to get a firm commitment to attend the next meeting.

Collect Membership Dues

When recruiting new members, either when going door to door or at meetings, get a commitment by collecting a small amount as membership dues. Many community-based organizations recommend charging such a fee to create a sense of ownership and commitment

Consumer Action's Lead Poisoning Project in San Francisco is assaulting lead poisoning by training trainers about the problem. Project Director Neil Gendel feels that the group's efforts can be most effective if they work with organizations and networks already providing services to families and their children. The Project is educating staff at community-based organizations (CBOs) in low and moderate-income minority neighborhoods, who, in turn, educate parents in their communities about the issue. The goal is to help these communities to educate themselves about having healthy children and decent housing.

A local toxic collector group, which teaches families about household hazardous waste, was trained to add lead poisoning awareness to their efforts. Another group reaches residents through a local church. The pastor educates his parishioners about lead poisoning during the mass and at coffee hour, with the help of an outreach person from the CBO and a nurse from a local hospital. Other organizations get the word out through established institutions, such as daycare centers, or through special events, such as a children's health fair.

The Project also works with public agencies and policy makers. It has helped get legislation passed as well as create citizen advisory committees that work to ensure that the new lead poisoning prevention measures actually get implemented. It oversees local governmental entities engaged in construction and maintenance activities in public facilities that might create lead hazards for small children (public housing, parks, recreation facilities, city-funded preschools) and sees to it that proper precautions are taken. It has convinced city agencies to provide lead poisoning information and services to families and children, urged school districts to train teachers about the issue, and educated local recreation and parks site management staff, encouraging them to pass along the information to parents.

The Project also found funding for CBOs from HUD and the CDC. The programs that the Project has initiated now have a life of their own and will benefit low and moderate-income communities for years to come.[3]

and to help in covering necessary costs of running the organization, such as paper, postage, copying, etc. A sliding scale can be used so as not to exclude those for whom it would be difficult to pay $5 or $10 a year.

Carrying out a Campaign

Define Your Issue or Goal

Pin down one specific objective you want to tackle first. You need to have both a STRATEGY (an overall game plan) and specific TACTICS (individual steps or actions you will take over the course of the campaign).

Choose Tactics that Support Your Cause

Your actions should provide you positive visibility in the media and attract new members, as well as be consistent with the overall mission and goals of the group. Write the plan down, and organize a schedule that works.

Find a Handle

Define some moral, political, economic, or legal grounds you can use to support your position. Is a public agency failing to take simple, inexpensive steps that would help people protect their families from lead poisoning? Is a lead poisoning protection law being disobeyed?

Formulate Concrete Demands

Choose goals that will make a difference but that are actually achievable with the resources you have, people power and money. Goals should be measurable. There should be short-term goals, which will give the organization positive reinforcement and credibility, as well as more ambitious long-term goals. Start small and work your way up.

Build a Coalition

There is strength in numbers. If you can join forces with other organizations with compatible goals, you might all profit. Establish relationships with organizations involved with children's issues, for example, or environmental justice, housing, or special education. Search out organizations that could bring something to your effort. Ask yourself how YOUR organization could help them, and ask for their cooperation on that basis. You can each support the other by turning out at events, signing letters pushing for legislation, and maybe even recruiting active participants.

Take Action

Define what you want to accomplish with a particular action, so that you can measure whether it has succeeded. Direct action is designed to show public support for a particular cause, and to influence a DECISION-MAKER, usually a public official, to take a particular action. Specific types of action that are generally taken by organizations working for social change include:

- Petitioning
- Picketing
- Rallying
- Letter writing
- Phone-in campaigns
- Public hearings
- Lawsuits
- Press releases
- Exposés in the media
- Paid advertising
- Demonstrations (candlelight vigils, caravans, sit-ins, parades, or marches)

- Boycotts
- Shareholder resolutions

Invite the Media

The impact of any action or event you stage is magnified manyfold by media coverage. Local press is always looking for good community stories. Supply them with a compelling issue as well as some strong visuals (signs, charts, large numbers of participants) and you will get the word out to the public.

Celebrate Victories

Work hard, but have fun too. Even the smallest victory deserves celebration. It helps to keep the group together and the energy level up.

When the City of New York began sandblasting the Williamsburg Bridge in the summer of 1992, neighborhoods on both the Brooklyn and Manhattan sides were showered with toxic lead paint fragments and dust. Yards, sidewalks, and playgrounds were contaminated, so that children could not play outside safely. Residents were irate.

A number of local organizations, along with a number of concerned public officials and private citizens, decided to take action. With the assistance of Matthew Chachere and Lucy Billings, attorneys at Bronx Legal Services, they brought a lawsuit to halt the sandblasting.

Chachere and Billings argued that the City could not undertake the lead removal work without first going through a process to ensure that it would not be a public health hazard. A New York State law requires that governmental entities carefully study and report on the potential impact of any major projects that could have significant environmental repercussions. Since sandblasting a bridge with lead paint might expose the public to toxic lead debris and dust, it should be covered by this requirement.

The court agreed. It ordered that the work be halted until the City completes an Environmental Impact Statement. Before any of the work can resume, the City must show that it is safe for the public. The ruling affects not only the Williamsburg Bridge but any of the other 838 city-owned bridges which may be scheduled for this type of maintenance work in the future.

Chachere is also fighting lead poisoning through a number of class-action lawsuits (actions brought on behalf of a number of separate individuals and groups who are all affected by the same illegal action). (He is now working out of Northern Manhattan Development Corporation, because of a 1996 Congressional prohibition against legal services bringing class-action lawsuits.) He represents the New York City Coalition to End Lead Poisoning in an action initiated in 1985 seeking to compel the City to enforce its 1983 law requiring removal of lead paint from privately owned multifamily residential buildings. In another class action, he is representing the interests of tenants in federally assisted housing in compelling landlords to maintain property free of lead paint. In a third class action, he is helping families with young children push the City and New York State to ensure that preschool, day care, and kindergarten facilities are free of lead paint.[4]

Evaluate Actions and Campaigns

Whether you are successful or not, you can learn from the experience. Look at your original plan and evaluate what happened differently and why. As well as discussing this as a group, invite written comments, and welcome them anonymously. This might result in critical feedback that could help you become stronger and more effective.

For more information on organizing, see the resources listed in Appendix B under Organizing.

Funding Sources

There are a number of possible government funding sources for organizations that have an educational or public service mission.

Federal Government

CDC Grants.   The CDC (Centers for Disease Control and Prevention) provides funding to state and local health agencies for lead poisoning prevention programs. Although over the past few years this money has mostly been used to pay for screening children's blood for elevated lead levels, it is now available for other types of lead poisoning prevention efforts. Educational and outreach programs are also funded through CDC grants.

These agencies often make the grants available to local groups with lead poisoning prevention goals. *To find out if your group could take advantage of this funding source, contact your local health department or your state lead program, listed in Appendix A.*

HUD Grants.   The U. S. Department of Housing and Urban Development also has a number of programs that provide money for lead poisoning prevention. Funds can be used to pay for public awareness programs and actual abatement of lead hazards in low-income homes, sometimes covering the testing of blood-lead levels for children living in the homes involved.

Grants are given to state and local governments. *To find out about the availability of funds in your area, contact your local health department or your state lead program, listed in Appendix A.*

EPA Grants.   There are a number of programs at the U. S. Environmental Protection Agency that provide funding for lead poisoning prevention programs. *To find out about EPA grant programs, contact your regional office of EPA, listed in Appendix A.*

Private Foundations

A number of private foundations have awarded grants to nonprofit organizations that are carrying out lead poisoning prevention programs. They generally want to see that the organization has a well-established network in the community, as well as the skills and experience to be successful in what it proposes to do. If you have a new organization, you might want to join forces with a well-established community group.[5]

CHAPTER NINETEEN

Public Policy

The toxicity of lead has been known for thousands of years. In past centuries, it was believed that lead was dangerous only when people were exposed to large amounts, such as when they handled quantities of lead in their work, or when they drank wine cooked in solid lead pots, where the liquid would pick up very high concentrations. Only the most severe cases of lead poisoning were recognized, those that resulted in comas, convulsions, and death.

By the 1920s, scientists began recognizing the alarming frequency of childhood lead poisoning and the effects of the disease on the central nervous system of children.

In the early 1930s, efforts to prohibit the use of lead in interior paint were successfully opposed by the U. S. lead pigment industry. Meanwhile, a number of other countries either banned or severely restricted this use of the toxin.

In 1935, Baltimore became the first city in the United States to address the problem with environmental investigations and lead screening programs.

During the 1950s, lead poisoning rose, due to deteriorating lead-based house paint as well as increasing emissions from automobiles burning leaded fuel. More local lead screening programs were conducted to better understand the problem. Gradually, the focus began to turn from DETECTING lead-poisoned children to PREVENTING lead poisoning by reducing the sources of environmental exposure to lead.

In 1955, most paint manufacturers voluntarily reduced the lead content of house paint to 1%. In 1963, that level was reduced to 0.5%.

Finally, in the 1970s, the federal government responded to the crisis with legislation.

In 1971, the Lead-Based Paint Poisoning Prevention Act prohibited federally owned or assisted residential properties from being painted with lead-based paints. That law also funded screening, treatment, and abatement efforts in 25 states. Such programs were again funded through the Lead Contamination Control Act of 1988.

Since 1971, the Food and Drug Administration has been strengthening limits for how much lead may leach into food from ceramics. Later efforts focused on lead hazards in cans and the foil on wine bottles.

In 1973, the federal government began phasing out leaded gasoline.

In 1977, the Consumer Product Safety Commission banned any paint with more than 0.06% lead content to be manufactured or sold for residential use.

In 1979, a study by Dr. Herbert Needleman at the University of Pittsburgh showed that blood levels of lead that were considered safe even a few years earlier could affect the development of a child's brain.[1] This work was strongly controverted at first.[2] Today, however, it is generally accepted that common everyday exposures to lead threaten the health and well-being of children.

In 1986, lead pipes and solder were banned for use in installation and repair of residential plumbing.

In 1988, the federal government ordered states to examine and remedy lead contamination from school drinking fountains.

In 1991, the Lead and Copper Rule reduced the level of lead considered to be safe for drinking water from 50 ppb to 15 ppb. Over the last few years, the EPA has required water suppliers to test for lead in households in the communities they serve and to take action to reduce the levels of lead if they were too high.

In 1992, the Residential Lead-Based Paint Hazard Reduction Act (Title X) was adopted. The law focuses federal resources on preventing lead poisoning by reducing lead-based paint hazards. Federal information services have increased. States are required to put training and certification programs into place for lead abatement contractors. Owners of property must give information about lead poisoning to purchasers and renters of housing. The federal government must make any federally owned, insured, or assisted homes lead-safe. Detailed guidelines set out a strategy of risk assessment and hazard control in homes with lead paint.

In spite of all of these efforts to prevent lead poisoning, many potentially dangerous uses of lead continue to be allowed without adequate safeguards. Lead from gasoline and residential paint remains a threat in our environment, although they are no longer being used. Our housing is a long, long way from being safe from the millions of tons of lead-based paint that remains on our walls. The task of protecting ourselves and our children from lead poisoning is far from finished.[3]

CURRENT POLICY DEBATES

How Much Lead Is Safe?

On the one hand, blood lead levels have been declining over the past couple of decades. On the other hand, our awareness is growing about the damage that can be done to the brain by what were formerly considered safe levels of lead. As a result, some experts see lead poisoning as a problem that we pretty much have controlled, and others see it as one that we have not done anywhere near enough about.

More sophisticated scientific research has been able to show dangers from lead exposure at lower and lower levels. Whereas in the 1970s it was not considered dangerous to have a blood lead level of 40 μg/dl, it is now known that as little as 10 μg/dl can be harmful. Today the U. S. government has set 10 μg/dl as the LEVEL OF CONCERN.

But how can we be sure that even that level is safe? Not everyone agrees. One expert points out that the levels of lead in most people today are at least tens, if not hundreds, of times higher than BACKGROUND levels, or levels before people were ever exposed to lead from mining and industry. It would be a very unlikely coincidence if the threshold for toxicity just happened to be at the levels that are common today. In fact scientific studies have shown adverse effects of lead at levels lower than 10 μg/dl. It is likely that any amount of lead has the potential to do damage, and that we should make every effort to keep our exposure to lead as low as possible.[4]

Some experts explain that the levels we consider acceptable at a given point in time are largely based on EPIDEMIOLOGICAL considerations. That is, we look at what the average level is, and, knowing that lead is toxic, we choose a level that seems enough out of the ordinary as one to be attentive to. In the mid-1990s the average blood lead level was 2.4 μg/dl. The level of 10 μg/dl is enough above average that it should alert parents to take precautions, check out sources, and retest to protect the child.[5] This does not mean that a child with this level of lead will suffer any specific injury, nor that a child whose level is beneath this will necessarily be totally safe from injury.

Other advocates defend the level of 10 μg/dl as a health-based measure. The level was not set arbitrarily, or simply in response to the levels in the population, but rather in response to scientific evidence that children may be harmed by as little as 10 μg/dl of lead in their blood.

Lead-Safe versus Lead-Free

Some advocates insist that every child has the right to live in a home that is LEAD-FREE. As long as there is lead-based paint on the walls of homes, there is a potential danger to public health. Even if the paint is intact today, it will eventually deteriorate or be disrupted in such a way as to become accessible, and harmful, to children. Lead is a toxin and should not be found in housing, period.

Others believe that what is realistically achievable is that our homes be LEAD-SAFE. Only when the paint is disrupted or deteriorated does it pose a danger to a child. The vast majority of the children living in the 83% of homes built before 1978 containing lead paint are not in fact lead poisoned. Controlling only those areas of paint that actually present such a hazard is all that is necessary. While this usually will involve securely covering or removing lead paint (or painted components) in some cases a home can be made lead safe with careful house cleaning and other low- or no-cost approaches.

The current federal policy is to permit lead hazards to be controlled by means other than removing or permanently covering lead paint (abatement) for federally financed, insured, or assisted housing. Each state can set its own policy on this matter. The issue has been, and probably will continue to be, very hotly debated.

Lead-free advocates argue that even though interim controls cost less, you are not saving anything in the long run if they have to be repeated periodically to be protective. They feel that it makes better economic sense to remove the hazard once and for all. In order to work, interim controls are dependent on monitoring, which may or may not be carried out in any given case. In addition, many approaches are ineffective if structural problems are not first addressed, most notably water leaks and other sources of moisture. And even at their best, there is not enough validated experience with interim controls to know how effective they are.

Lead-safe advocates suggest that given the fact that funds are limited, it makes more sense to take steps to give the greatest number of people the greatest degree of protection. They see removing all the lead in a timely fashion from the approximately two-thirds of U. S. homes containing lead-based paint as impossible because of the expense involved. The amount it would cost to completely remove the lead from one house might pay for measures to make a number of homes lead-safe.

If abatement were required but not financed by the government, many families simply could not afford to keep their homes. Landlords also may have to abandon rental property because they cannot afford full-scale abatement of property that is bringing in only low to moderate rental income.

Blanket requirements for removing lead from housing may also fail on occasion to address the source of a specific lead poisoning. Although the vast majority of severe lead poisoning cases are caused by lead paint, there are also many cases caused by other sources.

In addition, removing paint without taking the necessary precautions and cleaning up well can make the situation much worse. Unfortunately, many property owners have trouble finding a competent, responsible contractor, and work is often done in an unsafe manner.

Universal versus Targeted Screening

The federal government is changing its recommendation from UNIVERSAL screening, where every child would be screened for lead poisoning, to one which would allow local authorities either a UNIVERSAL or TARGETED approach, where children would only be tested if they lived in a high-risk area or were assessed to be at risk according to specific criteria. The recommendation which the CDC issues will be directed towards state and local health officials, and is a guideline, not a strict requirement. Each state, county, or municipality will be free to formulate its own policy in response to the local situation and level of risk.

Advocates of universal lead screening feel that it is important to identify every lead-poisoned child, not just most of them. Even in areas that have predominantly new housing, there can be homes with lead paint. In addition, children MIGHT be lead poisoned from sources other than paint no matter where they live. The cost of each test is only a few dollars and the damage that could be done by lead is substantial.

Screening every child will give us more information about lead poisoning. And the better we understand it, the better we can prevent it, on the public health level.

Proponents of targeted screening explain that there are limited resources that can be dedicated to lead screening. If screening is done in all areas with high incidence or high risk of lead poisoning, and additionally for all children who are at risk because of their personal situation, then we will catch more lead poisoning cases for less money.

Although the federal government has been recommending since 1991 that every child be screened, we are a long way from universal screening. In fact, fewer than half of all American children from 1 to 6 years old are screened. Even in states where healthcare providers are legally required to screen children they often do not. Targeted-screening advocates suggest that some healthcare providers may be less resistant to this less rigid guideline, and may end up actually screening more children who are in fact at increased risk, and identifying a higher percentage of poisoned children.

Training and Licensing of Contractors, Risk Assessors, and Inspectors

Any work that involves disrupting a surface with lead-based paint can create lead hazards. Specialized training is needed for a contractor to do this work safely and effectively. Likewise, to ensure accurate assessment and measurement of lead hazards, those who evaluate those hazards must be knowledgeable and competent. There is now a great shortage of well-trained lead abatement and evaluation contractors. Federal law requires states to set up programs to train and certify contractors for lead hazard control and evaluation work. If a state does not set up such a program by 1998, then the federal government will.

Some advocates recommend extending high-quality training programs to other contractors whose work may involve disrupting lead paint, such as those who do remodeling or some types of maintenance work. Some states are more responsive to the need for training and certification than others. Lead poisoning prevention advocates have been able to facilitate the establishment of training and certification programs in a number of states.

Liability of Property Owners

Property owners can be held legally responsible for the damage done to a child by being exposed to lead in rented housing in certain circumstances. The conditions under which this liability is found by a court are inconsistent and unpredictable.

Because of this unpredictability, property owners find it harder and harder to get liability insurance. In some cases, this results in abandoning property. In others, landlords say they are reluctant to control lead hazards because it is not clear what is adequate and what is not under the law.

A federal task force has recommended that states address this problem by adopting provisions protecting property owners from liability for injury from lead poisoning if they have met specific standards for controlling lead hazards.

Critics warn that this may encourage inadequate lead hazard control unless the standards that must be met are truly protective of children's safety.

Public Funding Levels for Lead Poisoning Prevention Programs

It is clear that the price of lead poisoning is very high. Not only is a lot of human suffering caused by lead poisoning, but hard economic costs are also associated with the disease. The lowered IQs of millions of individuals result in lower productivity and earnings. The learning disabilities that are caused by damage to the brain result in increased expenses for special needs educational programs, which are publicly funded.

The Strategic Plan

A 1991 federal report calculated that the benefits to society—just the ECONOMIC benefits—of abating all housing built before 1950 would by far outweigh the costs. The CDC's *Strategic Plan for the Elimination of Childhood Lead Poisoning* urged increased public funding for lead abatement and more aggressive screening of lead-poisoned children as well as research in many areas related to controlling lead sources and screening.[6]

Some advocates question why the necessary funds to fulfill the goals set out in 1991 have not been forthcoming and blame this failure on lobbying by the real estate and insurance industries.

Short-Term Measures to Help

Until all housing is lead-free, advocates urge public agencies to provide much needed services to enable parents to better protect their children from lead poisoning, such as:

- More screening services free of charge
- SAFE HOUSES for families to stay in while their homes are being made lead-safe
- More funding for evaluating and controlling lead hazards
- Creation and enforcement of lead safety requirements for rental property

The Responsibility of Industry

There is a great deal of evidence that the lead pigment manufacturers were well aware of the danger that lead posed to young children as early as the 1920s.[7] Yet they continued manufacturing lead pigment and marketing it for use in residential paint with no warnings. This industry benefitted financially while many children were poisoned, are being poisoned, and will continue to be poisoned from lead-based paint.

Many advocates feel that the lead pigment industry should be held responsible for remedying the situation as much as possible, by paying medical costs and other expenses for families with lead-poisoned children and/or covering the cost of safely removing lead-based paint from homes.

Market Share Liability

A major obstacle to winning a legal action against one of these manufacturers is the impossibility of showing which company actually manufactured the lead-based paint, or the pigment in that paint, in a particular home that was painted 40 years ago or more.

Applying a MARKET SHARE LIABILITY theory would solve this dilemma. Advocates argue that since you cannot distinguish which of several manufacturers is liable, the burden should be shared by all of them according to the share of the market they had at the time the paint was sold. This argument has been rejected in some states, but is being presented in other states.

State legislatures are also being asked to enact laws that specifically would allow courts to accept this theory of liability.

Lead Trust Fund

A bill that has been considered by the U. S. Congress would create a source of money to help pay for removing the lead from low-income families' homes. The law has been called the Lead-Based Paint Abatement Trust Fund Act or the Lead Abatement Trust Fund Act. The theory behind the trust fund is that the fairest way to pay for cleaning up lead hazards is to put the burden on the industry that profited from lead in the first place, lead producers and importers.

Each year, for 10 years, $1 billion would be raised by imposing a fee of 45 cents for every pound of lead removed from any U. S. lead smelter or imported into the country, alone or in a lead product.

This money would be distributed by the U. S. Department of Housing and Urban Development to state and local governments. Locations with higher rates of poverty and of lead-paint hazards would receive larger shares. In order to receive grants, local and state governments would have to provide MATCHING FUNDS, or funds of their own, for running the lead abatement work. States could pass along the funds to agencies of local governments that have lead paint abatement laws.

Abatement work would always be done by certified abaters, and only 20% of the work paid for could be emergency measures. Priority would be given to removing lead hazards from owner-occupied and rental housing where pregnant women and young children live. Day-care centers would also be eligible for financial help.

Although many organizations and individuals have urged their senators and representatives in Congress to support the law, lead producers and importers have been pushing those same legislators to vote against it. They are afraid that if they had to pay a fee for every pound of lead they produced, the price of lead and products containing lead, most significantly car batteries, would go up, and they would end up losing business because people would not buy as much. Business might be lost to companies outside the United States with cheaper labor and lower environmental standards, and to CHOP-SHOP battery rebuilders who would neither pay the tax nor be controlled by environmental regulations.

It is true that prices would increase. The price of a car battery, for example, would increase by about $8.00. Proponents of this plan explain, however, that other factors would more than compensate. A congressional committee has studied the question and concluded that the demand for most lead products would not be affected. In addition, since there would be more money available for lead abatement, there would be 25,000 additional jobs created for abatement workers. So the law would help, not hurt, the economy.[8]

Although the present climate in the U. S. Congress is not conducive to this type of environmentally progressive legislation, if and when the situation changes, such a bill may be reintroduced.

OUR ROLE IN PUBLIC POLICY

Just as it is natural to avoid or refuse to recognize a stressful situation on a personal level (as discussed in Chapter 9), so it is normal to want to close our eyes to serious social crises and flaws in our political system. Some problems seem overwhelming, and each of us feels powerless to effect any real change.

In theory, the basis of the democratic system is that each individual has an equal voice. In reality, more powerful industries and special interest groups are better represented in policy-making than is the general interest of the public. Their economic benefit in a particular policy may be more clear and immediate than the harm to the public, which may be more generalized, longer term, and therefore little protested. Industries whose profit margins depend on the existence of a particular policy benefit economically by committing a chunk of that profit margin toward perpetuating that policy.

The general public may feel powerless against these well-funded business interests. But when people get together and voice their needs clearly and forcefully, things can change (as discussed in Chapter 18).

We are not powerless if we take action.

Endnotes

CHAPTER 1

[1] Debra J. Brody *et al.*, "Blood Lead Levels in the U. S. Population," *JAMA—The Journal of the American Medical Association* 272 (1994): 277–283.

[2] J. Julian Chisolm, Jr., "What Lead Does to Kids," *NEA Today* Nov. 1993: 13; Peter A. Baghurst *et al.*, "Environmental Exposure to Lead and Children's Intelligence at the Age of Seven Years; The Port Pirie Cohort Study," *The New England Journal of Medicine* 327 (1992): 1279.

[3] Centers for Disease Control (CDC), U. S. Department of Health and Human Services, *Strategic Plan for the Elimination of Childhood Lead Poisoning* (1991): 1.

[4] Brody *et al.*, 281.

[5] Mary H. Cooper, "Lead Poisoning," *CQ Researcher* 2 (1992): 538, citing Environmental Defense Fund.

[6] *Facts on File* (1992): 978C2; Susan Cummings and Lynn Goldman, "Even Advantaged Children Show Cognitive Defects from Low-Level Lead Toxicity," *Pediatrics* 90 (1992): 995–997.

[7] 25% of poor white children and 55% of poor African-American children had elevated blood lead levels in the mid-1980s. Agency for Toxic Substances and Disease Registry (ATSDR), U.S. Depart-

ment of Health and Human Services, *The Nature and Extent of Lead Poisoning in Children in the United States: A Report to Congress* (1988): 4. From 1988–1991 over 28% of poor African Americans from 1–5 years old had elevated blood lead levels, compared to about 10% of poor whites and about 4.5% of middle- and upper-income whites. Brody *et al.*, 282.

[8]See, e.g., Steven Waldman, "Lead and Your Kids," *Newsweek* 15 July 1991: 42–48.

[9]Rebecca Rex, personal interview, April 1996.

[10]National Research Council (NRC), *Measuring Lead Exposure in Infants, Children, and Other Sensitive Populations* (Washington: National Academy Press, 1993): 146.

[11]NRC, 63.

[12]David Bellinger and Kim Dietrich, "Low-Level Lead Exposure and Cognitive Function in Children," *Pediatric Annals* 23 (1994): 601; Baghurst *et al.*, 1279; David Bellinger, "Neurodevelopmental Effects of Low-Level Lead Exposure in Children," Reference Materials Vol. II, Association of Trial Lawyers of America (ATLA) 1996 Annual Convention, Boston: 1277; NRC 40–72.

[13]NRC, 32.

[14]Sandra Shaheen, Ph.D., memo to the author, July 1996.

[15]Herbert L. Needleman *et al.*, "The Long-Term Effects of Exposure to Low Doses of Lead in Childhood: An 11-Year Follow Up Report," *The New England Journal of Medicine* 322 (1990): 83–88; Herbert L. Needleman, "Childhood Exposure to Lead: A Common Cause of School Failure," *Phi Delta Kappan* September 1992: 36.

[16]Joel Schwartz and David Otto, "Lead and Minor Hearing Impairment," *Archives of Environmental Health* 46 (1991): 300–305; Chisolm, 13.

[17]Chisolm, 13; NRC, 63.

[18]Herbert L. Needleman *et al.*, "Bone Lead Levels and Delinquent Behavior," *JAMA—The Journal of the American Medical Association* 275 (1996): 363–369; William G. Sciarillo *et al.*, "Lead Exposure and Child Behavior," *American Journal of Public Health* 82 (1992): 1356–1360.

[19]Shaheen, memo.

[20]Centers for Disease Control (CDC), U. S. Department of Health and Human Services, *Preventing Lead Poisoning in Young Children* (1991): 9; NRC, 82.

[21]NRC, 71.

[22]Joel Schwartz, C. Angle, and H. Pitcher, "Relationship Between Childhood Blood Lead Levels and Stature," *Pediatrics* 77 (1986): 281–288. "Why Lead May Leave Kids Short," *Science News* 29 Aug. 1992: 143; "Lead's Reduced Stature," *Science News* 21 Sept. 1991: 189.

[23]CDC *Preventing Lead Poisoning* 9; NRC, 33.

[24]NRC, 32; CDC *Preventing Lead Poisoning* 9.

[25]NRC, 32.

[26]NRC, 147.

[27]D. Barltrop, "Transfer of Lead to the Human Foetus," *Mineral Metabolism in Pediatrics*, D. Barltrop and W. L. Burland, eds. (Oxford–Edinburgh: Blackwell Scientific, 1974): 135–151.

[28]ASTDR, 6.

[29]Mary Jean Brown, David Bellinger, and Julia Matthews, "In Utero Lead Exposure," *Maternal Child Nursing* 15 (1990): 94–96; NRC, 35–39.

[30]Howard Hu, "Knowledge of Diagnosis and Reproductive History Among Survivors of Childhood Plumbism," *American Journal of Public Health* 81 (1991): 1070–1072.

[31]Ellen Silbergeld, "Lead in Bone, Implications for Toxicology during Pregnancy and Lactation," *Environmental Health Perspectives* 91 (1991): 63–70.

[32]"Milk May Impair Fertility in Women ... as Lead Can in Men," *Science News* 146, 12 March 1994: 175, citing *Toxicology and Applied Pharmacology*, Feb. 1994.

[33]Howard Hu *et al.*, "The Relationship of Bone and Blood Lead to Hypertension," *JAMA—The Journal of the American Medical Association* 275 (1996): 1171–1176.

[34]Rohko Kim *et al.*, "A Longitudinal Study of Low-Level Lead Exposure and Impairment of Renal Function" *JAMA—The Journal of the American Medical Association* 275 (1996): 1177–1181; CDC, *Preventing Lead Poisoning* 9.

[35]NRC, 35.

CHAPTER 2

[1] National Research Council (NRC), *Measuring Lead Exposure in Infants, Children, and Other Sensitive Populations* (Washington: National Academy Press, 1993): 18.

[2] Bureau of Mines, U. S. Department of the Interior, *Mineral Commodity Summaries* (1975): 88; Bureau of Mines, U. S. Department of the Interior, *Mineral Commodity Summaries* (1990): 96; William Woodbury, *LEAD—1991* (U. S. Department of the Interior Bureau of Mines, 1993): 19.

[3] U. S. Environmental Protection Agency, *Report of the National Survey of Lead-Based Paint in Housing* (1995): 2–3.

[4] U. S. Consumer Product Safety Commission, "CPSC Finds Lead Poisoning Hazard for Young Children in Public Playground Equipment," *News from CPSC* 1 Oct. 1996.

[5] Richard Lansdown and William Yule, *Lead Toxicity: History and Environmental Impact* (Baltimore: Johns Hopkins University Press, 1983): 136.

[6] U. S. Environmental Protection Agency, *National Air Pollution Emission Estimates* 1940–1990 (1991): 61.

[7] Karen L. Florini and Ellen K. Silbergeld, "Getting the Lead Out," *Issues in Science and Technology* 9, Summer 1993: 39.

[8] *Federal Register* 59 (9 June 1994): 29753.

[9] *Federal Register* 60 (23 June 1995): 32587; *Hazardous Materials Intelligence Report* 15, 17 June 1994: 4.

[10] NRC, 119.

[11] Centers for Disease Control (CDC), U. S. Department of Health and Human Services, *Preventing Lead Poisoning in Young Children.* (1991): 22.

[12] U. S. Consumer Product Safety Commission, "CPSC Announces Recalls of Imported Crayons Because of Lead Poisoning Hazards," *News from CPSC*, 5 April 1994; *Boston Globe*, 6 April 1994: 3.

[13] Lansdown and Yule, 175–176.

[14] *Federal Register* 59 (9 March 1994): 11122.

[15] "Safety Alert! … New Source of Lead Poisoning Identified!" *The Refinishers News* (June 1995).

[16] U. S. Consumer Product Safety Commission, "CPSC Finds Lead Poisoning Hazard for Young Children in Imported Vinyl Miniblinds," *News from CPSC*, 25 June 1996.

[17] Sharon O'Brien Carter, R.N., Statewide Coordinator for Case Management Services, Massachusetts State Childhood Lead Poisoning Prevention Program, personal interview, 17 July 1996.

[18] "Lead Intoxication Associated with Chewing Plastic Wire Coating—Ohio," *Morbidity and Mortality Weekly Report* 42, 25 June 1993: 465–467; "Elevated Blood Lead Levels Associated with Illicitly Distilled Alcohol—Alabama 1990–1991," *Morbidity and Mortality Weekly Report* 14, 1 May 1992: 294.

CHAPTER 3

[1] Joseph Ponessa, Ph.D., Rutgers Cooperative Extension, personal interview, June 1996; Laboratory Study of Lead Cleaning Efficacy, U. S. Environmental Protection Agency, Office of Pollution Prevention and Toxics, Chemical Management Division, Technical Programs Branch, 1997.

[2] *The Merck Index: An Encyclopedia of Chemicals and Drugs* (Rahway, NJ: Merck & Co., Inc., 1976), 119; Christopher R. Milar and Paul Mushak, "Lead Contaminated Housedust: Hazard, Measurement and Decontamination," in *Lead Absorption in Children*, by J. Julian Chisolm, Jr. (Urban & Schwarzenberg, 1982): 147.

[3] Maurci Jackson, CLEO (Children's Lead Education Outreach) Coloring Book.

CHAPTER 4

[1] Committee on Environmental Health, American Academy of Pediatrics (AAP), "Lead Poisoning: From Screening to Primary Prevention," *Pediatrics* 92 (1993): 181.

[2]David Bellinger, "Neurodevelopmental Effects of Low-Level Exposure in Children," Reference Materials Vol. II, Association of Trial Lawyers of America (ATLA) 1996 Annual Convention, Boston: 1284–1285

[3]Sandra Shaheen, "Neuromaturation in Behavior Development: The Case of Childhood Lead Poisoning," *Developmental Psychology* 20 (1984): 542–550.

[4]John W. Graef, M.D., Children's Hospital, Boston, personal interviews, August 1996.

[5]Ibid.

[6]Kim Fuelling, Executive Director of the Association of Parents to Prevent Lead Exposure, personal interview, April 1996.

[7]Melissa J. Ritchie, Assistant Director APPLE (Association of Parents to Prevent Lead Exposure) (Ohio), personal interview, April 1996.

[8]Mary Jean Brown, R.N., Massachusetts Department of Public Health, personal interview, 31 July, 1996.

[9]David Guthrie, Centers for Disease Control and Prevention, U. S. Department of Health and Human Services, personal interview, May 1996.

[10]Brown interview.

[11]Graef interview.

[12]Brown interview.

[13]Centers for Disease Control (CDC), U. S. Department of Health and Human Services, *Preventing Lead Poisoning in Young Children* (1991): 55.

[14]National Research Council (NRC), *Measuring Lead Exposure in Infants, Children, and Other Sensitive Populations* (Washington: National Academy Press, 1993): 203.

[15]NRC, 6, 227; CDC *Preventing Lead Poisoning* 54.

[16]National Lead Information Center, "CDC Lead Screening Guidance Revised," *Lead Inform* 1 (Summer 1996).

[17]CDC *Preventing Lead Poisoning* 44–45.

[18]Environmental Protection Agency, *Seasonal Rhythms of Blood-Lead Levels: Boston, 1979–1983* (1995).

[19]Centers for Disease Control (CDC), U. S. Department of Health and Human Services, "State activities for prevention of lead poisoning among children—United States, 1992," *JAMA—The Journal of the American Medical Association* 269 (1993): 1614.

[20]In New York, for example, only 54% of 1- and 2-year olds were screened in 1995 although pediatricians are required by law to screen all children at these ages. *New York Times* 20 Sept. 1996.

[21]Alliance To End Childhood Lead Poisoning, *A Guide To Medicaid for Childhood Lead Poisoning Prevention Programs and Other Public Health Providers* (1993): 8.

[22]AAP, 179–180.

CHAPTER 5

[1]Chapter based on U. S. Department of Housing and Urban Development (HUD), *Guidelines for the Evaluation and Control of Lead-Based Paint Hazards in Housing* (1995).

[2]Marianna Koval, Lead Safe Homes, Inc., personal interview, 30 Aug. 1996.

CHAPTER 6

[1]Agency for Toxic Substance and Disease Registry (ATSDR), U. S. Department of Health and Human Services, *Toxicological Profile for Lead* (1993): 129; John W. Graef, M.D., Children's Hospital, Boston, personal interviews, August 1996.

[2]ATSDR, 114; Eva May Nunnelly Hamilton, Eleanor Noss Whitney, and Frances Seinkeiwicz Sizer, *Nutrition: Concepts and Controversies* (St. Paul: West Publishing Co., 1985): 337–338.

[3]Graef interview; D. Pincus and C.V. Saccar, "Lead Poisoning," *American Family Physician* 19 (1979): 120–124.

[4]ATSDR, 97–99; National Research Council (NRC), *Measuring Lead Exposure in Infants, Children, and Other Sensitive Populations* (Washington: National Academy Press, 1993): 127, 146.

[5]U. S. Department of Agriculture, Human Nutrition Information Service, "The Food Guide Pyramid" (1992).

[6]D. Baltrop and H. E. Khoo, "The Influence of Dietary Minerals and Fat on the Absorption of Lead," *Science Total Environment* 6 (1976): 265–274; Kathryn R. Mahaffrey, Ph.D., "Nutritional Factors in Lead Poisoning," *Nutrition Reviews* 39 (1981): 353–362.

[7]Maurci Jackson, CLEO (Children's Lead Education Outreach) Coloring Book.

[8]Hamilton *et al.*, Appendix H: Table of Food Composition and Appendix I: The RDA Tables.

[9]James D. Sargent, "The Role of Nutrition in the Prevention of Lead Poisoning in Children," *Pediatric Annals* 23 (1994): 640.

[10]Graef interview; Robert A. Goyer, "Nutrition and Metal Toxicity," *American Journal of Clinical Nutrition* 61 (suppl.) (1995): 648S.

[11]Hamilton *et al.*, Appendix H, Appendix I; Carper, 412–413.

[12]Mary Jean Brown, R.N., Massachusetts Department of Public Health, personal interview, 31 July 1996.

[13]Ibid.

[14]Ibid.

[15]Hamilton *et al.*, 337–338; Jean Carper, *Jean Carper's Total Nutrition Guide* (New York: Bantam Books, 1987): 412–413.

[16]Goyer, 648S; Graef interview.

[17]Hamilton *et al.*, Appendix H, Appendix I.

CHAPTER 7

[1]Jonathan Bader, Wisconsin Nutrition Project, Inc., personal interview, April 1996.

[2]Centers for Disease Control (CDC), U. S. Department of Health and Human Services, *Preventing Lead Poisoning in Young Children* (1991): 53–54.

[3]John W. Graef, M.D., Children's Hospital, Boston, personal interviews, August 1996.

[4]Ibid.; CDC, 55.

[5]Graef interview.

[6]Melissa Ritchie, personal interview, April 1996.

[7]CDC, 55–59, Graef interview.

[8]CDC, 55–59.

[9]Graef interview.

[10]Ibid.

[11]Ibid.

[12]Ibid.

[13]Holly A. Ruff *et al.*, "Declining Blood Lead Levels and Cognitive Changes in Moderately Lead-Poisoned Children," *JAMA—The Journal of the American Medical Association* 269 (1993): 1641–1646.

[14]Graef interview.

[15]David Bellinger, Ph.D., Children's Hospital, Boston, memo to author, 8 Aug. 1996.

[16]Deborah E. Glotzer, "Management of Childhood Lead Poisoning: Strategies for Chelaton," *Pediatric Annals* 23 (1994): 608.

CHAPTER 8

[1]World Health Organization, *Environmental Health Criteria* 165: *Inorganic Lead* (1995).

[2]Section written in collaboration with Sandra Shaheen, Ph.D., Longwood Neuropsychology, Boston.

[3]Section based on interviews with Karen Tewhey, Special Education/Mental Health Coordinator, ABCD Head Start, August 1996.

[4]20 *U. S. Code*, sec. 1400 *et seq.*; Public Law 94-142.

[5]Robert Reid and Antonis Katsiyannis, "Attention-Deficit/Hyperactivity Disorder and Section 504," *Remedial and Special Education* 16 (1995): 45.

[6]29 *U. S. Code*, sec. 794, Public Law 93-112, § 504.

[7]The section on public school services was based in part on an interview with Audrey Seyffert, Administrator of Pupil Services, Natick (MA) Public Schools, 8 July 1996.

CHAPTER 9

[1]Richard S. Lazarus and Susan Folkman, *Stress, Appraisal and Coping* (New York: Springer, 1984).

[2]Margaret Sauser, founder of UPAL (United Parents Against Lead) of MI, personal interview, April 1996.

[3]Rita B. May, R.N., Mothers of Lead Exposed Children (MOLEC), Missouri, personal interview, April 1996.

[4]Parents of lead-poisoned child, New York City, personal interviews, Sept. 1996.

[5]Kathy Maloof, LISCW, Massachusetts Department of Public Health, personal interview, 28 Aug. 1996; Beth Holleran, LICSW, Children's Hospital, Boston, personal interview, 21 Aug. 1996.

CHAPTER 10

[1]Mary H. Cooper, "Lead Poisoning," *CQ Researcher* 2 (1992): 528. Data from the Centers for Disease Control; National Research Council (NRC), *Measuring Lead Exposure in Infants, Children, and Other Sensitive Populations.* (Washington: National Academy Press, 1983): 140.

[2]Cooper, 536.

[3]U. S. Environmental Protection Agency, *Report on the National Survey of Lead-Based Paint in Housing: Base Report* (1995).

[4]Sharon C. Park and Douglas C. Hicks, "Appropriate Methods for Reducing Lead-Paint Hazards in Historic Housing," *Preservation Briefs* 37 (1995): 2.

[5]Adapted from U. S. Department of Housing and Urban Development (HUD), *Guidelines for the Evaluation and Control of Lead-Based Paint Hazards in Housing* (1995), citing P. E. Marino *et al.*, "A Case Report of Lead Paint Poisoning During Renovation of a Victorian Farmhouse," *American Journal of Public Health* 80 (1990): 1183–1185.

[6]HUD *Guidelines* 4-4.

CHAPTER 11

[1]U. S. Department of Housing and Urban Development (HUD), *Guidelines for the Evaluation and Control of Lead-Based Paint Hazards in Housing* (1995): 3–7.

[2]Mary H. Cooper, *Lead Poisoning,"* CQ Researcher* 2 (1992): 53S.

[3]U. S. Department of Housing and Urban Development (HUD), *Comprehensive and Workable Plan for the Abatement of Lead-Based Paint in Privately Owned Housing: Report to Congress* (1990): xvii.

[4]HUD *Guidelines* 3–7.

[5]HUD *Comprehensive and Workable Plan* xvii–xviii.

[6]Environmental Protection Agency (EPA), *Residential Sampling for Lead: Protocols for Dust and Soil Sampling, Final Report* (1995): 15–24; HUD *Guidelines* App. 13.1-6–13.1-7.

[7]HUD *Guidelines* App. 13.1-1.

[8]Marco Kaltofen, P.E., Boston Chemical Data, personal interview, Sept. 1996.

[9]U. S. Environmental Protection Agency (EPA), "Sampling House Dust for Lead: Basic Concepts and Literature Review," (1995): 6-2.

[10]Kaltofen interview.

[11]U. S. Environmental Protection Agency (EPA), "A Field Test of Lead-Based Paint Testing Technologies: Summary Report" (1995).

[12]Kaltofen interview.

[13]Ibid.

[14]Ibid.

[15]Ibid.

[16]Section based on HUD *Guidelines*.

[17]Section written in collaboration with Marianna Koval, Lead Safe Homes, Inc., Brooklyn, New York.

CHAPTER 12

[1]See generally Sherry Harowitz, "High Cost of Getting Lead Out of the House," *Kiplinger's Personal Finance Magazine*, Aug. 1991: 72; Elizabeth Razzi, "New Leads on Lead," *Kiplinger's Personal Finance Magazine*, Jan. 1988: 92; International Brotherhood of Painters and Allied Trades, *Getting the Lead Out* (undated): 8; U. S. Department of Housing and Urban Development (HUD), *Guidelines for the Evaluation and Control of Lead-Based Paint Hazards in Housing* (1995), 3–9.

[2]Dennis Livingston, Director, Community Resources, Inc., personal interview, 15 Aug. 1996.

[3]Residential Lead-Based Paint Hazard Reduction Act of 1992, 42 *U. S. Code* § 4851 *et. seq.*

[4]42 *U. S. Code* § 1014.

[5]U. S. Department of the Treasury, Internal Revenue Service, "Medical and Dental Expenses," IRS Publication 502; Rev. Rul. 79-66, 1979-1 CB 114.

[6]Dennis Livingston, *Maintaining a Lead-Safe Home*, Community Resources (1997): 36.

[7]Owner-occupant of rental property in Everett, MA, personal interview, Sept. 1996.

[8]Chapter based primarily on the HUD *Guidelines*, Chapters 3, 8 and 9.

CHAPTER 13

[1]Sharon C. Park and Douglas C. Hicks, "Appropriate Methods for Reducing Lead-Paint Hazards in Historic Housing," *Preservation Briefs* 37 (1995); Massachusetts Historic Commission, *Historic Buildings and the Lead Paint Hazard* (undated).

[2]Chapter based on U. S. Department of Housing and Urban Development (HUD), *Guidelines for the Evaluation and Control of Lead-Based Paint Hazards in Housing* (1995): 11–15.

CHAPTER 14

[1]"Blood Lead Levels in Children and Pregnant Women Living Near a Lead-Reclamation Plant," *JAMA—The Journal of the American Medical Association* 266 (1991): 647; *Federal Register* 53 (30 June 1988): 24787.

[2]Centers for Disease Control (CDC), U. S. Department of Health and Human Services, *Preventing Lead Poisoning in Young Children* (1991): 19; National Research Council (NRC), *Measuring Lead Exposure in Infants, Children, and Other Sensitive Populations* (Washington: National Academy Press, 1993): 122.

[3]U. S. Department of Housing and Urban Development (HUD), *Guidelines for the Evaluation and Control of Lead-Based Paint Hazards in Housing* (1995): 12-49; *Federal Register* 60 (11 Sept. 1995): 47251–47252.

[4]Childhood Lead Poisoning Act, Minn. Stat. Ann. § 144.9501 *et seq.* (1996).

[5]U. S. Environmental Protection Agency (EPA), "Residential Sampling for Lead: Protocols for Dust and Soil Sampling: Final Report," (1995): 6–14; HUD *Guidelines* App. 13.3.

[6]Michael Weitzman *et al.*, "Lead-Contaminated Soil Abatement and Urban Children's Blood Lead Levels," *JAMA—The Journal of the American Medical Association* 269 (1993): 1647–1654

[7]U. S. Environmental Protection Agency, Criteria and Assessment Office, *Urban Soil-Lead Abatement Demonstration Protection: Integrated Report* (1993).

[8]U. S. Environmental Protection Agency (EPA), *Is Your Yard Lead Proof?* (undated); EPA, *Controlling Lead in Soil: Soil Abatement Specifications* (EPA New England, undated); California Department of Health Services, Childhood Lead Poisoning Prevention Program, "Lead In Soil" (undated); HUD *Guidelines*: 12-49–12-54

[9]U. S. Department of Agriculture Extension Service, Soil and Plant Tissue Testing Laboratory, "Good Gardening Practices to Reduce the Lead Risk" (revised Nov. 1990); *Worldwide Limits for Toxic and Hazardous Chemicals in Air and Water*, ed. Marshall Gutty (Park Ridge, NJ: Noyes Publ., 1994): 457.

[10]Jay Burnett, "Is Your Garden Leaded?" *Organic Farming* Nov. 1992: 16–18.

[11]Beatrice Trum Hunter, "Dietary Lead: Problems and Solutions," *Consumers' Research* (1992): 18–19.

[12]U. S. Department of Agriculture Extension Service.

[13]EPA, *Is Your Yard Lead Proof?*

CHAPTER 15

[1]U. S. Department of Agriculture, Food and Drug Administration, "Reducing Exposure to Lead from Ceramic Ware," *FDA Backgrounder* (undated); *Federal Register* 58 (21 June 1993): 33865.

[2]Judith E. Foulke, "Lead Threat Lessens, but Mugs Pose Problem," *FDA Consumer* 27 (April 1993): 19–23.

[3]Russell Flegal *et al.*, "Lead Contamination in Food," *Food Contamination from Environmental Sources*, Jerome O. Nriagu and Mila S. Simmons, eds. (New York: John Wiley & Sons, Inc., 1988).

[4]*Federal Register* 58 (21 June 1993): 33860.

[5]Judith E. Foulke, "Toddler's Blood Test Leads to Juice Recall," *FDA Consumer* (Dec. 1992): 41–42.

[6]"Two Agencies Look at Lead in Wine," *FDA Consumer* (Nov. 1991): 2; "Wine, Getting the Lead Out," *Science News* (21 Sept. 1991): 189.

[7]Bruce R. Appel *et al.*, "Potential Lead Exposures from Lead Crystal Decanters," *American Journal of Public Health* 82 (1992): 1671–1673.

[8]Richard Lansdown and William Yule, *Lead Toxicity: History and Environmental Impact* (Baltimore: Johns Hopkins University Press, 1983): 170.

[9]J. Flattery *et al.*, "Lead Poisoning Associated with Use of Traditional Ethnic Remedies—California, 1991–1992," *Morbidity and Mortality Weekly Report* 42 (1993): 521–524.

[10]Ron V. Sprinkle, "Leaded Eye Cosmetics: A Cultural Cause of Elevated Lead Levels in Children," *Journal of Family Practice* 40 (1995): 358.

[11]Bernard P. Bourgoin *et al.*, "Lead Content in 70 Brands of Dietary Calcium Supplements," *American Journal of Public Health* 83 (1993): 1155–1160. Refer to article for amount of lead in specific calcium supplements.

[12]"Pewter Baby Cups Recalled," *FDA Consumer* 26 (Nov. 1992): 3–4.

[13]Beatrice Trum Hunter, "Dietary Lead: Problems and Solutions," *Consumers' Research* (May 1992): 21–22.

[14]These items are considered *adulterated* and so prohibited if they leach more than 0.5 ppm of lead. Large ceramic bowls may leach up to 1 ppm, small bowls up to 2 ppm, and plates and saucers up to 3 ppm. *Federal Register* 57 (6 July 1992): 29735.

[15]*Federal Register* 59 (12 Jan. 1994): 1638.

[16]*Federal Register* 58 (21 June 1993): 33863.

[17]*Federal Register* 58 (21 June 1993): 33860.

[18]These levels are 80 ppb for fruit juice and 250 ppb for other food products. *Federal Register* 58 (1 April 1993): 17233.

[19]*Federal Register* 61 (8 Feb. 1996): 4816.

[20]Foulke, "Lead Threat Lessens," 20.

CHAPTER 16

[1]*Federal Register* 56 (7 June 1991): 26470.

[2]*Federal Register* 56 (7 June 1991): 26466.

[3]U. S. Environmental Protection Agency (EPA), Memorandum from Lawrence Jensen, Assistant Administrator for Water, EPA, 29 Sept. 1987, in *Lead Poisoning: Hearings before the Subcommittee on Health and the Environment of the Committee on Energy and Commerce, U. S. House of Representatives* (1991): 98.

[4]*Federal Register*, 26465.

[5]Ibid., 26466.

[6]Ibid.

[7]EPA, Jensen memo, 98.

[8]New England Water Works Association (NEWWA), *Basic Chemistry of Corrosion Control Treatment to Meet the SWDA Lead and Copper Rule* (1995): 12.

[9]National Research Council (NRC), *Measuring Lead Exposure in Infants, Children, and Other Sensitive Populations* (Washington: National Academy Press, 1993): 129.

[10]U. S. Environmental Protection Agency (EPA), Office of Prevention, Pesticides and Toxic Substances, "Environmental Fact Sheet: Lead Leaching from Submersible Well Pumps" (April 1994); John H. Cushman, Jr., "U. S. Urges Users of New Well Pumps to Drink Bottled Water," *New York Times*, 19 April 1994.

[11]*Federal Register* 54 (10 April 1989): 14317.

[12]Michael Shannon and John Graef, "Hazard of Lead in Infant Formula" (letter), *The New England Journal of Medicine* 326 (1992): 137.

[13]*Federal Register* 56 (7 June 1991): 26460, 40 C.F.R. § 141–142 (1993).

[14]*Federal Register* 56 (7 June 1971): 26487. See statement of Jeffrey Wennberg, in *Lead Poisoning: Hearings* 563, for discussion of lead time and complications involved in implementing corrosion control.

[15]*Federal Register* 56 (7 June 1991): 26488.

[16]See *Standard Handbook of Environmental Engineering*, Robert A. Corbitt, ed. (McGraw-Hill, 1990): 5-124–5-125.

[17]*Federal Register* 56 (7 June 1991): 26466.

[18]National Fire Protection Association, *National Electrical Code Handbook* (1996): 174–175.

[19]"Water-Treatment Devices," *Consumer Reports* Feb. 1993: 79–82; "Fit To Drink?" *Consumer Reports* Jan. 1990: 27–43; National Toxics Campaign Fund, "A Consumer's Guide to Protecting Your Drinking Water" (undated).

CHAPTER 17

[1]This chapter is based on: Neil Leifer, Thornton, Early & Naumes, Boston, personal interview, 19 April 1996; Burton A. Nadler, Petrucelley and Nadler, personal interview, 21 May 1996; Benjamin Hiller, Moquin and Daley, personal interview, 30 May 1996; Harvey Weitz, presentation, Association of Trial Lawyers of America (ATLA) 1996 Annual Convention, Boston; Sonja Larson, J.D., "Landlord's Lia-

bility for Injury or Death of Tenant's Child from Lead Paint Poisoning," *American Law Reports 5th* 19: 405–438.

CHAPTER 18

[1] Maurci Jackson, Executive Director of United Parents Against Lead, personal interview, April 1996.

[2] Dennis Livingston, Director, Community Resources, Inc., personal interview, Oct. 1996.

[3] Neil Gendel, Project Director, Lead Poisoning Prevention Project of Consumer Action, personal interview, May 1996.

[4] Matthew Chachere, Northern Manhattan Improvement Corporation, personal interview, Oct. 1996.

[5] This chapter is based on Andrew Brengle, Carol Rougvie, and Jane Gallagher, "Detoxifying Your Home: Protecting Your Family and Community" (HOPE Resource Center, 1992); Gary Cohen and John O'Connor, eds., *Fighting Toxics: A Manual for Protecting Your Family, Community, and Workplace* (Washington: Island Press, 1990); Kim Bobo, Jackie Kendall, and Steve Max, *Organizing for Social Change; A Manual for Activists in the 1990s* (Minneapolis: Seven Locks Press, 1991); People Organizing to Demand Environmental Rights (PODER), *Lead Poisoning Prevention Community Organizing Manual* (undated).

CHAPTER 19

[1] Herbert L. Needleman *et al.*, "Deficits in Psychologic and Classroom Performances of Children with Elevated Dentine Blood Lead Levels," *New England Journal of Medicine* 300 (1979): 689–695.

[2] See Thomas A. Lewis, "The Difficult Question of Herbert Needleman," *National Wildlife* (April/May 1995): 20–25.

[3] Section based on Richard Rabin, "Warnings Unheeded: A History of Child Lead Poisoning," *American Journal of Public Health* 79 (1989): 1668–1674. Citations for laws are in Appendix H.

[4] David Bellinger, "Neurodevelopmental Effects of Low-Level Lead Exposure in Children," Reference Materials Vol. II, Association of Trial Lawyers of America (ATLA) 1996 Annual Convention, Boston: 1281; John Rosen, "Health Effects of Low Lead Exposure Levels," *American Journal Diseases of Children* 146 (1992): 1278; Joel Schwartz, "Beyond Loel's Values and Vote Counting Methods for Looking at Shape and Strengths of Associations," *Neurotoxicology* 14 (1993): 237.

[5] John W. Graef, M.D., Children's Hospital, Boston, personal interviews, August 1996.

[6] Centers for Disease Control (CDC), Department of Health and Human Services, *Strategic Plan for the Elimination of Childhood Lead Poisoning* (1991).

[7] Karen L. Florini *et al.*, *Legacy of Lead: America's Continuing Epidemic of Childhood Lead Poisoning* (Environmental Defense Fund, 1990).

[8] Karen L. Florini and Ellen K. Silbergeld, "Getting the Lead Out," *Issues in Science and Technology* 9 (1993): 34.

State-by-State Resources

Information about lead poisoning organizations was obtained in large part from a directory published by the Alliance to End Childhood Lead Poisoning (listed in Appendix B under *Advocacy*).

ALABAMA
State Childhood Lead Poisoning Prevention Program: 334-242-5661

Regional Office of EPA: 404-347-4727
USEPA, Region 4
345 Courtland Street, NE
Atlanta, GA 30365
for information on certification and training for lead inspectors, risk assessors, and abatement contractors, lead in drinking water, lead in soil, waste disposal, or any EPA programs

State Contact for Information on Lead in Drinking Water:

Joe Allen Power, Chief, Public Water Systems, Department of Environmental Management—205-271-7700

Private Organizations Working on Lead Poisoning Prevention:

WACC: Institute for Human Development
PO Box 809
Eutaw, AL 35462
phone: 205-372-3344
fax: 372-2243
contact: Carol P. Zippert
area served: County
services offered: Organizing, education, and economic development

State Trial Lawyers Association:

Don J. Gilbert
AL Trial Lawyers Association
770 Washington Avenue, Suite 270
Montgomery, AL 36104

ALASKA
State Childhood Lead Poisoning
Prevention Program: 907-465-5152

Regional Office of EPA: 206-553-1200
USEPA, Region 10
1200 Sixth Avenue
Seattle, WA 98101
for information on certification and training for lead inspectors, risk assessors, and abatement contractors, lead in drinking water, lead in soil, waste disposal, or any EPA programs

State Contact for Information on Lead in Drinking Water:

David Khan, Department of Environmental Conservation, Drinking Water & Waste Water Section—907-465-5317

Organizations Working on Lead Poisoning Prevention:

Alaska Health Project
218 East 4th Avenue
Anchorage, AK 99501
phone: 907-276-2864, 800-478-2864 (AK)
fax: 279-3089
contact: Dan Middaugh
area served: State of Alaska
services offered: Technical assistance, funding information, organizing, education, direct action, and advocacy

State Trial Lawyers Association:

Debra Gravo
AK Academy of Trial Lawyers
540 L St., Suite 206
Anchorage, AK 99501

ARIZONA
State Childhood Lead Poisoning
Prevention Program: 602-542-7307

Regional Office of EPA: 415-744-1124
USEPA, Region 9
75 Hawthorne Street
San Francisco, CA 94105
for information on certification and training for lead inspectors, risk assessors, and abatement contractors, lead in drinking water, lead in soil, waste disposal, or any EPA programs

State Contact for Information on Lead in Drinking Water:

Mike Kleminski, Program Development & Outreach Unit, Drinking Water Section, Arizona Department of Environmental Quality—602-207-4641

Organizations Working on Lead Poisoning Prevention:

**AriZona Public Interest Research Group
(AZPIRG)**
PO Box 32474
Tucson, AZ 85751
phone: 520-722-3888
fax: 296-7644
contact: Brian R. Fagin, Esq., Executive Director
area served: State of Arizona
services offered: Information for parents, community education, research, and public policy advocacy

Maricopa County Organizing Project
1818 South 16th Street, Suite 418
Phoenix, AZ 85034
contact: Tupac Enrique
phone: 602-254-5230
fax: 252-6094
area served: Maricopa County
services offered: Advocacy, research, organizing, education, and direct action

State Trial Lawyers Association:

Linda L. Schlegel
AZ Trial Lawyers Association
1161 East Camelback Road
Phoenix, AZ 85016

ARKANSAS
State Childhood Lead Poisoning Prevention Program: 501-661-2534

Regional Office of EPA: 214-665-7244
USEPA, Region 6
First Interstate Bank Tower
1445 Ross Avenue, 12th Floor, Suite 1200
Dallas, TX 75202-2733
for information on certification and training for lead inspectors, risk assessors, and abatement contractors, lead in drinking water, lead in soil, waste disposal, or any EPA programs

State Contact for Information on Lead in Drinking Water:

Bobby Makin, Asst. Director, Arkansas Department of Health, Drinking Water Engineering—
501-661-2623

State Trial Lawyers Association:

Carol Utley
AR Trial Lawyers Association
225 East Markham, Suite 200
Little Rock, AR 72201

CALIFORNIA
State Childhood Lead Poisoning Prevention Program: 510-450-2441

Regional Office of EPA: 415-744-1124
USEPA, Region 9
75 Hawthorne Street
San Francisco, CA 94105
for information on certification and training for lead inspectors, risk assessors, and abatement contractors, lead in drinking water, lead in soil, waste disposal, or any EPA programs

State Contact for Information on Lead in Drinking Water:

S. Kimberly Belshe, Director, Department of Health Services—916-657-1425

Organizations Working on Lead Poisoning Prevention:

Asian Neighborhood Design
461 Bush, Suite 400
San Francisco, CA 94108
phone: 415-982-2959
fax: 296-9066
contact: Maurice Miller
area served: San Francisco Bay Area
services offered: Provides housing; conducts organizing and education for tenants, particularly in low-income communities

California Communities Against Toxics (CCAT)
3815 50 Street, West
Rosamond, CA 93560
phone: 805-256-2101
fax: 256-0674
contact: Stormy Williams
area served: State of California
services offered: Networking and education

California League of Conservation Voters
10951 West Pico Boulevard, Suite 201
Los Angeles, CA 90064
phone: 310-441-1675
fax: 441-1685
contact: Candace Inagi, Urban Affairs Coordinator
area served: State of California
services offered: Advocacy; information on lead poisoning issues, lead-related legislation, legislators' voting records, and candidates' opinions

California Public Interest Research Group
926 J Street, Suite 113
Sacramento, CA 95814
phone: 916-448-4516
fax: 448-4560
contact: Mary Raferty
area served: State of California
services offered: Information for parents, community eduction, and advocacy

California Rural Legal Assistance Center on Race, Poverty and the Environment
631 Howard, Suite 300
San Francisco, CA 94105
phone: 415-777-2752
fax: 543-2752

contact: Luke Cole
area served: State of California
services offered: Information for parents, advocacy, legal and technical assistance

Communities for a Better Environment

605 W. Olympic Boulevard, Suite 850
Los Angeles, CA 90015
phone: 213-486-5114
fax: 486-5139
contact: Carlos Porras, So. California Director
area served: Southern California, primarily Los Angeles urban community
services offered: Information for parents, community education, and advocacy; referrals for lead screening, abatement, and other services

Concerned Citizens of South Central Los Angeles

4707 S. Central Avenue
Los Angeles, CA 90011
contact: Melodie Dove
phone: 213-846-2500
fax: 846-2508
area served: South Central Los Angeles
services offered: Advocacy, research, organizing, education, direct action, and housing

Del Rey Residents Concerned for Clean Air and Water

5091 Del Avenue
Del Rey, CA 93616
phone: 408-888-2612
contact: Mary Lou Martinez
area served: Del Rey neighborhood
services offered: Advocacy, research, organizing, education, direct action, and community outreach

Lead Poisoning Organizing Project

2244 Cazador Drive
Los Angeles, CA 90065
contact: Linda Kite
phone: 213-222-4495
fax: 222-4495
area served: Los Angeles
services offered: Information for parents, community education, and advocacy

Lead Poisoning Prevention Project of Consumer Action

116 New Montgomery Street, Suite 233
San Francisco, CA 94105
phone: 415-777-9648
fax: 777-5267
contact: Neil Gendel
area served: San Francisco Bay Area
services offered: Community organizing and education, mobilizing local agency resources to make public facilities lead safe for children and to educate parents about protecting children against lead hazards; publications include "Guide to Help Prevent the Lead Poisoning of Children in San Francisco," and "Kids at Risk," in Cantonese, Spanish and English

Lead Safe California

100 Pine Street, 26th Floor
San Francisco, CA 94111
contact: Ellen Widess
phone: 415-397-9401
fax: 397-5159
area served: State of California
services offered: Policy advocacy, clearinghouse and technical assistance on legal, regulatory, and scientific issues relating to lead hazards and childhood lead poisoning

People United for a Better Oakland (PUEBLO)

132 East 12th Street
Oakland, CA 94606
phone: 510-452-2010
fax: 452-2017
contact: Gwen Hardy
area served: Oakland
services offered: Information for parents, community education, and advocacy

PODER (People Organizing to Demand Environmental Rights)

474 Valencia Street, #155
San Francisco, CA 94103
phone: 415-431-4210
fax: 431-8525
area served: San Francisco
services offered: Information for parents, community education, advocacy, training specializing in grass-roots organizing; publications available to the public include: *Unidos Contra el Plemo*

(*United Against Lead*), a photonovel about how community residents organized neighbors to prevent lead poisoning, and *Lead Poisoning Prevention Community Organizing Manual*

San Francisco Tenants' Union
558 Capp Street
San Francisco, CA 94110
phone: 415-282-6622
fax: 282-6622
contact: Ted Gullicksen
area served: San Francisco
services offered: Information for parents and tenants and advocacy, specializing in safe and affordable housing

St. Peter's Housing Committee
474 Valencia St., Suite 156
San Francisco, CA 94103
phone: 415-487-9203
fax: 487-9022
contact: Gloria Lopez, Director
area served: San Francisco Mission District and Spanish-speaking residents of San Francisco
services offered: Information for parents, community education, advocacy regarding lead problems, and counseling advocacy regarding tenants' rights, including habitability

West County Toxics Coalition
1019 Macdonald Avenue
Richmond, CA 94801
phone: 510-232-3427
fax: 232-4111
contact: Lucille Allen
area served: Richmond
services offered: Information for parents and community outreach

State Trial Lawyers Association:

Diane Rito
San Francisco Trial Lawyers Association
World Trade Center, Suite 207
San Francisco, CA 94111

Nancy Drabble
Consumer Attorneys of CA
980 9th Street, Suite 200
Sacramento, CA 95814

COLORADO
State Childhood Lead Poisoning Prevention Program: 303-692-3539

Regional Office of EPA: 303-293-1603
USEPA, Region 8
999 18th Street, Suite 500
Denver, CO 80202-2405
for information on certification and training for lead inspectors, risk assessors, and abatement contractors, lead in drinking water, lead in soil, waste disposal, or any EPA programs

State Contact for Information on Lead in Drinking Water:

Jerry Biberstine, Section Chief, Colorado Department of Health, Water Quality Control Division, Drinking Water Branch—303-692-3546

State Trial Lawyers Association:

John A. Sadwith
CO Trial Lawyers Association
1888 Sherman Street, #370
Denver, CO 80203

CONNECTICUT
State Childhood Lead Poisoning Prevention Program: 860-509-7745

Regional Office of EPA: 617-565-3420
USEPA, Region 1
John F. Kennedy Federal Building
One Congress Street
Boston, MA 02203
for information on certification and training for lead inspectors, risk assessors, and abatement contractors, lead in drinking water, lead in soil, waste disposal, or any EPA programs

State Contact for Information on Lead in Drinking Water:

Gerald Iwan, Chief, Water Supplies Section, Department of Public Health & Addictive Services—203-240-9262

Organizations Working on Lead Poisoning Prevention:

Bridgeport Child Advocacy Coalition (BCAC)
475 Clinton Avenue
Bridgeport, CT 06605
phone: 203-368-4291
fax: 368-1239
contact: Marilyn Ondrasik
area served: Bridgeport
services offered: Information for parents, research, planning, community education, and advocacy

Connecticut Citizen Research Group/ Action Group
45 South Main Street
West Hartford, CT 06107
phone: 203-561-6006, Safe House—860-525-1834
fax: 561-6018
contact: Tammy Greaton
area served: State of Connecticut
services offered: Information for parents, emergency shelter, and community education

Connecticut Lead Project
555 Windsor Street
Hartford, CT 06120
phone: 203-280-0133
fax: 527-3305
contact: Dawn Amore
area served: Hartford, Waterbury, New Britain, Windham, Meriden
services offered: Coordination of activities of various agencies, advocacy

El Hogar del Futuro, Inc.
645 Park Street
Hartford, CT 06106
phone: 203-249-0348
contact: Anna Morales
area served: Hartford
services offered: Training and support for families to self-manage co-op housing

Keep Kids Lead Free, Inc.
Stamford Health Department
888 Washington Boulevard
Stamford, CT 06904
phone: 203-977-5701
fax: 367-1225

contact: Ana Cordova-Goodring
area served: Stamford
services offered: Education, community education, and advocacy

Yale Lead Program
333 Cedar Street
PO Box 208064
New Haven, CT 06510-8064
phone: 203-764-9106
fax: 764-9110
contact: Fay Godbolt
area served: New Haven
services offered: Information for parents, advocacy, and family social services, including lead screening, medical care, and case management

State Trial Lawyers Association:

Neil Ferstrand
CT Trial Lawyers Association
96 Oak Street
Hartford, CT 06106

DELAWARE
State Childhood Lead Poisoning Prevention Program: 302-739-4735

Regional Office of EPA: 215-597-9800
USEPA, Region 3
841 Chestnut Building
Philadelphia, PA 19107
for information on certification and training for lead inspectors, risk assessors, and abatement contractors, lead in drinking water, lead in soil, waste disposal, or any EPA programs

State Contact for Information on Lead in Drinking Water:

Ed Hallock, Division of Public Health—302-739-5410

State Trial Lawyers Association:

Michael Rost
DE Trial Lawyers Association
715 King Street, 2nd Floor
Wilmington, DE 19801

DISTRICT OF COLUMBIA
**State Childhood Lead Poisoning
Prevention Program: 202-727-9870**

Regional Office of EPA: 215-597-9800
USEPA, Region 3
841 Chestnut Building
Philadelphia, PA 19107
*for information on certification and training for
lead inspectors, risk assessors, and abatement contractors, lead in drinking water, lead in soil, waste
disposal, or any EPA programs*

*Organizations Working on Lead Poisoning
Prevention:*

**Americans Against Childhood Lead
Poisoning**
PO Box 301
Burke, VA 22009-0301
phone: 703-978-3190
fax: 978-5357
contact: Fariba Nazemi
area served: States of Virginia and Maryland, and
District of Columbia
services offered: Educates expectant mothers and
households with young children, inspects houses
for lead, and advocacy

**Association of Community Organizations
for Reform Now (ACORN)**
739 8th Street, SE
Washington, DC 20003
phone: 202-547-9292
fax: 546-2483
contact: Chris Leonard
area served: Washington, DC
services offered: Information for parents, community education, and advocacy

DC Coalition to End Lead Poisoning
% Alice Hamilton Occupational Health Center
1310 Apple Avenue
Silver Spring, MD 20910
phone: 202-543-0005
fax: 565-4391
contact: Brian Christopher
area served: Washington, DC
services offered: Information for parents, worker

lead abatement training, community education
and organizing, and local advocacy

State Trial Lawyers Association:

Kathy Huggins
Trial Lawyers Association of Metro DC
1100 Connecticut Ave., NW #800
Washington, DC 20036

FLORIDA
**State Childhood Lead Poisoning
Prevention Program: 904-488-3385 or
488-9228**

Regional Office of EPA: 404-347-4727
USEPA, Region 4
345 Courtland Street, NE
Atlanta, GA 30365
*for information on certification and training for
lead inspectors, risk assessors, and abatement contractors, lead in drinking water, lead in soil, waste
disposal, or any EPA programs*

*State Contact for Information on Lead in
Drinking Water:*

Tom Douglas, Department of Environmental
Protection—904-488-3935

State Trial Lawyers Association:

Scott Carruthers
Academy of FL Trial Lawyers
218 South Monroe Street
Tallahassee, FL 32301

GEORGIA
**State Childhood Lead Poisoning
Prevention Program: 404-657-6534**

Regional Office of EPA: 404-347-4727
USEPA, Region 4
345 Courtland Street, NE
Atlanta, GA 30365
*for information on certification and training for
lead inspectors, risk assessors, and abatement contractors, lead in drinking water, lead in soil, waste
disposal, or any EPA programs*

State Contact for Information on Lead in Drinking Water:

David Shirley, Program Coordinator, School Safety & Environmental Services, Georgia Department of Education   404-656-2454

Organizations Working on Lead Poisoning Prevention:

Southern Organizing Committee for Economic and Social Justice
PO Box 10518
Atlanta, GA 30310
phone: 404-755-2855
fax: 755-0575
contact: Connie Tucker
area served: The South
services offered: Research, organizing, education, and direct action

State Trial Lawyers Association:

Brenda Brayton
GA Trial Lawyers Association
1250 Hurt Building
50 Hurt Plaza SE
Atlanta, GA 30303-2916

HAWAII
State Childhood Lead Poisoning Prevention Program: 808-832-5860

Regional Office of EPA: 206-553-1200
USEPA, Region 10
1200 Sixth Avenue
Seattle, WA 98101
for information on certification and training for lead inspectors, risk assessors, and abatement contractors, lead in drinking water, lead in soil, waste disposal, or any EPA programs

State Contact for Information on Lead in Drinking Water:

William Wong, Hawaii State Department of Health, Environmental Management Division, Safe Drinking Water Branch—808-586-4258

Organizations Working on Lead Poisoning Prevention:

Ke Kua'aina Hunauna Hou
Star Route 265
Kaunakakai, HI 96748
phone: 808-558-8393
contact: Colette Y. Machado
services offered: Research, organizing, education, and direct action

State Trial Lawyers Association:

Loren D. Leibling
Consumer Attorneys Association
1088 Bishop Street
Honolulu, HI 96813

Robert Toyofuku
Hawaii Trial Lawyers Association
1088 Bishop Street, Suite 1111
Honolulu, HI 96813

IDAHO
State environmental health contact: 208-332-5544

Regional Office of EPA: 206-553-1200
USEPA, Region 10
1200 Sixth Avenue
Seattle, WA 98101
for information on certification and training for lead inspectors, risk assessors, and abatement contractors, lead in drinking water, lead in soil, waste disposal, or any EPA programs

State Contact for Information on Lead in Drinking Water:

Eldon Nelson, Idaho Department of Education—208-334-3300

Organization Working on Lead Poisoning Prevention:

Idaho Conservation League
PO Box 844
Boise, ID 83701
phone: 208-345-6933
fax: 344-0344

contact: Rick Johnson
services: Works to protect Idaho's land and clean water resources through citizen action

State Trial Lawyers Association:

Kay Shields
ID Trial Lawyers Association
PO Box 1777, 1517 West Hays
Boise, ID 83701

ILLINOIS
State Childhood Lead Poisoning Prevention Program: 217-782-0403

Regional Office of EPA: 312-886-6003
USEPA, Region 5
77 West Jackson Boulevard
Chicago, IL 60604-3590
for information on certification and training for lead inspectors, risk assessors, and abatement contractors, lead in drinking water, lead in soil, waste disposal, or any EPA programs

State Contact for Information on Lead in Drinking Water:

George Michael Brandt, Chief, Illinois Department of Public Health—217-782-3517

Organizations Working on Lead Poisoning Prevention:

Bethel New Life, Inc.
7 North Keeler
Chicago, IL 60624
phone: 773-826-7474
fax: 826-7484
contact: Robin Dixon
area served: Chicago/West Garfield Park
services offered: Information for parents, community education and advocacy. Medical, legal, housing assistance to low-income residents

Children and Youth 2000
220 South State Street, Suite 1210
Chicago, IL 60604

phone: 312-922-2000
fax: 922-2277
contact: Martha Quinn
area served: Chicago
services offered: Education and advocacy; staffs a speakers' bureau project on lead poisoning

Lead Education and Awareness Project (LEAP)
3 South 237 Briarwood Drive
Warrenville, IL 60555
phone: 773-260-9550
fax: 668-9617
contact: Cynthia Lowrie
area served: Nonmetropolitan areas of Illinois
services offered: Information for parents, contractor referral service, and advocacy

Lead Elimination Action Drive (LEAD)
2125 West North Avenue
Chicago, IL 60647
phone: 773-292-4990
fax: 292-0333
contact: John Knox
area served: Chicago
services offered: Information for parents, community education, and organizing

Parents Against Lead (PAL)
1438 East 52nd Street
Chicago, IL 60615-4122
phone: 773-324-7824
fax: 324-7560
contact: Maurci Jackson
area served: State of Illinois
services offered: Information for parents, community education, and advocacy

State Trial Lawyers Association:

James M. Collins
IL Trial Lawyers Association
110 W. Edwards Street
PO Box 5000
Springfield, IL 62705

INDIANA
State Childhood Lead Poisoning Prevention Program: 317-233-1232

Regional Office of EPA: 312-886-6003
USEPA, Region 5
77 West Jackson Boulevard
Chicago, IL 60604-3590
for information on certification and training for lead inspectors, risk assessors, and abatement contractors, lead in drinking water, lead in soil, waste disposal, or any EPA programs

State Contact for Information on Lead in Drinking Water:

T.P. Chang, Chief, Drinking Water Branch, Indiana Department of Environmental Management—317-233-4222

State Trial Lawyers Association:

Michealle B. Wilson
IN Trial Lawyers Association
150 West Market Street, Suite 210
Indianapolis, IN 46204

IOWA
State Childhood Lead Poisoning Prevention Program: 515-242-6340

Regional Office of EPA: 913-551-7020
USEPA, Region 7
726 Minnesota Avenue
Kansas City, KS 66101
for information on certification and training for lead inspectors, risk assessors, and abatement contractors, lead in drinking water, lead in soil, waste disposal, or any EPA programs

State Contact for Information on Lead in Drinking Water:

Dennis Alt, Supervisor, Water Supply Section, Iowa Department of Natural Resources—515-281-8998

State Trial Lawyers Association:

Scott Brown
IA Trial Lawyers Association

218 6th Avenue, Suite 526
Des Moines, IA 50309

KANSAS
State Childhood Lead Poisoning Prevention Program: 913-296-0189, 296-1343, or 296-6215

Regional Office of EPA: 913-551-7020
USEPA, Region 7
726 Minnesota Avenue
Kansas City, KS 66101
for information on certification and training for lead inspectors, risk assessors, and abatement contractors, lead in drinking water, lead in soil, waste disposal, or any EPA programs

State Contact for Information on Lead in Drinking Water:

Dave Waldo, Kansas Department of Health and Environment—913-296-5503

Organizations Working on Lead Poisoning Prevention:

LeadBusters, Inc.
U. Kansas Medical Center
2002 West 39th Street, Suite 1029
Kansas City, KS 66160
phone: 913-438-LEAD or 588-7153
fax: 588-7160
contact: Larry Rubin
area served: Greater Kansas City (western Missouri, eastern Kansas)
services offered: Speakers bureau, education, curriculum development, grant development, research, training, advocacy, community empowerment, hazard control management programs, information and referral

State Trial Lawyers Association:

Terry Humphrey
Kansas Trial Lawyers Association
700 SW Jackson, Suite 706
Topeka, KS 66603-3731

KENTUCKY
State Childhood Lead Poisoning Prevention Program: 502-564-2154

Regional Office of EPA: 404-347-4727
USEPA, Region 4
345 Courtland Street, NE
Atlanta, GA 30365
for information on certification and training for lead inspectors, risk assessors, and abatement contractors, lead in drinking water, lead in soil, waste disposal, or any EPA programs

State Contact for Information on Lead in Drinking Water:

John T. Smither, Branch Manager, Div. of Water, Div. of Environmental Protection—502-564-3410

State Trial Lawyers Association:

Penny Gold
KY Academy of Trial Attorneys
12700 Shelbyville Road
Louisville, KY 40243

LOUISIANA
State Childhood Lead Poisoning Prevention Program: 504-568-5070

Regional Office of EPA: 214-665-7244
USEPA, Region 6
First Interstate Bank Tower
1445 Ross Avenue, 12th Floor, Suite 1200
Dallas, TX 75202-2733
for information on certification and training for lead inspectors, risk assessors, and abatement contractors, lead in drinking water, lead in soil, waste disposal, or any EPA programs

State Contact for Information on Lead in Drinking Water:

T. Jay Ray, Administrator, Louisiana Department of Health and Hospitals, Office of Public Health, Safe Drinking Water Program—504-568-5100

Organizations Working on Lead Poisoning Prevention:

Deep South Center for Environmental Justice
7325 Palmetto Street, PO Box 45-B
Xavier University of Louisiana
New Orleans, LA 70125
phone: 504-483-7340
fax: 488-7977
contact: Beverly Wright
area served: Southeastern Louisiana
services offered: Technical assistance in research, education, and training

Gulf Coast Tenants' Organization
1866 North Gayoso Street
New Orleans, LA 70119
phone: 504-949-4919
fax: 949-0422
contact: Pat Bryant
services offered: Leadership and organizing training, advocacy, research, education, and direct action

North Baton Rouge Environmental Association
421 Springfield Road
Baton Rouge, LA 70807
phone: 504-775-0341
fax: 774-2928
contact: Florence T. Robinson
area served: North Baton Rouge
services offered: Advocacy, research, organizing, education, and direct action

United Parents Against Lead of Louisiana (UPAL)
3317 Beech Drive
Gretna, LA 70056
phone: 504-393-0744
fax: 393-0744
contact: Sherrell Duggan
area served: State of Louisiana
services offered: Information and resources for parents

State Trial Lawyers Association:

Leah Guerry
LA Trial Lawyers Association

PO Drawer 4289
Baton Rouge, LA 70821

MAINE
**State Childhood Lead Poisoning
Prevention Program: 207-287-5690**

Regional Office of EPA: **617-565-3420**
USEPA, Region 1
John F. Kennedy Federal Building
One Congress Street
Boston, MA 02203
*for information on certification and training for
lead inspectors, risk assessors, and abatement contractors, lead in drinking water, lead in soil, waste
disposal, or any EPA programs*

*State Contact for Information on Lead in
Drinking Water:*

Phil Kemp, Assistant Toxicologist, Maine Bureau
of Health—207-287-5378

*Organizations Working on Lead Poisoning
Prevention:*

**Committee for the Prevention of
Childhood Lead Poisoning**
389 Congress Street, Room 307
Portland, ME 04101
phone: 207-874-0833
fax: 864-8913
contact: Mary Ann Amrich
area served: Portland
services offered: Public education and advocacy

State Trial Lawyers Association:

Lucy Stinson
ME Trial Lawyers Association
PO Box 428
Augusta, ME 04332-0428

MARYLAND
**State Childhood Lead Poisoning
Prevention Program: 410-631-3847**

Regional Office of EPA: **215-597-9800**
USEPA, Region 3
841 Chestnut Building

Philadelphia, PA 19107
*for information on certification and training for
lead inspectors, risk assessors, and abatement contractors, lead in drinking water, lead in soil, waste
disposal, or any EPA programs*

*State Contact for Information on Lead in
Drinking Water:*

Boyd Grove, Public Drinking Water Program,
Maryland Department of the Environment—410-
631-3706

*Organizations Working on Lead Poisoning
Prevention:*

**Americans Against Childhood Lead
Poisoning**
PO Box 301
Burke, VA 22009-0301
phone: 703-978-3190
fax: 978-5357
contact: Fariba Nazemi
area served: States of Virginia and Maryland, and
District of Columbia
services offered: Educates expectant mothers and
households with young children, inspects houses
for lead, and advocacy

CLEARCorps Baltimore
409 N. Patterson Park Avenue
Baltimore, MD 21231
phone: 410-675-4685
fax: 327-0410
e-mail: mrobbin@gl.umbc.edu
contact: Michael Robbins
area served: Baltimore
services offered: community education and lead
abatement of vacant units, through the CLEAR-
Corps (Community Lead Education and Reduction Corps) project, established under an Ameri-
Corps grant from the Corporation for National
Service

**Coalition to End Childhood Lead
Poisoning and Parents Against Lead**
28 East Ostend Street
Baltimore, MD 21230-4209
phone: 410-727-4226, 800-370-5323
fax: 410-727-6775
e-mail: leadfree@msn.com

contact: Ruth Ann Norton
area served: National
services: Offers extensive information and direct outreach services as well as lead-safe initiatives. Early intervention, prevention, education, and outreach services; lead-safe housing analysis and advocacy; resource identification and referral. Publishes guide to lead poisoning prevention in Maryland, "Get The Lead Out! Community Guide To Lead Poisoning Prevention."

Community Resources
28 East Ostend Street
Baltimore, MD 21230
phone: 410-727-7837
fax: 706-0295
contact: Dennis Livingston
area served: Region
services offered: Design and implementation of projects that focus on solving environmental problems with community-controlled economically sustainable programs

United Parents Against Lead of Maryland (UPAL)
700 North Gilmore
Baltimore, MD 21217
phone: 410-728-6176
fax: 728-6176
contact: Cassandra Yelverton
area served: State of Maryland
services offered: Support and information for parents, community education, and advocacy

State Trial Lawyers Association:

Janelle Cousino
MD Trial Lawyers Association
1018 North Charles Street
Baltimore, MD 21201

MASSACHUSETTS
State Childhood Lead Poisoning Prevention Program: 617-753-8401

Regional Office of EPA: 617-565-3420
USEPA, Region 1
John F. Kennedy Federal Building
One Congress Street
Boston, MA 02203

for information on certification and training for lead inspectors, risk assessors, and abatement contractors, lead in drinking water, lead in soil, waste disposal, or any EPA programs

State Contact for Information on Lead in Drinking Water:

Phyllis Madigan, Department of Public Health, Lead Poisoning Prevention—617-522-3700, x363

Organizations Working on Lead Poisoning Prevention:

Dorchester Bay Economic Development Center
phone: 617-825-4200
services offered: One Stop Deleading Center— community-based center for information on deleading loans and methods

Dudley Street Neighborhood Initiative
513 Dudley Street
Roxbury, MA 02119
contact: Trish Settles
phone: 617-442-9670
fax: 427-8047
area served: Roxbury/Dorchester
services offered: Testing, analysis, and education on lead in soil for gardeners

Lead Action Collaborative
% Boston Globe Foundation
PO Box 2378
Boston, MA 02107
phone: 617-929-2893
fax: 929-2041
contact: Mariella C. Tan Puerto
area served: Boston
services offered: Fund-raising, technical assistance, and advocacy

Lena Park Community Development Corporation
150 American Legion Highway
Dorchester, MA 02124
phone: 617-288-7398
fax: 436-0999
contact: Kyle McKinney
area served: Boston
services offered: Information for parents, counsel-

ing, housing, social services intake and referral, and advocacy

Massachusetts Association of CDCs
197 Portland Street
Boston, MA 02114
phone: 617-523-7002
fax: 523-5409
contact: Joe Kreisberg
area served: State of Massachusetts
services offered: Supports community development corporations

Mass Affordable Housing Alliance (MAHA)
1773 Dorchester Avenue
Dorchester, MA 02124
phone: 617-265-8995
fax: 265-7503
contact: Hillary Frank
area served: State of Massachusetts
services offered: Information for parents, community education, and advocacy, specializing in safe and affordable housing

Task Force on Child Lead Poisoning
8 Sawin Street
Arlington, MA 02174
phone: 617-646-3889
fax: 727-4581
contact: Richard Rabin
area served: Boston
services offered: Obtaining funding for deleading, advocacy

United Parents Against Lead of Massachusetts (UPAL)
1-A Terrace Street
Roxbury, MA 02121
phone: 617-442-1617
contact: Laverne Jacobs Robinson
area served: State of Massachusetts
services offered: Support and information for parents, community education, advocacy

State Trial Lawyers Association:

Barbara Sullivan
Massachusetts Academy of Trial Attorneys
15 Broad Street, #415
Boston, MA 02109

MICHIGAN
State Childhood Lead Poisoning Prevention Program: 517-335-9242

Regional Office of EPA: 312-886-6003
USEPA, Region 5
77 West Jackson Boulevard
Chicago, IL 60604-3590
for information on certification and training for lead inspectors, risk assessors, and abatement contractors, lead in drinking water, lead in soil, waste disposal, or any EPA programs

State Contact for Information on Lead in Drinking Water:

Jim Cleland, Acting Chief, Michigan Department of Public Health, Div. of Water Supply—517-335-8326

Organizations Working on Lead Poisoning Prevention:

Core City Neighborhoods (CCN)
3301 23rd Street
Detroit, MI 48208
phone: 313-894-8431
fax: 894-5983
contact: Brian Watts
area served: Detroit
services offered: Information for parents, community education, economic development

Flint–Genesee United for Action, Justice and Environmental Safety
6901 W. Boulevard Drive
Flint, MI 48505
phone: 810-785-9901
contact: Janice O'Neal
area served: Flint, Genesee
services offered: Advocacy, research, organizing, education, and direct action

United Parents Against Lead of Michigan (UPAL)
54126 CR 657
Paw Paw, MI 49079
phone: 616-668-8183
contact: Margaret Sauser
area served: State of Michigan

services offered: Support and information for parents and community education

State Trial Lawyers Association:

Jane R. Bailey
MI Trial Lawyers Association
501 South Capitol Avenue, #405
Lansing, MI 48933-2327

MINNESOTA
State Childhood Lead Poisoning Prevention Program: 612-215-0927

Regional Office of EPA: 312-886-6003
USEPA, Region 5
77 West Jackson Boulevard
Chicago, IL 60604-3590
for information on certification and training for lead inspectors, risk assessors, and abatement contractors, lead in drinking water, lead in soil, waste disposal, or any EPA programs

State Contact for Information on Lead in Drinking Water:

Bruce Olfen, Supervisor, Special Services, Minnesota Department of Health—612-627-5167

Organizations Working on Lead Poisoning Prevention:

People of Phillips
East Franklin Avenue, South
Minneapolis, MN 55404
phone: 612-874-1711
fax: 874-7605
contact: "Doc" Davis
area served: Minneapolis
services offered: Information for parents, community education, and advocacy

The Sustainable Resources Center
1916 Second Avenue South
Minneapolis, MN 55403
phone: 612-870-4255
e-mail: SueSR@aol.com
contact: Sue Gunderson
area served: Minneapolis metropolitan area
services offered: Community education, lead risk assessment and lead abatement, through the

CLEARCorps (Community Lead Education and Reduction Corps) project, established under an AmeriCorps grant from the Corporation for National Service

State Trial Lawyers Association:

Richard Martin
MN Trial Lawyers Association
706 2nd Avenue South
140 Baker Building
Minneapolis, MN 55402

MISSISSIPPI
State Childhood Lead Poisoning Prevention Program: 601-960-7463 or 961-5171

Regional Office of EPA: 404-347-4727
USEPA, Region 4
345 Courtland Street, NE
Atlanta, GA 30365
for information on certification and training for lead inspectors, risk assessors, and abatement contractors, lead in drinking water, lead in soil, waste disposal, or any EPA programs

State Contact for Information on Lead in Drinking Water:

Joseph Brown, Director, Bureau of Environmental Protection, Mississippi Department of Health—601-960-7518

State Trial Lawyers Association:

David F. Gates
MS Trial Lawyers Association
PO Box 1992
Jackson, MS 39205

MISSOURI
State Childhood Lead Poisoning Prevention Program: 573-751-6102

Regional Office of EPA: 913-551-7020
USEPA, Region 7
726 Minnesota Avenue
Kansas City, KS 66101

for information on certification and training for lead inspectors, risk assessors, and abatement contractors, lead in drinking water, lead in soil, waste disposal, or any EPA programs

State Contact for Information on Lead in Drinking Water:

Michael Carter, Bureau of Environmental Epidemiology—314-526-4911

Organizations Working on Lead Poisoning Prevention:

Mothers of Lead Exposed Children (MOLEC) and United Parents Against Lead of Missouri (UPAL)
PO Box 8142
Kansas City, MO 64112
phone: 913-538-1531
contact: Shanea McGeehan
area served: Kansas City
services offered: Information for parents, community education, and advocacy

State Trial Lawyers Association:

Linda S. Simon
MO Association of Trial Attorneys
PO Box 1792
Jefferson City, MO 65102

MONTANA
State Childhood Lead Poisoning Prevention Program: 406-723-0041

Regional Office of EPA: 303-293-1603
USEPA, Region 8
999 18th Street, Suite 500
Denver, CO 80202-2405
for information on certification and training for lead inspectors, risk assessors, and abatement contractors, lead in drinking water, lead in soil, waste disposal, or any EPA programs

State Contact for Information on Lead in Drinking Water:

Jim Melstad, Montana Department of Health, Environmental Services Water Quality Bureau, Public Water Supply Program—406-449-5256

State Trial Lawyers Association:

Russell B. Hill
MT Trial Lawyers Association
#1 North Last Chance Gulch
Helena, MT 59601

NEBRASKA
State Childhood Lead Poisoning Prevention Program: 402-471-0782 (toll free in NE 888-242-1100)

Regional Office of EPA: 913-551-7020
USEPA, Region 7
726 Minnesota Avenue
Kansas City, KS 66101
for information on certification and training for lead inspectors, risk assessors, and abatement contractors, lead in drinking water, lead in soil, waste disposal, or any EPA programs

State Contact for Information on Lead in Drinking Water:

Jack Daniel, Director, Division of Environmental Health and Housing Surveillance, Nebraska Department of Health—402-471-2541

State Trial Lawyers Association:

Stella Huggins
NE Associaton of Trial Attorneys
605 South 14th Street, #450A
Lincoln, NE 68508

NEVADA
State Childhood Lead Poisoning Prevention Program: 702-687-6615

Regional Office of EPA: 206-553-1200
USEPA, Region 10
1200 Sixth Avenue
Seattle, WA 98101
for information on certification and training for lead inspectors, risk assessors, and abatement contractors, lead in drinking water, lead in soil, waste disposal, or any EPA programs

State Contact for Information on Lead in Drinking Water:

Terry Hall, Nevada Health Protection Services—702-687-6615

State Trial Lawyers Association:

Victoria D. Riley
NV Trial Lawyers Association
406 North Nevada Street
Carson City, NV 89703

NEW HAMPSHIRE
State Childhood Lead Poisoning Prevention Program: 603-271-3970

Regional Office of EPA: 617-565-3420
USEPA, Region 1
John F. Kennedy Federal Building
One Congress Street
Boston, MA 02203
for information on certification and training for lead inspectors, risk assessors, and abatement contractors, lead in drinking water, lead in soil, waste disposal, or any EPA programs

State Contact for Information on Lead in Drinking Water:

Dr. Gerald Bourgeois, Deputy Commissioner, New Hampshire Department of Education—603-271-3144

State Trial Lawyers Association:

Jennifer Sodati
NH Trial Lawyers Association
PO Box 447
Concord, NH 03302-0447

NEW JERSEY
State Childhood Lead Poisoning Prevention Program: 609-292-5666

Regional Office of EPA: 908-321-6671
USEPA, Region 2
Building 5
2890 Woodbridge Avenue
Edison, NJ 08837-3679

for information on certification and training for lead inspectors, risk assessors, and abatement contractors, lead in drinking water, lead in soil, waste disposal, or any EPA programs

State Contact for Information on Lead in Drinking Water:

Water Supply Element, New Jersey Department of Environmental Protection—609-292-5550

Organizations Working on Lead Poisoning Prevention:

Donald Jackson Neighborhood Corporation
620 Clinton Avenue
Newark, NJ 07108
phone: 201-242-5057
fax: 642-7355
contact: Randall Alston
area served: Newark
services offered: Information for parents, community education, and advocacy

Mothers Get the Lead Out
509 Cedarcroft Avenue
Audubon, NJ 08106
phone: 609-546-6480
contact: Robin Dustman
area served: South New Jersey
services offered: Referrals, support, and information from parents who have dealt with lead poisoning in their children and want to share what they have learned

NJ Anti-Lead Poisoning Coalition
90 Martin Street
Paterson, NJ 07401
phone: 201-345-8616
fax: 345-6719
contact: Bob Roe
area served: New Jersey
services: Information for parents, community education, advocacy, neighborhood organization, and materials development

New Jersey Citizen Action
46 Paterson Street, 2nd Floor
New Brunswick, NJ 08901

phone: 908-246-4772
fax: 214-8385
contact: Ralph Scott
area served: New Jersey
services offered: Information for parents, community education, advocacy, and organizing to combat lead poisoning

New Jersey Head Start Association
224 East State Street
Trenton, NJ 08608
phone: 609-392-2772
contact: Cecile Dickey
area served: New Jersey
services offered: Education and advocacy for families of preschoolers in need

NJ Task Force on the Prevention of Lead Poisoning
385 Georges Road
Dayton, NJ 08625
phone: 908-329-3429
fax: 329-3429
contact: Bob Tucker
area served: New Jersey
services offered: Information for parents, community education, and advocacy

The South Jersey Lead Consortium
% Univ. of Medicine and Dentistry of New Jersey–School of Medicine
40 East Laurel Road, Suite 200 PCC
Stratford, NJ 08084
phone: 609-566-6225
fax: 566-6208
contact: Sally Henry
area served: South Jersey
services offered: Information for parents, community education, and advocacy

United Parents Against Lead of NJ (UPAL)
PO Box 8485
Newark, NJ 07108
phone: 201-371-2892
contact: Sakinah Boyette
area served: New Jersey
services offered: Information for parents

State Trial Lawyers Association:

Cornelius J. Larkin
ATLA—New Jersey
150 West State Street
Trenton, NJ 08608

NEW MEXICO
State Childhood Lead Poisoning Prevention Program: 505-827-3709

Regional Office of EPA: 214-665-7244
USEPA, Region 6
First Interstate Bank Tower
1445 Ross Avenue, 12th Floor, Suite 1200
Dallas, TX 75202-2733
for information on certification and training for lead inspectors, risk assessors, and abatement contractors, lead in drinking water, lead in soil, waste disposal, or any EPA programs

State Contact for Information on Lead in Drinking Water:

Robert Gallegos, Health Program Manager, Drinking Water Section, New Mexico Environmental Improvement Division—505-827-7536

State Trial Lawyers Association:

Peter C. Mallery
NM Trial Lawyers Association
PO Box 301
Albuquerque, NM 78103

NEW YORK
State Childhood Lead Poisoning Prevention Program: 518-473-4602

Regional Office of EPA: 908-321-6671
USEPA, Region 2
Building 5
2890 Woodbridge Avenue
Edison, NJ 08837-3679
for information on certification and training for lead inspectors, risk assessors, and abatement contractors, lead in drinking water, lead in soil, waste disposal, or any EPA programs

State Contact for Information on Lead in Drinking Water:

Bureau of Public Water Supply, New York Department of Health—518-458-6731

Organizations Working on Lead Poisoning Prevention:

Center for Occupational and Environmental Health
425 E. 25th Street
PO Box 643
New York, NY 10010
phone: 212-481-8790
fax: 481-8795
contact: Dawn Mays-Hardy
area served: New York City
services offered: Training for community health professionals

Chinese Progressive Association
83 Canal Street, Suite 304/305
New York, NY 10002
phone: 212-274-1891
contact: Mae Lee
area served: Chinese community of New York City
services offered: Bilingual education, outreach, and support for families dealing with lead poisoning

Citizens Committee for New York City
Neighborhood Resources Department
305 7th Avenue, 15th Floor
New York, NY 10001
phone: 212-989-0909
fax: 989-0983
area served: New York City
services offered: Information for parents, supports local neighborhood organizations

City of Buffalo Lead Hazard Control Project
313 City Hall
Buffalo, NY 14202
phone: 716-851-4240
fax: 851-5306
contact: Theresa Calvin
area served: City of Buffalo, with support services to targeted areas with high numbers of children under age six with elevated blood lead levels

services offered: Education to all city residents; support services to residents of targeted areas, including case management, relocation and abatement, and education

Developmental Disabilities Prevention Program/People, Inc.
1219 North Forest Road
Williamsville, NY 14221
phone: 716-634-8132/1709
fax: 632-4956
contact: Joan Harms
area served: Eight western New York counties
services offered: Information for parents, community education by medical, legal, and parent advocates; publishes preschool curriculum "Lead Has a Human Face"

Environmental Advocates
353 Hamilton Street
Albany, NY 12210
phone: 518-462-5526
fax: 427-0381
contact: Loretta Simon
area served: New York State
services offered: Public education; lobbying; information on state lead policy initiatives, legislation, and regulations; founding member and resource for Coalition for a Lead-Free New York

El Puente
211 South 4th Street
Brooklyn, NY 11211
phone: 718-387-0404
fax: 387-6816
contact: Monica Rivera
area served: Brooklyn
services offered: Information for parents

Jobs and Environment Campaign
530 East 13th Street
New York, NY 10009
phone: 212-529-1260
fax: 529-1260
contact: Manny Ness
area served: New York State
services offered: Information for parents, community education

Montefiore Medical Center Lead Poisoning Prevention Project
111 East 210th Street-Safe House
Bronx, NY 10467
phone: 718-547-2789
fax: 547-2881
contact: Megan Charlop
area served: New York City
services offered: Information for parents, community organization, leadership training

Northern Manhattan Improvement Corporation
76 Wadsworth Avenue
New York, NY 10033
phone: 212-822-8300
fax: 740-9646
contact: Matthew Chachere
area served: New York City
services offered: Information for parents, advocacy, and legal representation

NY City Coalition to End Lead Poisoning (NYCCELP)
PO Box 7682
New York, NY 10016
phone: 718-547-2789
fax: 547-2881
contact: Megan Charlop
area served: New York City
services offered: Advocacy

NY Public Interest Research Group (NYPIRG)
9 Murray Street, 3rd Floor
New York, NY 10007
phone: 212-349-6460
fax: 349-1366
contact: Catherine McVay Hughes
area served: New York State
services offered: Information for parents, community education, advocacy. Publishes *Get The Lead Out: NYPIRG's Handbook for Lead Poisoning Prevention*, containing extensive list of lead poisoning resources in New York State

NY State Healthy Schools Network
33 Central Avenue
Albany, NY 12210
phone: 518-462-5527

contact: Claire Barnett
area served: Primarily New York State, but takes calls from out of state
services offered: Policy advocacy; building occupant information and referral

Parents Against Lead in Schools (PALS)
215 East 5th Street
New York, NY 10003
phone: 212-420-1971
contact: Lydia Saltzman
area served: New York State
services offered: Information for parents, community education, advocacy

South Bronx Clean Air Coalition
384 East 149th Street, Room 330
Bronx, NY 10455
phone: 718-585-6480
contact: Joe Perez
area served: South Bronx
services offered: Educational outreach; community organizing; assistance in obtaining resources related to lead poisoning, including lead testing, de-leading, alternative housing, and legal counsel

United Parents Against Lead of New York (UPAL)
80 Riley Street
Buffalo, NY 14209
phone: 716-884-2411
contact: Rovenea Turner
area served: New York State
services offered: Information for parents, community education, advocacy

State Trial Lawyers Association:

Laurence R. Buxbaum
NY State Trial Lawyers Association
132 Nassau Street
New York, NY 10038

NORTH CAROLINA
State Childhood Lead Poisoning Prevention Program: 919-715-5381 or 733-2884

Regional Office of EPA: 404-347-4727
USEPA, Region 4

345 Courtland Street, NE
Atlanta, GA 30365
for information on certification and training for lead inspectors, risk assessors, and abatement contractors, lead in drinking water, lead in soil, waste disposal, or any EPA programs

State Contact for Information on Lead in Drinking Water:

Dr. Ronald Levine, State Health Director—919-715-4126

State Trial Lawyers Association:

Dick M. Taylor
NC Academy of Trial Lawyers
1312 Annapolis Drive
Raleigh, NC 27605

NORTH DAKOTA
State Childhood Lead Poisoning Prevention Program: 701-328-5188

Regional Office of EPA: 303-293-1603
USEPA, Region 8
999 18th Street, Suite 500
Denver, CO 80202-2405
for information on certification and training for lead inspectors, risk assessors, and abatement contractors, lead in drinking water, lead in soil, waste disposal, or any EPA programs

State Contact for Information on Lead in Drinking Water:

Sherwin Wanner, Environmental Engineer, Department of Health & Consolidated Laboratories—701-328-5210

State Trial Lawyers Association:

Sharon A. Gallagher
ND Trial Lawyers Association
105 3rd Avenue, NW
Mandan, ND 58554

OHIO
State Childhood Lead Poisoning Prevention Program: 614-466-5332

Regional Office of EPA: 312-886-6003
USEPA, Region 5
77 West Jackson Boulevard
Chicago, IL 60604-3590
for information on certification and training for lead inspectors, risk assessors, and abatement contractors, lead in drinking water, lead in soil, waste disposal, or any EPA programs

State Contact for Information on Lead in Drinking Water:

Daniel Chatfield, Manager, Community Environmental Management Program, Division of State Environmental Health Services, Ohio Department of Health—614-466-1450

Organizations Working on Lead Poisoning Prevention:

Association of Parents To Prevent Lead Exposure (APPLE) and United Parents Against Lead of Ohio (UPAL)
7278 Case Road
North Ridgeville, OH 44039
phone: 216-327-3166
fax: 226-0928
contact: Kim Fuelling
area served: Cleveland/northern Ohio
services offered: Information for parents and advocacy

Environmental Health Watch
4115 Bridge Avenue, #104
Cleveland, OH 44113
phone: 216-961-4646
fax: 961-7179
contact: Stuart Greenberg
area served: Cleveland
services: Information for parents, community education, and advocacy

Housing Directions of Greater Toledo
1326 Collingwood Boulevard
Toledo, OH 43602
phone: 419-243-8818
fax: 243-2024

contact: Dorothy Dean
area served: Greater Toledo
services offered: Information for parents and community education, specializing in housing

State Trial Lawyers Association:

Richard H. Mason
OH Academy of Trial Lawyers
395 E. Broad Street, No. 200
Columbus, OH 43215-3844

OKLAHOMA
State Childhood Lead Poisoning Prevention Program: 405-271-4471 or 271-7353

Regional Office of EPA: 214-665-7244
USEPA, Region 6
First Interstate Bank Tower
1445 Ross Avenue, 12th Floor, Suite 1200
Dallas, TX 75202-2733
for information on certification and training for lead inspectors, risk assessors, and abatement contractors, lead in drinking water, lead in soil, waste disposal, or any EPA programs

State Contact for Information on Lead in Drinking Water:

Michael Harrell, Oklahoma State Department of Health, Public Water Supply Division—405-271-5205

State Trial Lawyers Association:

Tony Borthick
OK Trial Lawyers Association
323 NE 27th Street
Oklahoma City, OK 73105-2798

OREGON
State Childhood Lead Poisoning Prevention Program: 503-248-5240

Regional Office of EPA: 206-553-1200
USEPA, Region 10
1200 Sixth Avenue
Seattle, WA 98101

for information on certification and training for lead inspectors, risk assessors, and abatement contractors, lead in drinking water, lead in soil, waste disposal, or any EPA programs

State Contact for Information on Lead in Drinking Water:

Chris Hughes, Oregon Health Division, Drinking Water Section—503-731-4317

State Trial Lawyers Association:

Charles Tauman
Oregon Trial Lawyers Association
1020 SW Taylor, Suite 400
Portland, OR 97205

PENNSYLVANIA
State Childhood Lead Poisoning Prevention Program: 717-783-8451

Regional Office of EPA: 215-597-9800
USEPA, Region 3
841 Chestnut Building
Philadelphia, PA 19107
for information on certification and training for lead inspectors, risk assessors, and abatement contractors, lead in drinking water, lead in soil, waste disposal, or any EPA programs

State Contact for Information on Lead in Drinking Water:

Jeff Gordon, Division of Drinking Water Management—717-772-4018

Organizations Working on Lead Poisoning Prevention:

Dignity Housing
7208 Germantown Avenue
Philadelphia, PA 19119
phone: 215-242-3140
fax: 242-3382
contact: Wayne E. Stokes
area served: Philadelphia
services offered: Provides affordable housing and life skills support to homeless families and individuals

Philadelphia Citizens for Children and Youth
7 Benjamin Franklin Parkway
Philadelphia, PA 19103
phone: 215-563-5848
fax: 563-9442
contact: Mary Goldman
area served: Philadelphia and southwestern Pennsylvania
services offered: Advocates for children on issues including lead poisoning, loans HEPA vacuum cleaners to families, distributes information on lead poisoning prevention methods and available services

Public Interest Law Center of Philadelphia
125 South 13th Street
Philadelphia, PA 19107
phone: 215-627-7100
fax: 627-3123
contact: Jerome Balter
area served: Philadelphia
services offered: Information, education, and advocacy

The Tenants' Action Group of Philadelphia
Lead Poisoning Prevention Program
21 South 12th Street, 12th Floor
Philadelphia, PA 19107
phone: 215-575-0700 ext. 254
fax: 575-0718
contact: Jennifer Evert
area served: Philadelphia
services offered: Outreach and education, advocacy

United Parents Against Lead of Pennsylvania (UPAL)
7722 Temple Road
Philadelphia, PA 19150
phone: 215-927-9906
fax: 927-9906
contact: Sharon Johnson
area served: State of Pennsylvania
services offered: Information and support for parents, community education, and advocacy

State Trial Lawyers Association:

Nancy Mulloy
PA Trial Lawyers Association

121 South Broad Street, Suite 800
Philadelphia, PA 19107-4594

Patricia M. Patterson
Philadelphia Trial Lawyers Association
121 South Broad Street, Suite 800
Philadelphia, PA 19107-4594

RHODE ISLAND
State Childhood Lead Poisoning Prevention Program: 401-277-2312

Regional Office of EPA: 617-565-3420
USEPA, Region 1
John F. Kennedy Federal Building
One Congress Street
Boston, MA 02203
for information on certification and training for lead inspectors, risk assessors, and abatement contractors, lead in drinking water, lead in soil, waste disposal, or any EPA programs

State Contact for Information on Lead in Drinking Water:

June Swallow, Chief, Div. of Drinking Water Quality, Rhode Island Department of Health—401-277-6867

Organizations Working on Lead Poisoning Prevention:

Childhood Lead Action Project/Get The Lead Out Coalition
421 Elmwood Avenue
Providence, RI 02907
phone: 401-785-1310
fax: 467-2507
contact: Roberta Aaronson
area served: Providence, Pawtucket, and Central Falls
services offered: Support and information, for parents education, advocacy

Church Community Housing Corporation
50 Washington Square
Newport, RI 02840
phone: 401-846-5114
fax: 849-7930

contact: Stephen P. Ostiguy
area served: Newport County
services offered: Provides safe, affordable housing for families, as well as information, education, and advocacy

Elmwood Neighborhood Housing Services

9 Atlantic Avenue
Providence, RI 02907
phone: 401-461-4111
fax: 461-2210
contact: Joan Carbone
area served: Rhode Island
services offered: Community education, outreach, and advocacy

State Trial Lawyers Association:

Nancy Striuli
RI Trial Lawyers Association
One Park Row
Providence, RI 02903

SOUTH CAROLINA
State Childhood Lead Poisoning Prevention Program: 803-734-4450 or 737-4061

Regional Office of EPA: 404-347-4727
USEPA, Region 4
345 Courtland Street, NE
Atlanta, GA 30365
for information on certification and training for lead inspectors, risk assessors, and abatement contractors, lead in drinking water, lead in soil, waste disposal, or any EPA programs

State Contact for Information on Lead in Drinking Water:

Robert E. Malpass, P.E., Chief, Bureau of Drinking Water Protection, Department of Health and Environment Control—803-734-5310

Organization Working on Lead Poisoning Prevention:

Charleston County Health Department
334 Calhoun Street
Charleston County Health Department

Charleston, SC 29401
phone: 803-724-5946
fax: 724-5962
contact: Steve Boxx
area served: Charleston
services offered: Screening, community education, lead risk assessment, and lead abatement, through the CLEARCorps (Community Lead Education and Reduction Corps) project, established under an AmeriCorps grant from the Corporation for National Service

State Trial Lawyers Association:

Linda Franklin
SC Trial Lawyers Association
PO Box 11557
Columbia, SC 29211

SOUTH DAKOTA
State Childhood Lead Poisoning Prevention Program: 605-773-3364

Regional Office of EPA: 303-293-1603
USEPA, Region 8
999 18th Street, Suite 500
Denver, CO 80202-2405
for information on certification and training for lead inspectors, risk assessors, and abatement contractors, lead in drinking water, lead in soil, waste disposal, or any EPA programs

State Contact for Information on Lead in Drinking Water:

Darren Busch, South Dakota Department of Water Quality and Natural Resources, Office of Drinking Water, Division of Land and Water Quality—605-773-3754

State Trial Lawyers Association:

Sarah Schwerdtfeger
PO Box 1154
201 Euclid Avenue, No. 4
Pierre, SD 57501

TENNESSEE
State Childhood Lead Poisoning
Prevention Program: 615-741-5683

Regional Office of EPA: **404-347-4727**
USEPA, Region 4
345 Courtland Street, NE
Atlanta, GA 30365
for information on certification and training for lead inspectors, risk assessors, and abatement contractors, lead in drinking water, lead in soil, waste disposal, or any EPA programs

State Contact for Information on Lead in Drinking Water:

David Draughon, Director, Division of Water Supply, Tennessee Department of Environment & Conservation—615-532-0191

State Trial Lawyers Association:

John Summers
TN Trial Lawyers Association
1903 Division Street
Nashville, TN 37203

TEXAS
State Childhood Lead Poisoning
Prevention Program: 800-422-2956

Regional Office of EPA: **214-665-7244**
USEPA, Region 6
First Interstate Bank Tower
1445 Ross Avenue, 12th Floor, Suite 1200
Dallas, TX 75202-2733
for information on certification and training for lead inspectors, risk assessors, and abatement contractors, lead in drinking water, lead in soil, waste disposal, or any EPA programs

State Contact for Information on Lead in Drinking Water:

Anthony E. Bennett, Texas Natural Resources—
512-239-6020

Organizations Working on Lead Poisoning Prevention:

People Organized in Defense of Earth and Her Resources (PODER)
55 North IH 35m #205B
Austin, TX 78702-5206
phone: 512-472-9921
fax: 472-9922
contact: Sylvia Ledesma
area served: Austin
services offered: Provides education, advocacy, and action for communities

United Parents Against Lead of Texas (UPAL)
7927 Midland Forest
Houston, TX 77088
phone: 713-448-4275
contact: Rebecca Rex
area served: Houston/southeast Texas
services offered: Information and referrals for families affected by lead poisoning

West Dallas Coalition for Environmental Justice
5105 Goodman Street
Dallas, TX 75211
phone: 214-330-7947
contact: Luis Sepulveda
area served: Dallas/Barrios
services offered: Information, education, and lobby

State Trial Lawyers Association:

Tommy Townsend
TX Trial Lawyers Association
PO Box 788
Austin, TX 78767-0788

UTAH
State Childhood Lead Poisoning
Prevention Program: 801-536-4000

Regional Office of EPA: **303-293-1603**
USEPA, Region 8
999 18th Street, Suite 500
Denver, CO 80202-2405
for information on certification and training for lead inspectors, risk assessors, and abatement con-

tractors, lead in drinking water, lead in soil, waste disposal, or any EPA programs

State Contact for Information on Lead in Drinking Water:

Gayle Smith, Director, Bureau of Drinking Water/Sanitation, Utah Department of Health—801-538-6159

State Trial Lawyers Association:

Lillian Garrett
UT Trial Lawyers Association
645 South 200 East #103
Salt Lake City, UT 84111

VERMONT
State Childhood Lead Poisoning Prevention Program: 802-865-7786

Regional Office of EPA: 617-565-3420
USEPA, Region 1
John F. Kennedy Federal Building
One Congress Street
Boston, MA 02203
for information on certification and training for lead inspectors, risk assessors, and abatement contractors, lead in drinking water, lead in soil, waste disposal, or any EPA programs

State Contact for Information on Lead in Drinking Water:

Acting Commissioner, Department of Health—802-863-7280

Organizations Working on Lead Poisoning Prevention:

Vermont Lead Safety Project and United Parents Against Lead of Vermont (UPAL)
14 Pleasant Street
Bristol, VT 05443
phone: 802-453-5617
fax: 453-5617
contact: Lesley Wright
area served: State of Vermont
services offered: Information, education, and advocacy

Vermont Public Interest Research Group (VPIRG)
43 State Street
Montpelier, VT 05602
phone: 802-223-5221
fax: 223-6855
contact: Jenny Carter
area served: State of Vermont
services offered: Information, education, and advocacy

State Trial Lawyers Association:

Jennifer J. Smith
Vermont Trial Lawyers Association
64 Main Street, Suite 28
Montpelier, VT 05602

VIRGINIA
State Childhood Lead Poisoning Prevention Program: 804-225-4455

Regional Office of EPA: 215-597-9800
USEPA, Region 3
841 Chestnut Building
Philadelphia, PA 19107
for information on certification and training for lead inspectors, risk assessors, and abatement contractors, lead in drinking water, lead in soil, waste disposal, or any EPA programs

State Contact for Information on Lead in Drinking Water:

Allen Hammer, Director, Division of Water Supply Engineering—804-786-5566

Organizations Working on Lead Poisoning Prevention:

Americans Against Childhood Lead Poisoning
PO Box 301
Burke, VA 22009-0301
phone: 703-978-3190
fax: 978-5357
contact: Fariba Nazemi
area served: States of Virginia and Maryland, and District of Columbia
services offered: Educates expectant mothers and

households with young children, inspects houses for lead, and advocacy

Lynchburg Lead Abatement Program
900 Church Street
Lynchburg, VA 24501
phone: 804-847-1572
fax: 845-7630
contact: Ernest Smith
area served: Lynchburg
services offered: Information, education, advocacy, specializing in lead-safe housing

Tinbridge Hill Neighborhood Council
94 Polk Street
Lynchburg, VA 24504-4927
phone: 804-847-8393
contact: Aubrey L. Barbour
area served: Lynchburg
services offered: Information, education, and community services

United Parents Against Lead of Virginia (UPAL)
1522 East 18th Street
Richmond, VA 23224
phone: 804-232-1238
contact: Zakia Shabazz
area served: State of Virginia
services offered: Information and support for parents, community education, and advocacy

State Trial Lawyers Association:

Jack Harris
VA Trial Lawyers Association
700 East Main Street, #1510
Richmond, VA 23219

WASHINGTON
State Childhood Lead Poisoning Prevention Program: 206-753-2556

Regional Office of EPA: 206-553-1200
USEPA, Region 10
1200 Sixth Avenue
Seattle, WA 98101
for information on certification and training for lead inspectors, risk assessors, and abatement con-
tractors, lead in drinking water, lead in soil, waste disposal, or any EPA programs

State Contact for Information on Lead in Drinking Water:

James Hudson, Washington Department of Health, Division of Drinking Water—206-753-9674

State Trial Lawyers Association:

Gerhard Letzing
WA State Trial Lawyers Association
1809 7th Avenue, #909
Seattle, WA 98101

WEST VIRGINIA
State Childhood Lead Poisoning Prevention Program: 304-558-7997

Regional Office of EPA: 215-597-9800
USEPA, Region 3
841 Chestnut Building
Philadelphia, PA 19107
for information on certification and training for lead inspectors, risk assessors, and abatement contractors, lead in drinking water, lead in soil, waste disposal, or any EPA programs

State Contact for Information on Lead in Drinking Water:

B. G. Pritt, Environmental Engineering Division, Office of Environmental Health Services, West Virginia State Department of Health—304-558-2981

State Trial Lawyers Association:

Norma Egnor
WV Trial Lawyers Association
PO Box 3968
Charleston, WV 25301

WISCONSIN
State Childhood Lead Poisoning Prevention Program: 608-267-0473

Regional Office of EPA: 312-886-6003
USEPA, Region 5

77 West Jackson Boulevard
Chicago, IL 60604-3590
*for information on certification and training for
lead inspectors, risk assessors, and abatement contractors, lead in drinking water, lead in soil, waste
disposal, or any EPA programs*

State Contact for Information on Lead in Drinking Water:

Robert Baumeister, Chief, Public Water Supply
Section—608-266-2121

Organizations Working on Lead Poisoning Prevention:

Wisconsin Citizen Action
152 West Wisconsin Avenue, Suite 308
Milwaukee, WI 53203
phone: 414-272-2562
fax: 274-3494
contact: Tonya M. Mantilla
area served: Wisconsin/Midwest
services offered: Grass-roots organizing, coalition
building, public education, creation of Community Lead Safe Zones and SAFE HOUSES

Wisconsin Council on Developmental Disabilities
722 Williamson Street
Madison, WI 53703
phone: 608-266-7707
fax: 267-3906
contact: Caroline Hoffman
area served: State of Wisconsin
services offered: Advocacy

Wisconsin Nutrition Project
1245 East Washington Avenue
Suite 76
Madison, WI 53703

phone: 608-251-4153
fax: 251-8545
contact: Jonathan Bader
area served: State of Wisconsin
services offered: Information to parents, community education, and advocacy, specializing in nutrition and health aspects

State Trial Lawyers Association:

Jane Garrott
WI Academy of Trial Lawyers
44 East Mifflin Street, #103
Madison, WI 53703

WYOMING
State Childhood Lead Poisoning Prevention Program: 800-458-5847 or 307-777-7957

Regional Office of EPA: 303-293-1603
USEPA, Region 8
999 18th Street, Suite 500
Denver, CO 80202-2405
*for information on certification and training for
lead inspectors, risk assessors, and abatement contractors, lead in drinking water, lead in soil, waste
disposal, or any EPA programs*

State Contact for Information on Lead in Drinking Water:

Dennis Hemmer, Director, Department of Environmental Quality—307-777-7192

State Trial Lawyers Association:

Marcia Rothwell Shanor
WY Trial Lawyers Association
2601 Central Avenue, #100
Cheyenne, WY 82001

Subject-by-Subject Resources

Resources are grouped under the following subject headings, presented alphabetically.

Advocacy
Ceramics
Drinking Water
Educational Materials/Curricula
Federal Grants
General Information on Lead Poisoning
Inspectors/Risk Assessors
Lead Industry
Lead Paint Hazard Control
  Historic Restoration
  Home Maintenance
  Home Renovation
  Rental Property
Legal
Mining/Smelting
Occupational Safety
Organizing
Product Safety
Soil
Special Education
Testing/Laboratory Analysis
Waste Disposal

ADVOCACY

Alliance To End Childhood Lead Poisoning
202-543-1147 (fax 543-4466)
277 Massachusetts Avenue, NE
Suite 200
Washington, DC 20002
(Don Ryan, Director)
Advocacy on national level. Alliance of national leaders in pediatrics, public health, environmental protection, affordable housing, education, civil rights, and children's welfare. Publications include: directory of local lead poisoning organizations and model state lead poisoning legislation.

Coalition to End Childhood Lead Poisoning and Parents Against Lead
410-727-4226 or 800-370-5323 (fax 410-727-6775)
28 East Ostend Street
Baltimore, MD 21230-4209
(Ruth Ann Norton, Director)
Offers extensive information and direct outreach services as well as lead-safe initiatives. Early intervention, prevention, and outreach services, lead-safe housing analysis and advocacy, resource identification and referral.

Conservation Law Foundation
617-350-0990 (fax 350-4030)
Lead Poisoning Prevention Project
62 Summer Street
Boston, MA 02110
(Stephanie Pollack, Director)
Advocacy on national level. Grassroots Assistance Program provides legal, technical, and strategic assistance to organizations working to fight lead poisoning. "Access to Leadlaws" is database of state and local laws and contacts. Publications include model state lead poisoning law.

National Center for Lead-Safe Housing
410-992-0712 (fax 715-2310)
The American City Building, Suite 205
10227 Wincopin Circle
Columbia, MD 21044
(Nick Farr, Director)
Research and policy development to make low and moderate housing safe from lead hazards.

United Parents Against Lead (UPAL)
773-324-7824 (fax 324-7560)
1438 East 52nd Street
Chicago, IL 60615
(Maurci Jackson, Director)
Network of parent support groups nationwide.

CERAMICS

Environmental Defense Fund (EDF)
212-387-3525
257 Park Avenue South
New York, NY 10010

Publishes brochure, "What You Should Know About Lead in China Dishes," also accessible through web site: http://www.edf.org/pubs/Brochures/ Lead in China.

Coalition for Safe Ceramicware
202-342-8450
3050 K Street NW, Suite 400
Washington, DC 20007

Food and Drug Administration (FDA)
301-443-3170
U. S. Department of Health and Human Services
Office of Public Affairs
5600 Fishers Lane
Rockville, MD 20857
Information about safety of containers. Offers reprints from "FDA Consumer Magazine," which has carried a number of articles concerning lead exposure from food and containers.

DRINKING WATER

EPA Safe Drinking Water Hotline
800-426-4791
Office of Water Resource Center
U. S. EPA
410 M Street, SW
Washington, DC 20460
Free publications, list of certified laboratories for water testing, list of water coolers containing lead.

National Drinking Water Clearinghouse (NDWC) 800-624-8301
West Virginia University
PO Box 6064
Morgantown, WV 26506-6064
Articles on drinking water issues mailed for $1 or faxed at higher prices.

National Technical Information Service (NTIS) 800-553-6847
U. S. Department of Commerce
5285 Port Royal Road
Springfield, VA 22161
Publications on a variety of technical areas, including those relating to controlling lead contamination in drinking water.

American Water Works Association (AWWA) 800-926-7337
6666 West Quincy Avenue
Denver, CO 80235
Publishes "Lead Control Strategies" and other titles at various prices.

Education Resources Information Center 614-292-6717
Access to EPA publications.

Bottled Water

International Bottled Water Association 800-WATER-11 (fax 703-683-4074)
113 North Henry Street
Alexandria, VA 22314-2973
Sets standards and tests for lead content in bottled water. Publishes list of complying brands.

Faucets

NSF International 800-NSF-MARK or 313-769-8010
http://www.nsf.org
3475 Plymouth Road
PO Box 130140
Ann Arbor, MI 48113-0140
Sets public health and performance standards for and certifies drinking water treatment systems and faucets, including for lead.

EDUCATIONAL MATERIALS/ CURRICULA

NLIC (National Lead Information Center) Clearinghouse 800-424-LEAD
"Lead Education Materials Database" contains descriptions of over 700 pieces of education and outreach materials, at various reading levels and including a number of languages. Information provided by phone, fax, or mail.

Office of Environment Health 617-534-5966 (fax 534-2372)
1010 Massachusetts Avenue, 2nd Floor
Boston, MA 02118
(contact: Abdi Yasuf)

Twenty-minute video, "Lead Paint Poisoning: The Thief of Childhood" with information and practical advice, available in English, French, Spanish, Cape Verdean Creole, Haitian Creole, and Vietnamese.

Education Development Center Inc. 617-969-7100 (fax 617-332-4318)
Lead Poisoning Prevention Project
55 Chapel Street
Newton, MA 02158-1060
(contact: John Wong)
ESL (English as a Second Language) lead poisoning curriculum.

Developmental Disabilities Prevention Program 716-632-4843 (fax 632-4956)
People Incorporated
3909 Genesee Street
Cheektowaga, NY 14225
(contact: Joan Harms)
Preschool curriculum, "Lead Has a Human Face."

FEDERAL GRANTS

HUD Office of Lead-Based Paint Abatement and Poisoning Prevention 202-755-1822
451 7th Street, SW, Room B-133
Washington, DC 20410
Lead abatement grants to cities, counties, and states.

U. S. Centers for Disease Control and Prevention (CDC) 404-842-6796
http://www.cdc.gov
255 East Paces Ferry Road, NE
Room 300, Mail Stop E-13
Atlanta, GA 30305
Lead poisoning prevention grants for state and local health departments.

U. S. Environmental Protection Agency (EPA)
(contact regional office, listed in Appendix A)
Environmental education grants.

GENERAL INFORMATION ON LEAD POISONING

**National Lead Information Center Hotline
800-LEAD-FYI (532-3394) or
202-833-1071
http://www.nsc.org/ehc/lead.htm**
(operated by the National Safety Council)
Free basic information packet to consumers on lead poisoning prevention, including list of state contacts.

**National Lead Information Clearinghouse
(NLIC) 800-424-LEAD (800-424-5323)**
1019 19th Street, NW
Suite 401
Washington, DC 20036
For hearing impaired TDD: 800-526-5456
fax: 202-659-1192
e-mail: ehc@cais.com
http://www.nsc.org/nsc/ehc/ehc.html
Technical information for lead abatement professionals or landlords, buyers, sellers of property with lead paint. Database with summary of educational materials from various sources. Newsletter on lead poisoning prevention issues: "Lead Inform."

**U. S. Environmental Protection Agency
(EPA) 202-260-2090**
401 M Street, SW
Washington, DC 20460
Gopher: gopher.epa.gov:70/11/Offices/
PestpreventToxic/Tosic/lead_pm
http://www.epa.gov/docs/lead_pm
Dial up: 919-558-0335
FTP: ftp.epa.gov (to log in, type "anonymous," use your internet e-mail address for password)

**Centers for Disease Control and
Prevention 404-639-3311**
Lead Poisoning Prevention Branch
4770 Buford Highway, NE
Building 101, Mail Stop 742
Atlanta, GA 30341

The Lead Line
Aulson Company
80 Foster Street
Peabody, MA 01960

Newsletter on developments in lead poisoning regulation, policy, technology, information.

The Lead Letter
311 McClellan Avenue
Mt. Vernon, NY 10553-2110
Newsletter on developments in lead poisoning regulation, policy, technology, information.

INSPECTORS/RISK ASSESSORS

**Your state lead poisoning program or
regional EPA office (in Appendix A)**

**The National Lead Information
Clearinghouse (NLIC)
800-424-LEAD (800-424-5323)**

**The Lead Listing 888-LEADLIST
http://www.leadlisting.org**

**The National Lead Abatement Council
(NLAC) 800-590-NLAC or 301-924-0804**
PO Box 535
Olney, MD 20832
Identifies trained lead service providers, state-by-state and contains general guidance to help the public select quality lead services.

**The Environmental Information
Association 770-986-2760**
1777 Northeast Expressway, Suite 150
Atlanta, GA 30129-2440

LEAD INDUSTRY

**Environmental Defense Fund (EDF)
202-387-3500**
1616 P Street, NW
Washington, DC 20036
Publishes "Hour of Lead: A Brief History of Lead Poisoning in the United States and the Efforts of the Lead Industry to Delay Regulation."

**Task Force on Child Lead Poisoning
617-646-3889 (fax 727-4581)**
8 Sawin Street
Arlington, MA 02174
(contact: Richard Rabin)
Information on the lead industry.

LEAD PAINT HAZARD CONTROL

U. S. EPA, Office of Pollution Prevention and Toxics 202-554-1404
401 M Street, SW
Washington, DC 20460
e-mail TSCA-Hotline@epamail.epa.gov
TDD 554-0551

HUD User
800-245-2691 or 301-251-5154
PO Box 6091
Rockville, MD 20850
Sells HUD publications, including "Guidelines for the Evaluation and Control of Lead-Based Paint Hazards in Housing," the basic source book for lead paint abatement and interim control, with detailed description of methods and standards used for HUD properties which serve as a model for hazard control work in private homes.

The Lead Listing 888-LEADLIST
http://www.leadlisting.org

The National Lead Abatement Council
PO Box 535
Olney, MD 20832
Identifies trained lead service providers, state-by-state, and contains general guidance to help the public select quality lead services.

Historic Restoration

Massachusetts Historical Commission
"Historic Buildings and the Lead Paint Hazard," available from:
Massachusetts State Bookstore
State House Room 116
Boston, MA 02133

National Park Service, U. S. Department of the Interior
"Preservation Brief 37: Appropriate Methods for Reducing Lead-Paint Hazards in Historic Housing"; "National Park Service's CRM (Cultural Resources Management) Bulletin," Volume 17, number 4 (containing an article on what to do about lead-based paint); and "The Secretary of the Interior's Standards for Rehabilitation and Guidelines for Rehabilitating Historic Buildings," available from:

Superintendent of Documents
U. S. Government Printing Office
Washington, DC 20402
or National Park Service Regional Offices.

Advisory Council on Historic Preservation
202-606-8503
1100 Pennsylvania Avenue, NW
Room 809
Washington, DC 20004
e-mail: achp@achp.gov

Home Maintenance

Community Resources
410-727-7837 (fax 706-0295)
28 East Ostend Street
Baltimore, MD 21230
(Dennis Livingston, Director)
Designs and implements projects that focus on solving environmental problems with community-controlled economically sustainable programs. Publishes "Maintaining a Lead Safe Home," a user-friendly, well-illustrated, clear and concise guide to lead-safe home repair and maintenance, including detailed information on hiring a contractor, dust sampling, cleanup, and other critical skills.

Home Renovation

"Reducing Lead Hazards When Remodeling Your Home," published by the EPA, is available through your state lead poisoning prevention program or regional office of the EPA.

Rental Property

ASTM (American Society for Testing and Materials)   610-832-9500
"Standard Guide for Prevention and Control of Lead-Based Paint Hazards in Rental Housing" explains duties of landlord and techniques available.

LEGAL

Mealey's Lead Litigation Reports
PO Box 446
Wayne, PA 19087-0446
Publishes updates on lead poisoning litigation.

Association of Trial Lawyers of America (ATLA) 202-965-3500 (fax 625-7084)
1050 31st Street, NW
Washington, DC 20007
Referral to ATLA Lead Paint Litigation Group member in your area regarding handling lead poisoning cases.

State trial lawyers associations (listed in Appendix A)

MINING/SMELTING

Idaho Conservation League 208-345-6933 (fax 344-0344)
PO Box 844
Boise, ID 83701
(Rick Johnson, Director)
Information on the effect of lead and other contaminants on land and water resources.

Mineral Policy Center 202-887-1872
1620 K Street, NW, Suite 808
Washington, DC 20006
(Susan Brackett, Communications Director)
Supports communities with concerns about mining issues.

People's Action Coalition 208-784-8891 (phone/fax)
PO Box 362
Kellogg, ID 83837
(Barbara Miller, Director)
Addresses cleanup of contamination and health intervention for communities affected by mining and smelting, in Pacific Northwest.

OCCUPATIONAL SAFETY

National Institute for Occupational Health and Safety 800-35-NIOSH

U. S. Occupational Safety and Health Administration (OSHA) 202-219-8615
Department of Job Safety and Health
202-219-8151
For information on respirators and protective clothing.

Local or regional OSHA offices.

ORGANIZING

The Center for Third World Organizing (CTWO) 510-533-7583 (fax 533-0923; internet: ctwo@igc.apc.org.)
1218 East 21st Street
Oakland, CA 94606
Organizer training and leadership development programs in communities of color; publishes newsletter, "The CTWO Times."

Island Press 800-828-1302
Box 7
Covelo, CA 95428
"Fighting Toxics: A Manual for Protecting Your Family, Community, and Workplace" is a full-length book on organizing for environmental protection.

The Midwest Academy 312-645-6010
225 West Ohio, Suite 250
Chicago, IL 60610
Provides training to organizations working for social change through citizen action. "Organizing for Social Change: A Manual for Activists" is the classic handbook on citizen action and organizing. It is available from:
Seven Locks Press 800-354-5348
PO Box 25689
Santa Ana, CA 92799

PODER (People Organized to Demand Environmental Rights) 415-431-4210
474 Valencia Street, Suite 155
San Francisco, CA 94103
"Lead Poisoning Prevention Community Organizing Manual" is a short, concise brochure on organizing specifically to fight lead poisoning.

PRODUCT SAFETY

Consumer Product Safety Commission (CPSC) 301-504-0580
Office of Information and Public Affairs
Washington, DC 20207
Internet:
Web site address: http://www.cpsc.gov

Gopher site address: cpsc.gov

e-mail address: info@cpsc.gov

List Server Service: listpro@cpsc.gov. *Sends product recall information automatically via internet e-mail. Send with your message: sub CPSCINFO-L (and your first and last name).*

Fax-on-Demand Service: 301-504-0051. *For new releases and certain other information, 24 hours, 7 days a week, dial on hand-set of fax and follow instructions.*

Consumer Hotline: 800-638-2772 (638-CPSC) (teletypewriter: 638-8270). *For prerecorded information, 24 hours, 7 days a week, staffed from 8:30 to 5:00.*

SOIL

U. S. Department of Agriculture Soil Conservation Service

local offices, and

Cooperative Extension Service

local offices

Can provide advice on what type of grasses and plants to use and how to prepare the soil.

U. S. EPA, Region 1
617-573-5770

JFK Federal Building

One Congress Street

Boston, MA 02203

(Ann Carroll, Lead Coordinator)

Publications: "Controlling Lead in Soils, Soil Abatement Specifications, EPA-NEW ENGLAND" (undated) and "Controlling Lead in Soils: Informational Report of the Lead in Soils Charrete" (August 16, 1995).

SPECIAL EDUCATION

The Council for Exceptional Children
703-620-3660

1920 Association Drive

Reston, VA 22091-1589

"Teaching Exceptional Children" (periodical).

CASE (Council of Administrators of Special Education, Inc.)
505-243-7622 (fax 247-4822)

Dr. Jo Thomason

615 16th Street, NW

Albuquerque, NM 87104

"Student Access: A Resource Guide for Educators, Section 504 of the Rehabilitation Act of 1973."

National Center for Learning Disabilities
212-687-7211

99 Park Avenue

New York, NY 10016

National Information Center for Children and Youth with Disabilities
703-893-6061 or 800-999-5599

PO Box 1492

Washington, DC 20013

Learning Disabilities Association of America 412-341-1515 or 341-8077

4156 Library Road

Pittsburgh, PA 15234

Children and Adults with Attention Deficit Disorder (CHADD) 954-587-3700

499 Northwest 70th Avenue, Suite 109

Plantation, FL 33317

Attention Deficit Information Network (AD-IN) 617-455-9895

475 Hillside Avenue

Needham, MA 02194

National Lead Information Clearinghouse 800-424-LEAD, ext. 738.

Maintains a list of neuropsychologists and special education researchers who work with lead poisoned children.

TESTING/LABORATORY ANALYSIS

NLIC (National Lead Information Clearinghouse) 800-424-LEAD

Provides a state-by-state list of laboratories approved by EPA's National Lead Laboratory Accreditation Program (NLLAP) and recommended for analyzing paint chips, dust wipes, and/or soil. Also information on specific XRF instruments.

American Association for Laboratory Accreditation 301-670-1377

656 Quince Orchard Road

Gaithersburg, MD 20878-1409
Laboratory accreditation program

**American Industrial Hygiene Association
703-849-8888**
2700 Prosperity Avenue, Suite 250
Fairfax, VA 22031
Laboratory accreditation program

**ASTM (American Society for Testing and
Materials) 610-832-9500**
Publishes standards for materials, products, systems, and services, including for sample collation and preparation and testing methods.

WASTE DISPOSAL

**Contact your regional EPA office, or
U. S. Environmental Protection Agency
(EPA) 202-554-1404 or 800-424-9346
Toxic Substances Control Hotline**
Information about federal regulations regarding hazardous waste disposal.

**National Conference of State Legislatures
(NCSL) 303-830-2200**
1560 Broadway, Suite 1700
Denver, CO 80202
Information about current state regulations regarding waste disposal and appropriate agencies in each state.

Occupations and Hobbies with Risk of Lead Exposure

HOBBIES

Ammunition making
Ceramics glazing
Ceramics making
Fishing weight making
Stained glass making

CONSTRUCTION/REPAIR WORK

Bridge, tunnel, elevated highway work
Cable stripping
Carpet laying/removing
Electrical work
Enameling
Lead soldering
Machining or grinding lead alloys
Paint stripping
Radiator repair
Residential lead paint removal
Roofing, siding, sheet metal work
Sanding of old paint

Welding
Wrecking and demolition work

MANUFACTURING/MINING/SMELTING

Ammunition and small arms
Battery manufacturing (primary and storage) or recovery
Bottle cap manufacturing
Brass, copper, or lead foundries
Cable covering manufacturing
Ceramic walls, floor, tiles, and glazing
Chemicals and chemical preparations
Communications equipment
Electronic component manufacturing
Fabricated metal products and structural metal
Fabricated rubber
Glass products (pressed and blown, or from purchased glass)
Industrial machinery and equipment
Insecticide manufacturing
Jewelry making

Lead production or smelting
Malleable iron foundries
Measuring and controlling devices
Metal fixtures and cans
Motor vehicles, parts, and accessories
Nonferrous rolling, drawing, and refining
Paint manufacturing
Plastics manufacturing
Plastics materials and resins
Plumbing fixture fitting and trim
Pottery products
Printing
Search and navigation equipment

Tanning
Transportation equipment
Valve and pipe fittings
Vitreous china food utensils

OTHER TYPES OF WORKERS AT RISK

Automobile mechanics
Dental technicians
Firing range instructors and janitors
Police officers
Scrap and waste handlers

Sources: "Lead in Your Life," *Prevention Magazine*, Sept. 1991, p. 111; Richard Rabin, Letitia Davis, and Daniel Brooks, "Lead at Work: Elevated Blood Lead Levels in Massachusetts Workers, April–October 1991," Massachusetts Executive Office of Labor, Aug. 1992, p. 4; David Rempel, "The Lead Exposed Worker," *JAMA—The Journal of the American Medical Association,* Vol. 262, 1989, p. 533; CDC, *Preventing Lead Poisoning in Young Children* (1991), p. 22.

Nutritional Values of Common Foods

	SERVING SIZE	FAT (g)	CALCIUM (mg)	IRON (mg)	VITAMIN C (mg)	ZINC (mg)
DAIRY PRODUCTS						
Cheese, American	1 oz	6	213	0.1	0	0.9
Cheese, cheddar	1 oz	9.4	205	0.2	0	0.9
Cheese, cottage	1 cup	10.2	136	0.4	0	0.8
Cheese, cream	1 oz	10	222	0.3	0	0.2
Cheese, Swiss	1 oz	8	270	0	0	1.1
Cream, sour	1 tbs	2.5	14	0	0.1	0
Half and half	1 tbs	1.7	16	0	0.1	0.1
Ice cream	1 cup	14	176	0.1	0.7	1.4
Milk, skim	1 cup	0.6	316	0.1	2.5	1.0
Milk, whole	1 cup	8.1	291	0.1	2.3	0.9
Sherbet (orange)	1 cup	3.8	103	0.3	3.9	1.3
Yogurt, fruit	8 oz	2.4	345	0.2	1.4	1.6
EGGS						
Fried	1	6.4	26	0.9	0	0.6

Note: some 0 values may actually be trace amounts.

	SERVING SIZE	FAT (g)	CALCIUM (mg)	IRON (mg)	VITAMIN C (mg)	ZINC (mg)
EGGS (*cont.*)						
Hard-cooked	1	5.6	28	1.0	0	0.7
Scrambled (with butter/milk)	1	7.1	47	0.9	0.1	0.7
FATS AND OILS	1 tbs					
Butter		11	4	0	0	0
Margarine		11.4	4	0	0	0
Mayonnaise		11	3	0.1	0	0
Salad dressing (blue cheese)		8	12	0	0.3	0
Salad dressing (French)		6.4	1.7	0.1	0	0
Salad dressing (Italian)		7.1	1.5	0	0	0
FRUITS AND FRUIT PRODUCTS						
Apple, raw	1 (5 oz)	0.5	10	0.3	7.8	0.1
Apple juice	8 oz	<1.0	15	1.5	0.2	1.0
Applesauce, sweetened	½ cup	0.3	5	0.5	2.2	0.1
Banana, raw	1 (4 oz)	0.6	7	0.4	10.3	0.2
Cantaloupe	½ (9.4 oz)	0.8	28	0.6	112.7	0.5
Cherries, sweet raw	10	0.7	10	0.3	4.8	0.1
Fruit cocktail, syrup	½ cup	0.1	8	0.4	2.4	0.2
Grapefruit, raw	½ (4.3 oz)	0.2	14	0.1	41.3	0.1
Grapes	10	0.1	3	0.1	1.0	0.1
Orange	1 (4.6 oz)	0.2	52	0.2	69.7	0.1
Orange juice, frozen	8 oz	<1.0	27	0.5	124	0.1
Peach, raw	1 (4 oz)	0.1	5	0.1	5.7	0.2
Pear, raw	1 (6 oz)	0.7	19	0.5	6.6	0.2
Pineapple, raw	1 slice (3 oz)	0.4	6	0.4	13.0	0.1
Raisins, seedless	1 cup	0.7	71	3.1	4.8	0.4
Strawberries, whole	1 cup	0.6	21	0.6	84.5	0.2
Watermelon, 10″	¹⁄₁₆	2.1	38	0.9	46.5	0.4
GRAIN PRODUCTS AND BAKED GOODS						
Bagel, plain	1	0.8	23.1	2.0	0	0.4
Bread, raisin	1 slice (0.9 oz)	0.7	27.3	0.8	0	0.2
Bread, white, enriched	1 slice (0.9 oz)	0.8	31.2	0.7	0	0.2

	SERVING SIZE	FAT (g)	CALCIUM (mg)	IRON (mg)	VITAMIN C (mg)	ZINC (mg)
GRAIN PRODUCTS AND BAKED GOODS (*cont.*)						
Bread, whole wheat	1 slice (0.9 oz)	0.8	25.7	0.8	0	0.5
Brownies	1 (1.2 oz)	4.6	12.1	0.8	0	0.2
Cake, angel food	1 slice (⅟12)	0.1	41.7	0.3	0	0.1
Cake, pound	1 slice (⅟10)	14.7	55	1.8	0.1	0.6
Cookies, choc. chip	1 (0.35 oz)	2.1	3.9	0.3	0	0.1
Corn flakes, enriched	1 cup	0.1	1	1.8	15.0	0.1
Crackers, graham	2	2.6	11.2	1.0	0	0.2
Crackers, saltines	4	1.4	2.5	0.6	0	0.1
Doughnut, cake type	1	7.8	16.8	0.8	0	0.2
Macaroni, cooked	1 cup	0.6	13.2	1.7	0	0.5
Macaroni & cheese	¾ cup (6.4 oz)	20.1	309.6	1.9	0.4	1.7
Oatmeal or rolled oats	1 cup	2.4	20	1.6	0	1.1
Pancake, plain	1 (2.6 oz)	5.7	182.3	1.1	0.4	0.5
Pie, apple	⅛ of 9″ pie	22	11	1.7	1.7	0.3
Pie, banana cream	⅛ of 9″ pie	13.8	85.4	1.3	3.3	0.6
Pie, cherry	⅛ of 9″ pie	20.3	15.8	1.7	1.3	0.3
Pie, lemon meringue	⅛ of 9″ pie	14.9	19.7	1.4	4.0	0.5
Pie, pecan	⅛ of 9″ pie	26.3	21.5	1.9	0.4	1.6
Pizza, cheese, thin	1 slice (2.2 oz)	6.2	148.3	1.3	6.8	0.7
Rice, brown, cooked	⅔ cup	0.8	15.7	0.8	0	0.7
Rice, white, cooked	⅔ cup	0.1	13.7	1.9	0	0.6
Rolls, hamburg/hot dog	1	2.4	43	1.2	0	0.3
Rolls, whole wheat	1	1.0	38.2	0.9	0	0.6
LEGUMES, NUTS, SEEDS						
Chick peas (garbanzo)	½ cup	1.9	60	1.9	0	1.1
Beans, Boston baked	½ cup	6.7	71.9	2.3	1.4	0.9
Beans, pinto, cooked	½ cup	0.3	39.9	1.3	0	0.6
Peanut butter	1 tbs	8.2	5.0	0.3	0	0.5

	SERVING SIZE	FAT (g)	CALCIUM (mg)	IRON (mg)	VITAMIN C (mg)	ZINC (mg)
LEGUMES NUTS, SEEDS (*cont.*)						
Peanuts, roasted in oil	1 oz	14.0	24.0	0.5	0	1.9
Soy milk	1 cup	6	20	0.8	0	0.2
Sunflower seeds	1 oz	14.1	33	1.9	0.4	1.4
Tofu	½ cup	3.9	117.8	1.3	0	0.7
MEAT, POULTRY, FISH						
Clams, breaded, fried	3 oz	7.4	76	5.6	6.6	1.8
Crab meat, canned	3 oz	2.1	38.2	1.7	0	3.7
Fish sticks	2 oz	5.5	18	0.6	0.7	0.3
Haddock, filet, baked	3 oz	3.2	25.7	0.7	1.6	0.8
Salmon, canned	3 oz	6.1	191	0.8	0	0.8
Sardines, canned in oil	3 oz	9.4	371	2.5	0	2.5
Shrimp, fried, breaded	3 oz	9.8	61	1.9	0	1.3
Shrimp, steamed/ boiled	3 oz	0.9	70.5	1.6	0	1.7
Tuna, canned in oil	3 oz	7	7	1.6	0	0.3
Tuna, canned in water	3 oz	0.8	17	1.7	0	0.4
Bacon, crisp	3 slices	9.4	2	0.4	6.4	0.7
Beef steak, T-bone (lean)	3 oz	8.8	6	2.6	0	4.6
Bologna	1 slice (23 g)	4.6	3	0.2	8	0.5
Ground beef	3 oz	17.6	9	2.1	0	4.4
Frankfurter, raw beef	1 (45 g)	13.2	6	0.6	11	0.9
Ham, canned roasted	3 oz	13	7	1.2	11.9	2.2
Lamb chop, trimmed	1 medium	26	16.2	1.7	0.0	3.5
Liver, beef, braised	3 oz	4.2	6	5.8	19.2	5.2
Roast beef, rib, lean	3 oz	12.2	9	2.2	0	5.9
Sausage, pork link	1 link (13 g)	4.1	4	0.2	0	0.3

	SERVING SIZE	FAT (g)	CALCIUM (mg)	IRON (mg)	VITAMIN C (mg)	ZINC (mg)
MEAT, POULTRY, FISH (*cont.*)						
Chicken breast, roasted	½ (3.5 oz)	7.6	14	1.0	0	1.0
Chicken drum-stick, fried 1		11.3	12	1.0	0	1.7
SUGARS AND SWEETS						
Candy, caramels	1 oz	3	42	0.4	0	0.1
Candy, milk chocolate	1 oz	9	55	0.4	0	0.3
Honey	1 tbs	0	1	0.1	0.2	0.1
Jams & preserves	1 tbs	0	4	0.1	1.7	0
Sugar, white, granulated	1 tbs	0	0	0	0	0
VEGETABLES						
Asparagus, cooked	½ cup	0.3	22	0.6	24.4	0.4
Beans, green snap, cooked	½ cup	0.2	29	0.8	6.0	0.2
Beans, lime, green, cooked	½ cup	0.3	27	2	8.6	0.1
Broccoli, cooked	½ cup, chopped	0.2	89	0.9	49	0.1
Cabbage, raw	½ cup, shredded	0.1	16	0.2	16.5	0.1
Carrots, raw	1 medium	0.1	19	0.4	6.7	0.1
Cauliflower, raw	½ cup	0.1	14	0.3	35.8	0.1
Celery, raw	1 stalk	0.1	15	0.2	2.5	0.1
Collards, cooked	½ cup, chopped	0.1	74	0.4	9.3	0.6
Corn, cream style	½ cup	0.5	4	0.5	11.8	0.7
Corn, cut, cooked	½ cup	1.1	2	0.5	5.1	0.4
Cucumber, raw	½ cup	0.1	7	0.1	2.4	0.1
Lettuce, iceberg	1 large leaf (¾ oz)	0	4	0.1	0.8	0.0
Mushrooms, raw	1	0.1	1	0.2	0.6	0.1
Onions, raw, chopped	1 tbs	0	2	0	0.8	0.0
Peas, frozen, booked	½ cup	0.2	19	1.3	7.9	0.8
Potato, baked	1	0.2	19	2.7	26.1	0.6

	SERVING SIZE	FAT (g)	CALCIUM (mg)	IRON (mg)	VITAMIN C (mg)	ZINC (mg)
VEGETABLES (*cont.*)						
Potatoes, French fried	10	4.1	5	0.8	4.8	0.2
Potatoes, mashed	½ cup	0.6	28	0.3	7	0.3
Potato salad	½ cup	10.3	24	1.8	12.5	0.4
Spinach, from frozen	½ cup	0.2	139	1.4	11.6	0.7
Squash, summer	½ cup	0.3	24	0.3	5	0.4
Sweet potatoes, in skin	½ cup	0.1	28	0.4	24.6	0.3
Tomatoes, raw	1	0.3	8	0.6	21.6	0.1
Tomato juice, canned	½ cup	0.1	10	0.7	22.3	0.2
MISCELLANEOUS						
Pickle, dill, 4″ (4.8 oz)	1	0.3	22.9	4.3	9.4	0
Popcorn, plain	1 cup	0.4	0.9	0.2	0	0.3
Potato chips	1 oz	13.1	7	0.4	2.4	0.2
Soup, cream of chicken	1 cup	7.4	34	0.6	0.2	0.6
Soup, tomato, canned	1 cup	1.9	13	1.8	66.5	0.2

Sources: "Home and Garden Bulletin" No. 72, Superintendent of Documents, U. S. Government Printing Office, Washington, DC 20402, reprinted and expanded in Eva May Nunnelly Hamilton *et al.*, *Nutrition: Concepts and Controversies* (Minneapolis: West Publishing Co., 1985); USDA revised "Handbook 8 and Food Consumption Survey," reprinted in Jean Carper, *Jean Carper's Total Nutrition Guide* (New York and Toronto: Bantam Books, 1987).

Medical Follow-up

RECOMMENDED MEDICAL INTERVENTION FOR ELEVATED
BLOOD LEAD LEVELS
(Source: Centers for Disease Control)

Class I—Blood lead level 0–9 micrograms per deciliter (µg/dl)

- Continue to assess risk at routine pediatric visits and check lead level if child's risk changes.

Class IIA—Blood lead level 10–14 µg/dl

- Recheck lead levels in 3–4 months until two consecutive results less than 10 µg/dl or three consecutive results less than 15 µg/dl. (This applies to all of the following classes).
- Provide risk reduction and nutrition information.

Class IIB—Blood lead level 15–19 µg/dl

- Provide case management which includes providing risk reduction and nutrition education.
- Take a history to assess high-dose sources of lead, and address exposure sources.

- Recheck lead level as outlined in IIA, or more frequently if needed.
- If blood lead level remains in this range on two consecutive tests, consider an environmental investigation if resources allow.

Class III—Blood lead level 20–44 µg/dl

- Provide case management which includes a complete medical evaluation, iron status, neurobehavioral assessment, and referral to local health program for environmental investigation.
- Identify lead hazards and abate them.
- Provide risk reduction and nutritional education.
- Recheck lead level as outlined in IIA, or more frequently as needed.

Class IV—Blood lead level 45–69 µg/dl

- Include all of the above steps in III.
- Begin medical treatment (chelation therapy) and environmental assessment within 48 hours.

Class V—Blood lead level 70 µg/dl and greater

- Medical emergency: begin medical treatment (chelation therapy) and environmental investigation immediately.

TIMETABLE FOR CONFIRMING CAPILLARY BLOOD LEAD RESULTS WITH A VENOUS BLOOD LEAD LEVEL

(Source: New York State Department of Health and the American Academy of Pediatrics)

Blood Lead Level	Timetable
Less than 15 µg/dl	Not needed
15–19 µg/dl	Within 1 month
20–44 µg/dl	Within 1 week
45–69 µg/dl	Within 48 hours
70 µg/dl and greater	Immediately

Summary of Abatement Methods

COMPARISON OF LEAD ABATEMENT STRATEGIES
[Source: *Federal Register* 55: 14588 (18 April, 1990)]

Replacement

Advantages

Permanent solution
Allows for upgrade
Can be integrated with modernization
No lead residue left behind on surfaces
Low risk of failing to meet clearance standards

Disadvantages

Replacement component may be of lesser quality than original
Replaced components may be high volume and considered hazardous waste
Certain installation requires skilled labor

Appropriate Applications

Many interior or exterior components
Deteriorated components
Highly recommended for windows, doors, and easily removed building components

Inappropriate Applications

Restoration projects
When historic trust requirements apply
Most walls, ceilings, and floors

Comments

- *Nonstandard replacement components may need to be ordered in advance*
- *Demolition may damage adjacent surfaces*

- *May result in increased energy efficiency, e.g., window replacement*

Encapsulation

Advantages

Low dust if surface preparation is minimal, may be faster than some other methods

Disadvantages

May not provide long-term protection
Requires routine inspection
May require routine maintenance
Quality installation critical for durability

Appropriate Applications

Exterior trim, walls, interior floors, walls, ceilings, pipes, balustrades, and some interior trim

Inappropriate Applications

When encapsulation is not appropriate for substrate and substrate condition

Comments
- *Must be durable*
- *Seams must be sealed to prevent escape of lead dust*
- *Safe, effective, and aesthetic encapsulants for interior trim need to be tested*
- *Repainting leaded surfaces and the use of contact paper and paper wall coverings should not be considered for abatement*

Paint Removal On-Site

Advantages

Low level of skill required, allows for restoration

Disadvantages

High dust generated
Lead residue may remain on substrate and may be difficult to remove
Potential difficulty in meeting clearance standards and protecting workers
Stripping agents are hazardous and require more precautions

Appropriate Applications

Should generally be used on limited surface areas and when replacement, encapsulation, and off-site removal are impractical
Chemical removers work best on metal substrates

Inappropriate Applications

Generally should not be done on large surface areas
Check with manufacturer regarding recommendations for use on various types of wood and metal substrates

Comments
The following are unacceptable methods:
- *Gas-fired open flame burning*
- *Grinding or sanding without HEPA filtration*
- *Uncontained water blasting*
- *Open abrasive blasting*

Paint Removal Off-Site

Advantages

Allows for restoration
Better finished product generally than on-site paint stripping

Disadvantages

Lead residue may remain on substrate and may be difficult to remove
Damage may occur during removal and reinstallation
Swelling of wood, glass breakage, and loss of glues and fillers may occur
Hardware left on components may be damaged

Appropriate Applications

Restoration projects, especially doors, mantels, easily removed trim, metal railings

Inappropriate Applications

Check with stripping contractor regarding metal substrates

Comments
- *Check with stripping company for timing of work and procedures for neutralizing and washing compounds*

EPA RECOMMENDATIONS FOR RESPONSE ACTIONS
FOR RESIDENTIAL LEAD-CONTAMINATED BARE SOIL

AREAS OF CONCERN	BARE SOIL LEAD CONCENTRATION	RECOMMENDED RESPONSE ACTIVITIES
Areas expected to be used by children, including: · residential backyards · day-care and school yards · playgrounds · public parks, and · other areas where children gather	400–5000 ppm	Interim controls to change use patterns and establish barriers between children and contaminated soil, including: · planting ground cover or shrubbery to reduce exposure to bare soil · moving play equipment away from contaminated bare soil · restricting access through planting, fencing, or other actions, and · controlling further contamination of area Monitor condition of interim controls (In public housing, public notice of contaminated common area by local agency)
	> 5000 ppm	Abatement of soil, including: · removal and replacement of contaminated soil, and · permanent barriers (In public housing, public notice of contaminated common areas by local agency)
Areas where contact by children is less likely or frequent	2000–5000 ppm	Interim controls to change use patterns and establish barriers between children and contaminated soil, including: · planting ground cover or shrubbery to reduce exposure to bare soil · moving play equipment away from contaminated bare soil · restricting access through planting, fencing, or other actions, and · controlling further contamination of area Monitor condition of interim controls (In public housing, public notice of contaminated common area by local agency)
	> 5000 ppm	Abatement of soil, including: · removal and replacement of contaminated soil, and · permanent barriers (In public housing, public notice of contaminated common areas by local agency)

COMPARISON OF LEAD-BASED PAINT ABATEMENT METHODS[a]

	Method										
	Removal							Enclosure			
Attributes	HEPA Needle Gun	Heat Gun	HEPA Vacuum Blast	HEPA Sand	Remove/Replace	Caustic Paste	Off-site Stripping	Plywood Paneling	Gypsum	Prefab Metal	Wood, Metal, Vinyl Siding
Skill Level	High	Moderate	High	Moderate	High	Moderate	Moderate	Moderate	Moderate	High	Moderate
Esthetics	Erodes surface	Gouges	Erodes surfaces	Gouges/roughens	Good	Gouges	Good	Good	Good	Good	Good
Applicability	Very low, limited to metal and masonry	Wide, can damage some components	Very low, limited to metal and masonry	Low, limited by surface contour	Wide, dependent on skill level	Wide, can damage some components	Low, limited to components	Wide, walls	Wide, walls and ceilings	Varied, limited by components	Wide, walls
Lead Presence	Removed	Largely removed	Largely removed	Largely removed	Removed	Largely removed	Largely removed	Remains	Remains	Remains	Remains
Hazardous Waste Generation	Moderate	Moderate	Moderate	Moderate	Potentially high, pending TCLP test	High	High, but maintained off-site	Low	Low	Low	Low
Weather Limitations	Moderate	High	Moderate	Moderate	Minimal	High	None	Minimal	Minimal	Minimal	Minimal
Applicable to Friction Surface	Some	Yes	Some	Some	Yes	Yes	Yes	No	No	Yes	No

	1	2	3	4	5	6	7	8	9	10	11
Speed of Methodology	Moderate	Slow	Slow	Slow	Moderate	Very slow	Can be slow, requires coordination	Moderate	Moderate	Moderate	Moderate
Training Required	High	Moderate	High	Moderate	High	Moderate	Moderate	High	High	High	High
Capital Required	High	Low	High	Moderate	Moderate	Low	Low	Low	Low	High	Moderate
Worker Protection Required	High	High	High	High	Moderate	High	Moderate	Low	Moderate	Low	Low
Finish Work Required	Tentatively high	Moderate	Tentatively high	Moderate	Low	Moderate	Moderate	Moderate	Moderate	High	High
Product Availability	Limited	Moderate	Limited	Limited	Wide	Moderate	Limited, strip shops decreasing	Wide	Wide	Limited	Wide
Durability	Long	Long	Long	Long	Long	Long	Long	Moderate	Moderate	Long	Long
Labor Intensity	High	High	High	High	High	High	Moderate	High	High	High	High
Overall Safety	Moderate	Moderate	Moderate	Moderate	Very high	Moderate	High-high	High	High	High	High
Surface Preparation	None	None	None	None	None	Minimal—adjacent areas	Minimal—hardware removal	Minimal	Minimal	Minimal	Minimal
Cost	High	High	High	High	High	High	High	Moderate	Moderate	High	Moderate

aAdapted from Dewberry and Davis, HUD Lead-Based Paint Federal Housing Administration (FHA) Abatement Demonstration Project.

APPENDIX G

Lead Hazard Control Products

Products are grouped according to the following categories. Specific products are presented in each category alphabetically by manufacturer.

Spot test kits
Paint removers and strippers
Lead-specific detergents and dust removal products
Encapsulants and enclosure systems
High-efficiency particulate air (HEPA) vacuum cleaners

Listings of water-treatment devices are available in *Consumer Reports*, February 1993.

Information was obtained from representations by manufacturers and distributors. We are not endorsing any specific product or guaranteeing the accuracy of this information, but simply presenting it as a starting point. Contact the listed numbers of manufacturers and distributors to get updated and more detailed information.

SPOT TEST KITS

Test kits vary by type and ease of application, what materials they can test, their accuracy, and price. Spot test kits use one of two chemicals to detect lead: sodium sulfide or sodium rhodozinate.

Sodium sulfide is more accurate and can detect lead at lower levels. It releases a noxious gas during use, however. It shows the presence of lead by turning a darker color. It is therefore not recommended for detecting lead in a dark-colored paint. It has a limited shelf life. Sodium sulfide indicates a positive result in response to other metals than lead. It is unlikely to incorrectly indicate the absence of lead, as long as it is used on light-colored paint.

Sodium rhodozinate, or rhodizonic acid, a chemical in red wine, is nontoxic. It shows the presence of lead by turning a pink color. It is therefore difficult to read the results for red paint. Sodium rhodozinate is sensitive to air and water, so is usually stored in glass. It has an unlimited shelf life if kept unmixed with water.

Spot Test Kits Using Sodium Rhodozinate

KnowLead
Carolina Environment   800-448-LEAD
PO Box 26661
Charlotte, NC 28221
www.knowlead.com
Suggested retail price: $15 (four tests).
Availability: Baby supply stores and toll-free number.
Description: Detects lead in or on any surface. Easy to use, quick results, indefinite shelf life.

Lead Zone
Enzone   800-448-0535
4800 SW 51st Bldg. 100
Davie, FL 33314
Suggested retail price: $5 (six tests).
Availability: Hardware and department stores.
Description: Easy to use, nontoxic.

LeadCheck Swabs
Hybri-Vet Systems, Inc.   800-24-CHECK
PO Box 1210
Framingham, MA 01701
Suggested retail price: $5–$10 (2–4 tests).
Availability: Home centers, hardware, and paint stores.
Description: Easy to use, indefinite shelf life.

Lead Tester   800-896-LEAD
www.leadtest.com
Suggested retail price: $10 (3 tests), $15 (6 tests).
Availability: Internet or toll-free number.
Description: Involves mixing of chemicals. Can be used for paint, dust, or soil.

Lead Alert Kit
Pace Environs   800-361-5323
207 Rutherglen Dr.
Cary, NC 27511
Suggested retail price: $13 (10 tests); $25 (40 tests).

Availability: Department stores, Home Depot, retail outlets, or toll-free number.
Description: Easy to use, 1 year shelf life.

Spot Test Kits Using Sodium Sulfide

Lead Detective Kit
Innovative Synthesis Corporation 617-965-5653
2143 Commonwealth Ave.
Newton, MA 02166
Suggested retail price: $35 (over 100 tests).
Availability: Direct mail from manufacturer.
Description: Limited shelf life.

Lead Inspector Kit
Michigan Ceramic Supply, Inc.   800-860-2332
4048 Seventh St.
PO Box 342
Wyandotte, MI 48192
Suggested retail price: $20 plus shipping and handling (100 tests).
Availability: Toll-free number.
Description: Can also be used to test pottery by letting sit 24 hours.

PAINT REMOVERS AND STRIPPERS

Caution: Products should be used only after proper training and with very careful attention to precautions in manufacturer's instructions.

Strippers vary by toxicity, ease of application and cleanup, and price. Caustic strippers must be well neutralized after use. The surface may appear to be adequately neutralized but still contain enough caustic to prevent paint (primer or encapsulant) from sticking well. Noncaustic strippers can be more expensive. Stripping may generate waste classified as toxic and require precautions for disposal.

AGP PGR (Paint and Graffiti Remover)
AGP Surface Control Systems   518-734-5880
Thunderbird Terr.
PO Box 388
Windham, NY 12496
Suggested retail price: $39/gallon (covers 200–300 square feet).
Availability: By phone only.
Description: For most painted surfaces or uncoated substrates. The process can be stopped to

leave certain undercoatings. Also removes paint from rugs and clothes.

Safety/precautions: No volatile chemicals, non-toxic, noncaustic, nonacidic, nonflammable.

Nu-Strip

Autre Products, Ltd.   800-624-7672
PO Box 676
Amesbury, MA 01913

Suggested retail price: $59/gallon (covers up to 200 square feet).

Availability: Toll-free number.

Description: Gel may be painted on. Can be used on windowsills.

Safety/precautions: Biodegradable, nontoxic stripper.

STS Norway

Cerama-Tech of N. Arizona   800-317-3857
3122 Larkwood Ave.
Bullhead City, AZ 86429
siramic@rippers.com

Suggested retail price: $55/gallon for 5-gallon container, but may be shipped in smaller volumes at higher unit price.

Availability: Toll-free number.

Description: Fast-acting stripper. Softens and removes 10–15 coats of paint in 10–15 seconds. Dissolves gum and removes stains.

Safety/precautions: Mild caustic, gloves recommended.

Peel Away Strippers and Paint Removers

Dumond Chemicals, Inc.   212-869-6350
1501 Broadway
New York, NY 10036

Suggested retail price: $20–$25 for 1½ gallons (covers 20–30 square feet depending on number of layers of paint). Smaller volumes at higher unit price.

Availability: Home Depot and paint stores.

Description: Thick alkaline paste and fibrous laminate to remove many layers of paint. The thick paste is applied to a surface, then covered with the laminate paper. It is removed the next day, with all of the layers of paint (up to 30) under it affixed. High-lime-content paste stabilizes lead to 5 parts per million. Residue is washed away with water, and neutralized with vinegar.

Safety/precautions: No volatile organic chemicals, no toxic fumes. Removed layers kept wet, so no harmful dust.

Back-To-Nature Paint Removers and Strippers

Dynacraft Industries   800-922-0621
4 Kinney Rd.
Englishtown, NJ 07726

Suggested retail price: Range from $15 to $57/gallon (for range of products that work at different speeds, remove different numbers of layers, are applied in different manners, and provide varying coverage).

Availability: Toll-free number.

Description: New products, specifically for non-contractors. Remove multiple layers of paint. One product goes on green and turns off-white to indicate it is ready to be removed. Aerosol product for stripping detailed woodwork.

Safety/precautions: Nontoxic, biodegradable, nonflammable, virtually odorless. All but one product is noncaustic.

Piranha Strippers I through V

Fiberlock Technologies, Inc.   800-342-3755
630 Putnam Ave.   (FIBERLK)
Cambridge, MA 02139-0802

Suggested retail price: $110–$235 for 5 gallons/100–125 square feet.

Availability: Toll-free number, paint stores, and safety supply distributors.

Description: Only in 5-gallon containers.

Safety/precautions: Caustic. Require protective gear and measures to apply. One product is biodegradable.

Control Solvent Gel

Grayling Industries, Inc.   800-635-1551
1008 Branch Dr.
Alpharetta, GA 30201

Suggested retail price: $225 for 5-gallon pail (1 gallon covers 15–30 square feet of most surfaces).

Availability: Toll-free number.

Description: One-year shelf life. Can be removed with scraper and wire brush after 1 hour. For surfaces with many coats of paint, multiple applications may be required.

Safety/precautions: Caustic, usually recommended for contractors. Disposable protective gear recommended, possibly including respiratory gear for certain conditions.

Lead-Seal Strippers and Paint Removers

International Protective Coatings 800-334-8796
725 Carol Ave.
Oakhurst, NJ 07755
Suggested retail price: $225 for 5-gallon pail (1 gallon covers 15–30 square feet for most surfaces).
Availability: Toll-free number.
Description: Line of products include: lead paint remover, paint and coatings remover, lead paint removal paste, concentrated neutralizer and "self-sealing" lead paint removal paste, in 5- or 55-gallon containers.
Safety/precautions: Water-based (nontoxic).

Kwick Kleen Encapsulate Paint Remover

Kwick Kleen Solvents, Inc.   800-457-9144
1202 Barnett St., PO Box 807
Vincennes, IN 47591
Suggested retail price: Around $19/gallon, or $50/5 gallons (each gallon covers about 20 square feet).
Availability: Toll-free number.
Description: Trowel product on, leave for 2 to 5 hours, and remove with all layers of paint. Homeowner version of product is intended for small areas like windowpanes and trim.
Safety/precautions: Caustic stripper, could cause corrosive fumes. Wearing gloves and protective clothing and face shield recommended, but respirator not required. Inner membrane of the rubbery exterior never dries, so no lead dust generated.

AmeriStrip Gel, Paste

Safe Alternatives Corporation of America, Inc.
27 Governor St.   800-474-4SAC (4722)
Ridgefield, CT 06877
Suggested retail price: $45–$51/gallon (covers 45–75 square feet depending on how many coats of paint are to be removed). $8 for 8-oz container.
Availability: Toll-free number.
Description: Penetrates five or six coats in 1 hour. Apply like jelly onto any surface, the gel stays soft and eats into paint. Leave on as long as necessary; remove with putty knife and copper or bronze brush.
Safety/precautions: Noncaustic, water-soluble, pH close to that of water, no bad odor. Leaves no

dust or chips. Gloves and safety glasses recommended for application.

Note: Methyl chloride strippers are still sold in some places. Although they are less expensive, their use is hazardous and strongly advised against.

LEAD-SPECIFIC DETERGENTS AND DUST REMOVAL PRODUCTS

Products vary as to how they remove residual lead/lead dust and price per square foot.

AGP Wipe-a-way Wallwash

AGP Surface Control Systems   518-734-5880
Thunderbird Terr.
PO Box 388
Windham, NY 12496
Suggested retail price: $15–$20/gallon.
Availability: By phone only.
Description: Designed for cleanup after using AGP stripper and encapsulant products.

GE-ICI Industrial Cleaner

Global Encasement Inc. 800-230-7296 (W. Coast)
3 Hanover Sq.   800-266-3982 (E. Coast)
New York, NY 10004
Suggested retail price: Call for information
Availability: Call toll-free number for nearest distributer.
Description: A water-soluble, nontoxic, noncorrosive, biodegradable concentrate.

LeadSorb

De-Lead Technologies   800-274-9746
Division of Somay Products, Inc.
4301 NW 35th Ave.
Miami, FL 33142-4382
Suggested retail price: $22/gallon for 5 gallons ($0.07–$0.45/square foot depending on type of surface).
Availability: Toll-free number.
Description: Penetrating liquid that dries to a rubberlike surface, then can be peeled away as a solid. More effective than detergent for removing lead dust; primarily used by contractors.

Ledisolv

Hin-Cor Industries   704-587-0744
PO Box 410945
Charlotte, NC 28241

Suggested retail price: $7 for 8-oz concentrate (enough to clean 600–800 square feet) or $50/gallon concentrate.

Availability: By phone; expected to be in hardware and paint stores.

Description: Lead-specific detergent, mild pH, completely biodegradable. Dissolves and suspends lead from lead compounds, allowing it to be washed away. Works better with hard water than TSP. Should be left on 10–15 minutes to work effectively. Used at 1:50 dilution ratio.

Lead-Away

Lead-Away   800-829-9244
271 Western Ave.
Lyon, MA 01904

Suggested retail price: $67/24-oz spray bottle.

Availability: Toll-free number.

Description: Phosphate wash.

805 TSP Final Wash

Sentinel Chemical Co., Inc.   800-373-0633
51 NE 77th Ave.   888-373-0633
Minneapolis, MN 55432
www.senpro.com
dkmchew@senpro.com

Suggested retail price: Call for information.

Availability: Toll-free number.

Description: Phosphate detergent. Primarily for contractors. To be used with gloves and safety glasses.

ENCAPSULANTS AND ENCLOSURE SYSTEMS

Products vary as to ease of use, toxicity, ability to adhere, price, and other factors. Look for "PS-16 Protocols" (a proposed safety standard in the industry), or a conditional 20-year guarantee.

Many paint-type encapsulants do not allow tint changes after they leave the factory, and cannot offer dark colors, because the extra pigments can undermine the chemical shielding properties of the encapsulants, which have twice or more the solid content as even the best paints. It is possible to paint over most of them. Tints and most colors may be ordered for most paint-type encapsulants.

Some paint-type encapsulants can be used with scrims or fabric meshes for extra toughness, durability, and abrasion resistance.

There are three basic types of coating-type encapsulants:

- Elastomerics, with high stretchability but less abrasion resistance
- Acrylics, including styrate acrylics, which are tighter (less porous) than elastomerics, but more expensive and better covering
- Epoxies, which provide the tightest coverage and can be lead-safe with much thinner coverage

Note on comparing cost per square foot: Some manufacturers offered wet and dry millimeter (mm) thickness, whereas others offered square feet per gallon coverage. If you know the wet mm thickness, the square feet per gallon can be calculated by dividing 1620 by the wet film thickness (1620/film thickness in wet mm = square feet per gallon). If you want to calculate the dry mm thickness to meet a safety rating for the type of encapsulant paint-type coating you are using, a mathematical rule of thumb is to divide 1620 by 200 square feet (1620/200 square feet = X mm dry).

The same amount of encapsulant covers more square feet of surface if the surface is smooth and less if it is rough.

Check with the particular manufacturers before mixing product applications from different companies.

Encapsulants

Protect Apoxy

AGP Surface Control Systems   518-734-5880
Thunderbird Terr.
PO Box 388
Windham, NY 12496

Suggested retail price: $92/1.8 gallons plus $76/2 gallons primer (covers ~360 square feet depending on surface).

Availability: By phone only.

Description: The only water-based urethane epoxy encapsulant. Mixed by customer. Very thin coating. Separate primer and encapsulant for outside surfaces. Training is required by manufacturer before use, both to ensure safety and to validate the 20-year guarantee.

Safety/precautions: No volatile chemicals, nontoxic, noncaustic, nonacidic, nonflammable. Environmentally and worker safe.

Cerama-Tech 100

Cerama-Tech of N. Arizona   800-317-3857
3122 Larkwood Ave.
Bullhead City, AZ 86429
siramic@rippers.com
Suggested retail price: $50/gallon (covers 80–250 square feet depending on surface).
Availability: Through toll-free number and e-mail.
Description: Water-soluble vinyl acrylic and ceramic coating applied like paint. Dries to a very hard finish. Light shades. Durable enough for roofs and boat bottoms. High insulating properties. Certified as fire retardant and as an asbestos encapsulant. No primer needed. Fifteen-year warranty against chipping, peeling, or flaking.
Safety/precautions: Noncaustic, nontoxic.

LeadStop Encapsulants

Certech (Certified Technologies)   800-433-1892
1624 Harmon Pl., Suite 209
Minneapolis, MN 55406
Suggested retail price: $50/gallon (covers 80–250 square feet depending on surface).
Availability: Toll-free number.
Description: Elastomeric encapsulant for interior/exterior; white only. Tint may be added, or encapsulant may be painted over. Flame retardant, creates a moisture vapor lock, impermeable to the leaching of lead through the encapsulant.
Safety/precautions: Contains anti-ingestive agent, Bitrex (bitter taste to prevent children from eating it).

Lead Block (or Lead Cover)

Coronado Paint Company   800-323-0633
Premier Division   847-439-4200
2250 Arthur Ave.
Elk Grove Village, IL 60007
Suggested retail price: $49/gallon (covers 50 square feet).
Availability: Toll-free number.
Description: Acrylic elastomeric resin encapsulant; no primer required. For interior or exterior use (not for exterior use in Massachusetts). Satin finish, white or pastel colors. No mixing required, unless tinting. At least two coats to achieve required (14–16 mm) dry film thickness.
Safety/precautions: Nontoxic, includes anti-ingestant.

Protect-A-Coat, Extra-Coat (Back-To-Nature Safe Encapsulants)

Dynacraft Industries   800-922-0621
4 Kinney Rd.
Englishtown, NJ 07726
Suggested retail price: $35/gallon (110 square feet for two-coat coverage, 200 square feet for extra-coat, because only one coat is needed).
Availability: Toll-free number.
Description: Synthetic rubber, water-based, penetrating encapsulant. Satin finish, white or clear. Can be used with mesh/scrim.
Safety/precautions: Nontoxic.

Elastikote

Elastikote   301-663-0415
34 S. Market St.
Frederick, MD 21701
Suggested retail price: Around $35/gallon.
Availability: By phone only.
Description: Styrate acrylic encapsulant with urethane. Can mix to any pastel color or solid color. Two coats recommended, to 7–9 mm. Conditional 20-year warranty.
Safety/precautions: Noncaustic, nontoxic.

Encap Systems Encapsulants

Encap Systems   800-732-9156
230 N. Central Ave.
Columbus, OH 48222
Suggested retail price: $0.30–$0.50/square foot depending on the surface.
Availability: Toll-free number.
Description: Acrylic-based encapsulants. Can be sprayed or rolled on.
Safety/precautions: Noncaustic, nontoxic.

L-B-C (Lead Barrier Compound, LeadMaster)

Fiberlock Technologies, Inc.   800-342-3755
630 Putnam Ave.   (FIBERLK)
Cambridge, MA 02139-0802
Suggested retail price: $30–$40/gallon (covers 45–100 square feet depending on surface and on product—one is thicker and sturdier).
Availability: Paint stores and safety supply distributors.
Description: Thermoplastic elastomerics, for indoor use; conditional 20-year warranty. Low cost per square foot.

Safety/precautions: Nonhazardous and low content of volatile organic compounds. Contains anti-ingestant.

Enclosure Systems

Plaster In a Roll, Faster Plaster Liner
Flexi-Wall Systems   800-843-5394 (contractors)
PO Box 89   864-843-3104 (homeowners)
Liberty, SC 29657
Suggested retail price: $8–$9/gallon Flexi-Wall Adhesive #500 (covers about 160 square feet) and $20–$17/gallon Flexi-Wall Anti-G Coating #400 (covers 480–900 square feet). Fabrics about $5–$9/square yard, depending on style and quantity purchased.
Availability: Paint stores.
Description: Gypsum-impregnated fabric coverings, used with adhesive that crystallizes plaster for a permanent bond to the wall. Very strong, high tensile strength, impact and abrasion resistant. Can't be pulled loose. Attractive product line. May be used to permanently cover deteriorated surfaces, or as surface preparation for more lead-specific encapsulant.

LeadLock
Global Encasement Inc. 800-230-7296 (W. Coast)
3 Hanover Sq.   800-266-3982 (E. Coast)
New York, NY 10004
http://www.encasement.com
e-mail: globenca@ix.netcom.com
Suggested retail price: Between $0.80 and $1.00 per square foot (primer and top coat together).
Availability: Toll-free number.
Description: 100% acrylic environmentally advanced protective coatings for interior and exterior use. Class A, fire resistant, no toxic effluent, U. L. listed, water-based, nontoxic, low VOC. Products fully compatible to form composite systems. Line includes a primer for reintacting damaged paint, a primer for rust or over metal, acrylic caulk, topcoat, and scrim reinforcement fabric.

Saf-T-Seal
I.C., Inc.   410-252-5650
9478 Deereco Rd.
Lutherville, MD 21093
Suggested retail price: $270/5 gallons (covers 200–600 square feet depending on surface).

Availability: By phone only.
Description: Water-based, odor-free sealer resistant to salt spray, weathering, and chemicals. Makes surfaces impermeable to water vapor, gases, and other causes of surface deterioration. One coat for smooth surfaces, two coats for porous ones, so could be used as a primer on grease-, oil-, and mold-free surfaces before another encapsulant, or as a final encapsulant. Goes on white, dries clear. Aromatic solvents can remove it. No mixing required; not for use on ferrous metals. One-year shelf life.

Lead-Seal
International Protective Coatings   800-334-8796
725 Carol Ave.
Oakhurst, NJ 07755
Suggested retail price: About $35/gallon.
Availability: Paint, hardware, and safety supply stores, or toll-free number.
Description: Copolymer urethane, water-based elastomeric encapsulant; "one coat, one-step system," spray, brush, or roll. Conditional 20-year warranty. Contains anti-ingestant.

Kapsulkote I and Kapsulkote II
Kapsulkote   800-328-5885
5301 Nations Crossings Rd.
Charlotte, NC 28217
Suggested retail price: $0.24–$0.30/square foot ($27.50/gallon for K-II, $34.50 for K-I).
Availability: Toll-free number.
Description: Water-based elastomeric encapsulants. K-I is for exteriors, is very elastic, and helps prevent oxidation of covered metal surfaces. K-II is for interiors. Not rubberlike, looks, feels, and acts like regular paint. Primer may be necessary. White, tintable on request. Passed PS-16; 20-year conditional warranty on interior encapsulant.

Newtex Encapsulant Products
Newtex Industries   800-836-1001
8050 Victor-Mendon Rd.
Victor, NY 14564
Suggested retail price: $0.40–$0.50/square foot.
Availability: Toll-free number or hardware stores.
Description: Strong, woven, wall covering that can be embedded with a paint-type encapsulant as a reinforcement material; more attractive range of finishes over encapsulants alone for a stronger

wall; can be applied to some walls (higher-traffic) and not others.

Saf-T-Shield

Proko Industries   800-423-8341
PO Box 264
501 S. Foote St.
Cambridge City, IN 47327
Suggested retail price: $19–$22/gallon for base plus $22–$27/gallon for top coat (50–90 square feet/gallon). Extra charge for tinting.
Availability: Toll-free number.
Description: Used together to prime and apply a water-based 100% acrylic elastomeric encapsulant. Available in most pastels, midtones, matte, semigloss. Includes anti-ingestant.

HIGH-EFFICIENCY PARTICULATE AIR (HEPA) VACUUM CLEANERS

HEPA vacuum cleaners have stronger suction, and filter incoming dust, including lead dust. OSHA and EPA standards for HEPA vacuum cleaners require 99.97% efficiency at filtering particles that are 0.3 micrometers in diameter. These vacuum cleaners also help to reduce bacteria and allergens in surrounding environments.

Note: Some products claim to have a HIGH EFFICIENCY, "HEPA-like," or S-CLASS HEPA FILTER (such as Meile). These are not as effective as an actual HEPA filter, which is a four-stage filter. If you are considering a vacuum that is not on this list, ask the manufacturer if it is specifically appropriate for cleaning lead dust.

Euroclean 932 HEPA-vac

Euroclean   800-545-HEPA
905 W. Irving Park Rd.
Itasca, IL 60143
Suggested retail price: $550–$600.
Availability: Toll-free number.
Description: 2½ gallon capacity, dry only, with domestic accessories. Lightweight, attractive design, two-stage motor, 30-foot cord, complete with tool kit. Conditional 3-year warranty on parts and labor, designed "for use in hazardous waste removal applications."

Fortress Industries G-10 HEPA-vac

Fortress Industries   800-526-2569

12451 US 27
DeWitt, MI 48820
Suggested retail price: $410, replacement filter $80–$90.
Availability: Toll-free number.
Description: Single-stage, single-speed, 10 gallon, complete with attachments. One of the lowest-priced true HEPA-vacs on the market with quality and durability.

Minuteman Lead Vacuum

Minuteman International, Inc.   708-627-6900
11 S. Rohlwing Rd.   (fax 627-1130)
Addison, IL 60101-4244
Suggested retail price: $535.
Availability: By phone.
Description: Six-gallon capacity, dry only, includes attachments. Minimal noise (74 db), durable tank.

Nikro

Nikro Industries, Inc.   800-875-6457
638 N. Iowa St.
Villa Park, IL 60181
Suggested retail price: From $400.
Availability: Toll-free number, safety supply stores.
Description: 6- and 15-gallon models. Not recommended for daily use.

Nilfisk

Nilfisk of America, Inc.   800-645-3475
300 Technology Dr.   (NILFISK)
Malvern, PA 19355
Suggested retail price: Around $800, replacement filter $120.
Availability: Toll-free number.
Description: "Cadillac of HEPA-vac industry." Tight fittings and seals for long-term safety and effectiveness. Industrial models feature optional vacuum-assisted power tools for dust-free sanding, grinding, drilling, and descaling. Wet/dry model allows spraying of lead-specific detergent and immediate vacuum recovery. High rating from *Consumer Reports*.

White Mop-Pullman-Holt HEPA-vac 45 PB

White Mop-Pullman-Holt   800-237-7582

10702 N. 46 St.
Tampa, FL 33617
Suggested retail price: $450. (Wet and dry vacuums available at higher cost.)
Availability: Toll-free number, safety supply stores.
Description: Economy dry vacuum, 10-gallon capacity, with attachments, 33 lb.

HEPA-vac rental
Lead-Away   800-829-9244
271 Western Ave.
Lyon, MA 01904
Suggested retail price: Around $50/day (depending on distance and term of use).
Availability: Toll-free number.
Description: Sale and rental of HEPA vacuums.

Federal Laws that Control Lead Poisoning

AIR

The Clean Air Act mandates the U. S. Environmental Protection Agency to set national standards for the quality of air and limits for toxic emissions into the air.

42 U.S.C. sec. 7401 et seq.

Limitation of Lead Content of the Air

The maximum amount of lead allowed in the air is 1.5 micrograms of lead per cubic meter of air.

40 C.F.R. sec. 50.12

Limitation of Lead Emitted into the Air by Industries

Limits are placed by the EPA on the amount of particulate matter and opacity that can be emitted from primary and secondary lead smelters. The EPA requires that the best possible control technologies be used to keep lead out of the air.

40 C.F.R. part 60, subparts L and R

References are to the *U.S. Code*, noted as *U.S.C.*, the *Code of Federal Regulations*, noted as *C.F.R.*, and the *Federal Register*, noted as *Fed. Reg.*

Limits are placed on emissions from lead-acid battery manufacturing plants.

40 C.F.R. part 60, subpart KK

Leaded Gasoline

The level of lead allowed in automobile gasoline is limited to 0.05 gram per gallon for unleaded gasoline and 0.1 gram per gallon for leaded gasoline.

40 C.F.R. part 80

Prohibition of Engines Requiring Leaded Gasoline

The manufacture or sale of engines requiring leaded gasoline (either motor vehicle or nonroad) is prohibited after model year 1992.

42 U.S.C. sec. 7553

FOOD

Cans

Under a proposed federal rule, lead may not be used in any cans containing food products.

Fed. Reg. 58 (6-21-93) 33860

Wine/Lead Capsules

The use of lead capsules for wine bottled after February 1996 is prohibited as an "adulteration."

Fed. Reg. 61 (2-8-96) 4816
21 C.F.R. part 89

Ceramics

Limits are placed on how much lead can leach from ceramicware sold in the United States, whether it is made here or imported. When a testing solution is placed in the piece for 24 hours, it must absorb less than:

pottery flatware (plates)	3 ppm
small hollowware (bowls)	3 ppm
large hollowware	1 ppm
cups and mugs	0.5 ppm

Fed. Reg. 57 (7-6-92) 29734
40 C.F.R. part 117

Decorative ceramics must be conspicuously labeled as such.

Fed. Reg. 59 (1-12-94) 1638
21 C.F.R. part 109

PAINT

Paint with more than 0.06% lead content (as a percentage of the solids in the paint or of the paint film) may not be used in households or sold in interstate commerce.

16 C.F.R. part 1303 and sec. 1500.17

Federally Associated Housing

Federally owned or assisted housing and Indian housing may not be painted with lead-based paint.

42 U.S.C. sec. 4831(b)

Certain TARGET federally owned or assisted housing, and Indian housing, must be tested for lead paint and any lead paint with more than 0.06% (1 mg/cm^2) lead must be removed.

42 U.S.C. sec. 4822
24 C.F.R. part 35

- *sec. 510.410 (rehab. loan program)*
- *sec. 570.608 (CD black grant program)*
- *sec. 850.35 (housing development grants)*
- *sec. 880, 881, and 882.109 (section 8)*
- *sec. 960.701 and 965 (subchapter h) (public housing)*

Prohibition of Certain Uses of Lead-Based Paint

Federal law prohibited the use of lead-based paint for cooking, eating, or drinking utensils in 1976.

42 U.S.C. sec. 4831(a)

Also banned is the use of lead-based paint on furniture, toys, and other articles intended for use by children since 1978.

42 U.S.C. sec. 4831(c)
16 C.F.R. part 1303 (1978)

TITLE X—LEAD PAINT POISONING PREVENTION LEGISLATION

TITLE X of the Community Housing and Development Act, also known as the Residential Lead-based Paint Hazard Reduction Act of 1992.

42 U.S.C. sec. 4822 et seq.

Disclosure

The federal law mandates the provision of information to buyers and renters (disclosure) about possible lead hazards in housing. These requirements apply to all pre-1978 of housing.

42 U.S.C. sec. 4852
40 C.F.R. 745
Fed. Reg. 61 (3-6-96) 9064

Training and Certification

The law mandates states to set up programs to train and certify individuals engaged in lead-based paint activities.

15 U.S.C. sec. 2682
40 C.F.R. sec. 745
Fed. Reg. 61 (8-29-96) 45778

Lead Paint Hazard Reduction

Although the Lead-based Paint Poisoning Prevention Act of 1988 acknowledged the need to remove lead-based paint from the country's housing in order to protect the public from lead poisoning, the 1992 law sets priorities so that resources are focused where they are most useful. It also puts greater emphasis on reducing the dangers caused by dust, which may be greater than those presented by paint in cases.

Title X gets more specific than the prior law in terms of how lead paint hazards will be reduced. First, a home is visited and evaluated for lead hazard from paint and dust. Then those hazards are reduced with either temporary or permanent means, or a combination of the two.

The Environmental Protection Agency (EPA) is required to set limits for lead in dust and soil. Eventually, the EPA will also set standards for lead hazard control activities. But until this happens, HUD is responsible for these standards.

15 U.S.C. sec. 2683

The law sets out specific methods that are acceptable for reducing lead paint hazards from federally associated housing, and specifies precautions that must be taken in lead paint associated work in residential property. Although these standards do not legally apply to private housing, they set the model and are reflected to one degree or another in state policies (and in the recommendations made in this book).

TOYS

Designation as Hazardous Substances

Children's products containing hazardous levels of lead are banned under the Federal Hazardous Substances Act.

Art Materials

Children's art materials lacking a statement of conformance with federal standards (ASTM D-4236) are prohibited as misbranded.

15 U.S.C. sec 1261

WASTE DISPOSAL

Superfund Designation

Lead is designated as a hazardous substance under SUPERFUND. Any discharge into the environment of over a designated amount requires it to be publicly reported, whether it be into the water, air, or ground.

CERCLA, the Comprehensive Environmental Response, Compensation, and Liability Act of 1980, 42 U.S.C. sec. 9602

Hazardous Waste

Any waste containing more than 0.5 milligram of lead per liter is designated as a HAZARDOUS WASTE and must be disposed of according to special federal requirements for hazardous waste disposal.

40 C.F.R. part 261.24

Solid Waste Incineration

Emission guidelines and performance standards have been adopted to drastically reduce the amount of lead dispersed into the air from the combustion of municipal waste.

40 C.F.R. part 60
Fed. Reg 60 (12-19-95) 653

Disposal of Lead into Water

Lead has been designated by the EPA as a "hazardous substance." This means that, by authority of the Clean Water Act, the EPA regulates how much of it can be dumped (discharged) into bodies of water that are, or could be, used for navigation.

Any industry discharging more than 10 pounds of most lead compounds, or over 1 pound of lead arsenate, must report the discharge to the EPA.

42 U.S.C. sec. 1251
40 C.F.R. part 116

WATER

Prohibition of Use of Lead Pipes, Solder, and Flux

Solder or flux (used to treat the pipe to be soldered) must contain less than 0.2% lead if it is used in the installation or repair of any public water system or drinking water system in any home or other building where tap water will be used for drinking (since 1986). Pipes and pipe fittings must contain less than 0.8% lead if they are used in any public water system or drinking water system in any home or other building where tap water will be used for drinking.

42 U.S.C. sec. 300g-6

Drinking Water Fountains

In 1988, federal law prohibited the sale of drinking water coolers that are either lead-lined or contain any parts with illegally high lead content. The law ordered manufacturers to repair, replace, or provide a refund for water coolers with lead-lined tanks. The EPA was required to distribute a list of water coolers containing lead to the states, by the end of January 1989. The states are ordered to distribute this to educational agencies, schools, and day cares. Each state is to establish its own program to remedy lead contamination of water in schools, including measures to repair, remove, or replace water coolers that contribute lead to drinking water, by the end of January 1990.

42 U.S.C. sec. 300j-21-25

Bottled Water

Bottled water may not contain over 0.005 milligram of lead per liter. This is the same as 5 parts per billion, 3 times as strict as the limit for tap water. This does not cover soda water or mineral water, but these may soon be covered by either this or another new standard.

Fed. Reg. (5-25-94) 26933

The Lead and Copper Rule

The Lead and Copper Rule establishes an action level for lead at 15 ppb and sets up requirements for water suppliers to monitor drinking water and take measures to reduce the lead content if necessary. The following table lists the requirements and time frames set out in the law.

42 U.S.C. sec. 300g-1
40 C.F.R. parts 141 and 142
Fed. Reg. 56 (6-7-91) 26460

The Safe Drinking Water Act of 1986 allows the EPA to set a maximum level for drinking water contaminants.

42 U.S.C. sec. 300 g et seq.

Large Systems
(serving more than 50,000 persons)

Monitoring
- Tap water testing   January 1, 1993

Corrosion Control (CC)

1. CC studies   July 1, 1994
2. State chooses CC method   January 1, 1995
3. CC installed   January 1, 1997
4. Follow-up sampling   January 1, 1998
5. State reviews and sets criteria   July 1, 1998
6. Water systems operate according to state criteria and continue to conduct tap sampling.

Medium Systems
(serving between 3300 and 50,000 persons)

Monitoring
- Tap water testing   July 1, 1993

Corrosion Control (CC)

1. Water system may propose CC   6 months after action level exceeded
2. State may require CC studies   12 months after action level exceeded
3. Or, state may require specific CC   18 months after action level exceeded
4. Complete CC studies   18 months after ordered
5. State designates CC method   6 months after CC study
6. Water system installs CC   24 months after CC designated
7. Follow-up sampling   6 months after CC designated
8. State reviews and designates criteria   6 months after sampling

Continued Monitoring
- Water systems operate according to water criteria and continue to conduct tap sampling.

Small Systems
(serving 3300 persons or less)

Monitoring
- Tap water testing   July 1, 1994

Corrosion Control (CC)

1. Water system may propose CC   6 months after action level exceeded
2. State may require CC studies   12 months after action level exceeded
3. State requires specific CC   24 months after action level exceeded
4. Complete CC studies   18 months after ordered
5. State designates CC method   6 months after CC study
6. Water system installs CC   24 months after CC designated
7. Follow-up sampling   36 months after CC designated
8. State reviews and designates criteria   6 months after sampling

Water systems operate according to water criteria and continue to conduct tap sampling.

Then, if necessary, for all size systems:

Source Water Treatment

1	System monitors water source and makes recommendations	6 months after action level is exceeded
2	State determines treatment	6 months after 1
3	Water system installs treatment	24 months after step 2
4	Tap and source water monitoring	36 months after step 3
5	State reviews and sets standards	6 months after step 4

Water system operates in compliance with state standards and continues monitoring.

Replace Lead Service Lines

- Replace 7% lead lines per year   begins when action level is exceeded

After both corrosion control and source water treatment are completed, the system can stop service line replacement if monitoring shows that action level is no longer exceeded.

Summary of Steps You Can
Take to Prevent Lead Poisoning

SCREENING

Have your child screened annually at least at ages 1 and 2, or more often if you are at increased risk.

NUTRITION

Feed your children a nutritious diet, with regular meals and healthy snacks, low in fat and high in calcium, iron, zinc, and vitamin C.

WORK OR HOBBY

Be careful not to bring home lead dust from work or hobby. If you are involved in some activity that brings you in contact with lead, change your clothes and remove your shoes before entering your family's living space, and launder your lead-contaminated clothes separately.

Always check the labels of any art supplies you use to see if they contain lead. If they do, be sure to use adequate ventilation and wash your hands well when you are finished, especially before eating or coming into contact with young children.

LEAD PAINT

Test the paint in your home if it was painted before 1978. Unless and until you know that you don't have lead paint in your home, take the following precautions:

Temporary Measures

Hard Surfaces
Wet mop floors and wash hard surfaces regularly.

Floor Coverings
Have floor coverings professionally cleaned or vacuum with a HEPA vac.

Hand Washing

Wash children's hands after playing outside and before eating.

Toys

Wash toys or pacifiers regularly.

Teething

Watch that your children don't chew on leaded surfaces; provide safe teething objects.

Hot Spots

Cover up any peeling or flaking paint so children can't reach it.

Emergency Repairs

Conduct emergency repairs on peeling surfaces, taking proper precautions.

Lead Hazard Control

Have lead paint hazards controlled by a certified lead abatement contractor, taking the necessary precautions:

- Methods should be used that create as little dust as possible.
- Family should not be present when the work is done.
- Workers should use protective clothing and equipment.
- Lead dust should be prevented from getting on your belongings or anywhere else in your home.
- Entire home should be cleaned very carefully afterwards.

HOME RENOVATION

Test the paint in your home before doing any renovation or remodeling that would disrupt painted surfaces, if your home was built before 1978. If lead is present, take the same precautions as for lead hazard control work.

SOIL

Test your soil for lead. Unless and until you know that you don't have lead in your soil, take the following precautions:

Children's Play Area

- Wash your children's hands when they come inside from playing outdoors.
- Encourage your children to play in grassy areas or a clean sandbox, rather than in the dirt.
- Keep your children away from the soil closest to your house by planting shrubs near there.
- Cover the soil in other areas of the yard by planting grass or other ground cover, or by spreading gravel or wood chips.
- Turn or sod the soil, as a temporary measure. This dilutes but does not remove the hazard.
- To solve the problem more permanently, remove the top 4–6 inches of soil and dispose of it in an approved landfill, or pave over it with concrete.

Garden

- Plant as far as possible from the road and from any buildings containing lead paint.
- Investigate prior uses of the land to determine if lead arsenate was ever used on the land (as an insecticide for fruit trees), or any demolition work done on buildings that might have existed on the land.
- If there is some lead, but the level is below 300 ppm, minimize lead ingested by:
  —Using at least 25% organic compost by volume, the more decayed and the less fibrous the better.
  —Using lime to get your soil to a pH of 6.5.
  —Keeping the soil moist and using mulch, to minimize dust.
  —Avoiding growing leafy crops and root crops; these absorb more lead than fruiting crops.
  —Removing outer leaves from any leafy crop and peeling root crops before eating.
  —Washing produce thoroughly with water and a small amount of vinegar (1%) or nontoxic liquid dishwashing detergent (0.5%) and then rinsing well before eating.

FOOD AND CONTAINERS

Ceramics
- Do not use old or imported ceramics for food unless they have been tested for lead.
- Avoid regular use of any ceramics for storing or serving acidic foods.
- Do not use any ceramic items that show a chalky gray residue after washing, or any marked "For Decorative Purposes Only."

Leaded Crystal
- Do not use leaded crystal regularly for drinking.
- Pregnant women and young children should avoid any use of leaded crystal.
- Do not use leaded crystal baby bottles.
- Do not store beverages in leaded crystal.

Cans
Restrict consumption of imported canned goods unless you know that lead solder was not used.

Foil on Wine Bottles
Wipe the rim with lemon juice or vinegar before removing the cork and before pouring any wine bottled before 1996.

DRINKING WATER

Test your drinking water for lead. Unless and until you know that you don't have lead in your water, do the following:

Flush Water
Let the water run until there is a noticeable change in temperature before using it for drinking or cooking.

Cold Water
Use cold water for drinking, cooking, and preparing baby formulas.

Service Lines
Ask your water supplier if you are served by lead pipes.

Loose Solder
Remove loose lead solder and debris from new plumbing by periodically removing strainer from taps and letting water run 3–5 minutes.

Solder in Plumbing
Check for lead solder.

Water Filter
Use a drinking water filtering device if necessary.

Index